Twentieth-Century Composers

AMERICAN MUSIC
SINCE 1910

TWENTIETH–CENTURY COMPOSERS

EDITED BY
ANNA KALLIN AND NICOLAS NABOKOV

Twentieth–Century Composers

American Music Since 1910

by Virgil Thomson

WITH AN INTRODUCTION BY
NICOLAS NABOKOV

Holt, Rinehart and Winston
NEW YORK   CHICAGO   SAN FRANCISCO

Library of Congress Catalog Card Number: 77–80367

First Holt Paperback Edition—1972

Sections of this book have appeared in the *New York Review
of Books*.

ISBN: 0–03–091484–1

Printed in the United States of America

The musical examples from *FOUR SAINTS IN THREE
ACTS* and *THE MOTHER OF US ALL*, copyright 1947
and 1948 by Virgil Thomson, are used by kind permission
of the publisher, G. Schirmer, Inc.

DESIGNER: HERB JOHNSON
DESIGN DIRECTION: BERRY EITEL
INSERT: C. GRIDLEY

Contents

Photographs follow pages 78 and 110.

vii

Introduction.
Twentieth-Century Makers
of Music

BY NICOLAS NABOKOV

This is not history nor is it a chronicle although perforce it deals
with chronology. It is rather an imaginary map of twentieth-century music. Like all maps it is divided into regions and these
regions represent loose cultural entities determined in turn by
ethnic and geographical cohesion.

All choices made by the authors of these volumes are personal
ones. They express personal views, personal agonisms and an-
tagonisms, personal tastes and judgments of value and of historical importance. But in so far as each author knows the musical
life of his region each volume can be relied upon as being a fair
albeit a personal description of what has happened to music in the
region of his particular concern during the twentieth century.

The language used in these books is intentionally unencumbered by a *fatras* of technical terms. It is I believe accessible to
the average reader and music lover. It will give him a more coherent and detailed picture of the "state of music"—to use the
title of a famous book—than if it were cluttered by technical
terms and followed the chronological evolutionary paths of music
history.

Do these books, these regional essays, concerned primarily

with the most important composers of the twentieth century lack historical value? I do not think so. Precisely because the views expressed in them are personal and hence obviously partisan, they may be a refreshing contribution to music history.

For however imaginary or even arbitrary a cartographic division may appear to be, it deals with concrete facts and with a great variety of musical happenings.

The regional divisions are limited to Europe and America; the reason is obvious. First we do not deal with non-Western musical traditions, however valuable and ancient they may be; second until the middle of this century there were no significant contributions from non-European and non-American regions. I am well aware that since the second half of this century there have appeared a number of gifted composers in Japan and elsewhere. Still all valuable twentieth-century music has so far been composed in Europe and Americas. New discoveries in musical language, stylistic changes, technical innovations, all of them stem from here and were later adopted or copied elsewhere.

But when does this century start? Surely not in 1900; datelines are arbitrary landmarks. They rarely coincide with a change of heart and mind or indicate the rise of a new style or of a new technique. The case of the Florentine musical Renaissance, or of Monteverdi's first operas in Venice at the turn of the seventeenth century, are convenient exceptions. Usually new centuries begin or end long before or after their datelines.

Yet no one will deny that there is such a thing as *l'esprit du siècle*. When we say "This is an eighteenth-century Italian opera," or "This is seventeenth-century Spanish court music," we know what we mean, and anyone acquainted with music history will understand what is being said. *L'esprit du siècle* is something intangible and yet concrete; it has little to do with dates or datelines. Sometimes it ripens late in the century (*vide* Mozart); sometimes it overlaps two centuries (*vide* Haydn). J. S. Bach and Handel wrote their grandiose works in the first half of the eighteenth century, but does their work represent the spirit of the *siècle des lumières*? Certainly not. Both Bach and Handel however extraordinary their achievements stand at the end, at the completion of a long stylistic evolution and of a historical period, whereas their contemporary Domenico Scarlatti for instance (all three were born in 1685) especially in his last, Spanish period points the way into the future and is far more daring and experimental than the two grand Germans.

Century crossings are like traffic crossings. Lights are announced in advance and arrows point in different directions; forward, backward, and sideways. In the case of twentieth-century music the greenest of all lights, whose arrow points straight into the future, is of course Claude Debussy. To a minor extent this is true of Alexander Scriabin, despite the Chopinesque and Lisztian gloss that covers so much of his early music.

Rimsky-Korsakov's arrow points sideways. He belongs only in part to our century and is of course one of its outstanding pedagogues and masters of orchestration. Finland's Sibelius, that hypertrophic symphonic bard so dear to Anglo-Saxon audiences of the 1930s, is the opposite of an innovator. Whether good or bad his music does not belong to our century's concerns and worries. Like the music of other symphony composers it represents the continuation of the nineteenth century in the midst of the twentieth. His light is red; the arrow points backward.

But what then is the *esprit* of our century? What does it consist of; what are its distinguishing signs? Can it be described, circumscribed, evaluated? Of course it can but only in a general, hazy way. Partly because it is not yet quite "fulfilled," partly because we ourselves are in the midst of it and lack perspective to look at it objectively.

One of our century's distinguishing features is fairly obvious —the quickening pace of change, the extraordinary profusion of experimentation, and (what could have been foreseen since Wagner) the concomitant breakdown of so-called "academic" rules and traditions. Rarely before in the short history of Western music has there been such an *accélération de l'histoire* to use the title of a famous essay by the French historian Daniel Halévy.

Another early discernible aspect of this century's musical production is its variety. Dozens of different aesthetic and technical trends (often contradictory) coexist peacefully (or not) and fill the publishing houses and blue-printing presses, or gather dust on conductors' shelves and piano-tops. Perhaps a more particular, sociological distinguishing mark of this century's music is its increasing urbanization. Although rural elements, materials, and folkloristic memories still linger in it, they are purely reflective. In one way or another all of twentieth-century music has served urban needs and reflected urban life and urban outlooks. There has been little *plein-air* stuff produced by the composers of this century. Our musical trouts do not hop around in brooks and mountain streams; they are flown in by airplane and served blue or sautéed in megalopolitan restaurants. As for our present-day advanced music it is recorded and fractured on tape, seasoned and peppered by electronic sound, and salted by computers. All of it addresses itself to city dwellers, not to rural folk.

With this general trend towards urbanization goes a constant search, a perpetual metamorphosis of the musical language. The fundamental change is brought about by the discovery of a new compositional technique devised in Vienna at the beginning of this century. It had of course been foreshadowed by earlier developments but never stated as a complete logical method for musical composition. It is based on atonality and uses as its structural principle *series* constructed out of autonomous, rootless, and equi-valid twelve tones of the chromatic scale. It discards once and forever the distinction between consonance and dissonance. Quite a number of composers have accepted this technique as soon as it was stated; others have staunchly rejected it; others again have gone further and have experimented with musical structures made of smaller particles than semitones. Curiously enough the Latin and the Slavic worlds remained impervious to the twelve-tone serial technique for a very long time. Only after World War II did serialism penetrate the French and Italian preserves where it has now been adopted by young composers and by a few older ones as part of an inevitable evolution of music.

Russia alone remains officially impervious to the serial technique, though unofficially it is I am told being used by many composers of the younger generation. Nowadays serial technique has penetrated other elements of the musical language such as metrical divisions, rhythm, dynamics, intensity of sound, and timbre. All of them undergo serial treatments in the works of some of the most able advanced composers.

Another important innovation that enriched the language of

twentieth-century music and enhanced its vocabulary is due to the discovery of electronic sound. The possibility of producing electronic sound has been known for quite some time, but the first usable instrument was built in 1920 by a Russian engineer (and amateur cellist) Lev Teremin. I remember seeing it and experimenting with it under Teremin's guidance in the 1920s. It looked like a movable antenna and could produce a great variety of sounds. What Teremin liked best about it—and I least—was its ability to imitate the sound of a cello. "You don't need to use your clumsy fingers on a string anymore," he would say. In 1928 Maurice Martenot presented his far more perfected electronic instrument to the Parisian public. It is endowed with a keyboard, has been widely used by composers, and is a mainstay of symphony orchestras.

But the use of integral electronic sound for musical composition has come about only after World War II and paralleled a general advance in electronics. In the late 1940s and early 1950s serviceable electronic studios devised especially for musical composition started to mushroom first in Europe, then in America, and in Japan. With this came at once a sizable production of purely electronic or partly electronic music. By now it is firmly rooted in our century's music as one of its important branches.

The last technical innovation and the latest one chronologically is the use of computers for musical composition. So far only a few composers have experimented successfully with it. But electronics and the computer might, I believe, realize the dream of a few early pioneers of this century who had hoped that "*all* sounds should be put at the disposal of composers." Now this hope is a reality. It is difficult to foresee what it will do to the art of music. It may of course change its nature as an art. It may make music a branch of technology or something belonging to the world of mathematics, physics, symbolic logic, and games of chance.

Chance (aleatoric) improvisation or invention within a given framework (as in Indian music) or without it, games with sound structures are now widely used by far-out composers all over the world. Games and "gaming" have long been missing in music; yet once upon a time in the fifteenth and sixteenth centuries they were an essential part of musical composition.

Because of mass communication music in our century has long

ceased to be the privileged pleasure of an educated elite and has become a consumers' commodity. It can now be pumped through any hole, at any time, into any space, like air into flat tires. It is unavoidably consumed by millions of people who do not even notice what they are consuming.

To the contemporary composer mass media are both a convenience and a challenge. A composer without tapes is nowadays an outcast. No one has time to study scores and read music. It has to be recorded otherwise it will not be accepted for further performances. Therefore tapes and records are indispensable to composers. On the other hand by making music available to an ever-broadening public, mass media (with their money-making habits) tend to accustom the public to a life in a comfortable "musical museum." It is I believe more difficult nowadays to change the museum habits of the mass public than it was when music belonged to an educated minority. Today's composer is faced with this challenge: centuries of "musical museums" look down at him as an intruder. But sooner or later these museum habits will have to give way or make room for new works of music. The longing for change in us is much too strong to be content with a perpetual past.

Our century has been filled or should I say pestered by a variety of "isms," passing trends and fads. Partly these "isms" reflected the spirit of change I referred to earlier; partly they were signs of instability and of a strange mass-immaturity; partly again they mirrored the mobility and inchoateness of our society. But a number of those "isms" such as impressionism, neoclassicism, expressionism, and its *Doppelgäenger* twelve-tone serialism, and even neo-Romanticism, have become broad international aesthetic movements resulting in lasting works of art.

Fast change brings with it also fast aging of styles, techniques, and aesthetic outlooks. The late Theodore Adorno discussed this in a remarkable essay called "On the Aging of New Music," first published I believe in 1954. In it he points to an irreversible process: on the one side he sees an ever-accelerating, self-devouring, and self-begetting quickening of civilization's pace; on the other side the loss of interest in ephemeral works of art. By the time these works reach their consumer they have lost their freshness, their meaning, and their value; they are worn before they are consumed.

I do not share all of Adorno's deductions but I do believe that his analysis is valid in one essential point: in order to become meaningful again music must rid itself of nineteenth-century habits, the clutches of historicism, and its immortality machine. Music should get itself defrocked like present-day priests and nuns who want to serve their community and enjoy life. It should forget about its nineteenth-century "beatification" (foretold by Goethe and accomplished by Wagner). The composer should stop being a public idol like a TV singer or a cinema actor. He should be again a juggler, a gamester, a trickster, and use all the newly developed techniques for his tricks and games. He should not compose for eternity, but for fleeting occasions and for the fun of it. He should then let his work disappear in Lethe, just as the thousands of seventeenth- and eighteenth-century operas, cantatas, and oratorios have fortunately disappeared. Only musicologists regret their absence.

In conclusion I should mention two important, unconnected, and contradictory events that took place in our century. The first concerns the world of ethics. A tragedy took place in this century and afflicted its composers and their music. I refer to the brutal repression of musical freedoms for extended periods of time in the heartlands of Europe. No one at the turn of this century could have foreseen that in its third decade and in the name of untenable, anachronistically absurd doctrines, composers and their music would be subject to persecution and banishment. The art of music is non-ideographic and hence *per se* is not able to transmit ideologies; and yet it is on ideological grounds that it was repressed, persecuted, forbidden, and put under harsh state controls. This is certainly not *l'esprit du siècle* but its shame and its scandal.

The other important event is the central subject of the first of this five-volume series—the rise to full maturity of American music.

Like the rise of Russian music in the nineteenth century, it has been preceeded by a period of gestation and followed, in an equally analogical way, by the discovery of its own, national "self." In the late twenties or early thirties Nadia Boulanger (the teacher of so many gifted American composers) used to say to them: "Watch out! American music is about to take off, just like Russian music did in the 1850s." Now it is in full bloom. But I will not venture any further upon the territory of Virgil Thomson.

All I want to say here is that this event may be of great importance to the future of musical composition. America is gradually becoming the homing ground for all kinds of musical activities and a guest-house for some of the world's best and most advanced minds in the field of the arts and especially music. It may well be that it will be music's true "New World," provided of course that its internal and external stresses do not shatter its body-politic to such an extent as to make life for the arts precarious or even impossible.

Twentieth-Century Composers

AMERICAN MUSIC SINCE 1910

1. America's Musical Maturity

In colonial times and during the first century of the republic, music in America grew abundantly and for the most part unguided. During the latter part of the nineteenth century a sort of adolescence had taken place, marked by attention to its educational needs and a preoccupation with its reproductive forces. In 1867 and '68 the New England Conservatory of Music, in Boston, and the Chicago Musical College were founded, their aim being to train performers in the best European tradition, at that time esteemed to be the German. And in 1872 a department of music was founded at Harvard University to train composers, its model being the English universities, where the writing of music was taught as a liberal art separable pedagogically and socially from its performers.

As early as 1842 the Philharmonic Society of New York was founded for performing symphonic repertory, a precedent to be followed later in the century by St. Louis (1880) Boston (1881) Chicago (1891) Cincinnati (1895) Philadelphia (1900) Minneapolis (1903) San Francisco (1911) and other cities. Opera companies also came into existence, singing German, French, and Italian repertory in those languages (though the Metropolitan Opera Company for its first seven years, from 1882 to '89, gave everything, including Bizet's *Carmen,* in German). And the organized touring of reputable artists, along with tented chatauqua seasons in country towns (named after the summer camps for culture held in Chatauqua, New York) and indoor "lyceum" courses for the winter, offered high-standard concerts which served equally to cultivate the layman's taste and to stand as models for those professionally aspiring. The gramophone industry too, by 1900, was beginning to distribute passable performances.

By that time also, composers were appearing whose technique, formed under German masters, was scarcely less competent than that of their similarly trained British colleagues. George W. Chadwick, Horatio Parker, and Edward MacDowell, all of whose lives crossed the century line, were the grandfathers of us all. As educated pioneers, they took title to professional status and passed it to their heirs. That title included right of access to the performing organizations. So that in the decades succeeding the first one of this century, performance of American works by the orchestras of New York, Boston, Chicago, and other cities came to be as acceptable to the public as it was instructive to the composer.

Our early great men, all the same—Chadwick and Parker and MacDowell—are merely ancestors. For all the charm and competence of their music, it is a pale copy of its continental models. Its thin perfume is of another time and place than twentieth-century America; and so, indeed, though more robust by far, is that of its contemporaries in operetta, Victor Herbert and Reginald de Koven. And for all that Chadwick and MacDowell had aspired, like Grieg and Smetana, to depict their country, they did so as European travelers might have done and no whit more convincingly than Dvořak, who during the 1890s spent three years in America, in his "New World" Symphony actually did do.

What separated these men from succeeding generations and even from their pupils was the fact that they had received their higher training and most of their artistic precepts in Germany. Now Germany during the latter part of the nineteenth century, as compared to the vigors arising in France and Russia, was musically a dying swan. It was in France between 1890 and 1914 that the new century, foreseen by Chabrier and Fauré, was being brought to birth in the work of Debussy, Ravel, Stravinsky, and Erik Satie. I realize that during these same decades Richard Strauss and Gustav Mahler were working in Vienna quite successfully and that in Spain Albéniz and in Russia Scriabin were producing original work. But nobody then or now could find in any of the music by these men much to build on. And Arnold Schoenberg, though certainly one of our century's founding fathers, did not become visible as such until around 1910.

As viewed from America, the musical prognosis for Europe was so clearly favorable to France that well before World War I the brighter young Americans had begun to go there for studies. And they came home orchestrating out of Berlioz rather than out of Wagner, adept at modal counterpoint, acquainted with the new harmonic freedoms and metrical subtleties, and habituated to structural and thematic usages other than those that had come to dominate German teaching. German study had unquestionably been of value to the rise of American musicians into a higher level of artistic behavior. Through its help they were leaving off the stiffness characteristic of provincial art and beginning to take on the ease of intercourse, the at-homeness with broader themes, that mark international good usage. It was through their French contacts, however, that they first tasted freedom.

The major problem, after technical mastery, that any maturing music has to face is that of nationalism. Lacking local masters to feed on—the Beethovens, the Mozarts, the J. S. Bachs—is there perchance a folklore than can serve as nourishment? Is the heritage of commercial popular music usable at all? Are you limited to local sources for expressing your time and place? What are your sources anyway? Obviously they must be looked at.

The collecting of Negro spirituals had begun in 1867, just after the Civil War. In 1910 John Lomax published his first volume of cowboy song-poetry and several of the actual tunes. In 1917 the English folklorist Cecil Sharp started publication of the Appalachian ballads. These particular researches, some possibly set off by Bela Bartók's similar work in Hungary and certainly by Sharp's own collecting in England, opened to composers a goldmine of nostalgic feelings and of melodies that would be exploited in the 1930s. By that time a vast library of American-language folklore had been assembled and identified, virtually all of it Anglo-Celtic in origin. Even the Negro spirituals, as we learn from the studies of Dr. George Pullen Jackson, were African only in the manner of their singing, both their words and their tunes having been adopted from Scottish and Scotch–Irish hymnody.

The very popular nineteenth-century songs of Stephen Foster, proclaiming the pathos of Negro life through Celtic melody, though widely sung had failed to generate an idiom. They were beautiful hybrids, but sterile. And their communication was limited, since Negroes, our chief carriers around the country of both melody and rhythm, have never found them appealing. The spirituals themselves, that other Scotch-African crossbreed, seem to have had in them more chromosomes, their contribution to the blues being clearly, I think, a dominant strain. Ragtime, a genre that came up in the late nineties, was weakening by 1914. Its accent was irresistibly American; but it never developed beyond its early congealment as a species of pianoforte virtuosity for the salon (or saloon), poor in musical invention and shallow as expression. Nor did it give birth to jazz; it was merely replaced by it.

The birth of the blues is commonly dated as 1909, the year in which W. C. Handy wrote his now classical *Memphis Blues,* though Gunther Schuller allows them a quarter-century of evolution before that. Jazz appeared contemporaneously as a way of playing dance music, an urban folk style that by 1912 to 1915 had become nationally circulated. Though jazz has from its beginnings used commercial pop-tunes for its variations, neither blues nor jazz actually came out of Tin Pan Alley, as we call our popular composers; and they have to this day remained largely independent of the monied distribution channels. There are jazz and blues recordings, of course; but they are often hard to come by and, unlike pop records, are a poor substitute for the real presence. The blues are a true folk art form, with a fixed meter of twelve four-four bars, generally grouped as three-line stanzas, expressing in the first person amorous or economic frustration.* For example:

> *Got the Saint Louis Blues, just as blue as I can be;*
> *That man got a heart like a rock cast in the sea,*
> *Or else he would not gone so far from me.*

---

* The South distinguishes two main moods, the "po' house blues" and the "who' house blues."

Jazz is instrumental, a communal improvisation in four-four time on some popular tune—usually a commercial one which the players have no qualms about turning inside out. Blues and jazz have from their beginnings lived happily together, and both have continued to evolve in subtlety. Both, in fact, are authentic forms with a literature, a history, a tradition of high style in performance, a world public, and no signs of senescence. They have nourished the commercial and stimulated our art music—Darius Milhaud's *La Création du monde* and George Gershwin's *Rhapsody in Blue*, to mention only two celebrated works.

In the intellectual music tradition, the decade between 1910 and 1920 saw the establishment at Harvard in Cambridge, Massachusetts and at Columbia University in New York of French-trained composers, chief among these Edward Burlingame Hill and Daniel Gregory Mason, teaching younger composers, and particularly teaching them to orchestrate in the French way. In 1916 Ernest Bloch, a Swiss whose earlier career had been led in Paris, came to the United States to compose and to teach (in New York, in Cleveland, in Berkeley, California). On the verge of the same year Edgard Varèse arrived, a pupil of Vincent d'Indy and of Albert Roussel, a friend of Busoni and Debussy, already at thirty-three a leader in the advance-guard.

Henry Cowell, in California, had been performing as early as 1912 piano pieces involving tone-clusters. And Charles Griffes, a French-style impressionist (though he had actually studied in Berlin) in the late 1910s came out of hiding (he had been teaching in a boys' school) with songs, piano pieces, some highly poetic orchestral compositions expertly scored, and a shockingly original piano sonata. Another hidden composer, Charles Ives, who had since 1900 been working mostly in secret, in 1919 actually published one of his larger works, the now famous "Concord" Sonata.

At the end of World War I, Hill in Boston, Mason in New York, John Alden Carpenter in Chicago, and John Powell from Virginia were the major American composers of French formation, Hill and Mason being, along with Bloch, teachers of the brighter young. Percy Goetschius (1853–1943), a German-schooled theorist of great learning, was the chief preceptor for music writing at New York's Institute of Musical Art between

1905 and 1925; but his influence did not survive the 1920s, though till eighty he continued to publish textbooks. Chadwick, Mac-Dowell, and Parker throughout the 1910s and '20s continued to be performed; but their influence was waning. The 1910–20 decade left us strong works by Bloch, by Cowell, by Ives, by Ruggles, by Griffes, perhaps by others. It also left us a French-based pedagogy of composition and, in Ives and Varèse, the example of an ambitious and hard-headed left-wing or experimental school. Both achievements have lasted well beyond mid-century. And it is thanks to them that American music has since 1920 pursued a development parallel to that of Europe and sometimes leading Europe, as in the case of John Cage during the 1950s.

If the 1910s were characterized not only by changes in the teaching of composition but also by the appearance of radically modernist composers, many of whom did not become known till later, the 1920s, on the other hand, saw a modernist movement organized for the presentation of its own works along with the latest creations from Europe. The International Composers' Guild, beginning in 1922, offered music by its chief promoters Edgard Varèse and Carlos Salzedo; and their concerts, which continued till 1927, included the work of Ruggles and other radical Americans along with foreign novelties by Milhaud, Berg, de Falla, Chavez, Malipiero, Ravel, Stravinsky, Schoenberg, and Webern. Its successor, the League of Composers, founded in 1923, continued a similar policy, included stage works, and after 1933 commissioned composers. The League's remarkably well-edited magazine, *Modern Music*, which covered contemporary music internationally, survived till 1947.

In the very early years of the 1920s, Griffes died and Ives ceased to compose. Cowell, Varèse, and George Antheil continued a modernist line as pioneers in the use of nonclassical sounds and of rhythmic innovation. Carl Ruggles was the author of short works high in dissonance content, achieved through chromatic atonality, that sustained a degree of tension among the interval relations unmatched by any music being written in Europe. To this day it has not lost its excitement; nor has that of Varèse. Cowell's best work, mostly composed after 1940, came to be less radical than its beginnings, evoking with tenderness

6

nineteenth-century rural America and sometimes, as an ethnographer, the traditional musics of Asia.

The 1920s saw also the founding of three remarkable music schools—the Juilliard in New York, the Curtis in Philadelphia, and the Eastman in Rochester, New York. It also saw the rise to fame of Nadia Boulanger in Paris as a teacher of Americans. Beginning in 1921 with Aaron Copland and myself, then Walter Piston, Roy Harris, and Elliott Carter, eventually nearly everybody of my generation studied with her. The American composers who have not passed through her studio mostly belong to a younger generation or to the twelve-tone school. Other exceptions are Samuel Barber, William Schuman, Lou Harrison, and John Cage.

The successful careers of Copland and of Roger Sessions also began in this decade, the end of it leaving American music with a beginning repertory of modernistic orchestral works, many of them recognizably American in feeling. The continuity of this production and the later symphonic contributions of Roy Harris, Randall Thompson, Walter Piston, and William Schuman proved the sound schooling and expressive powers of the American composers who matured in the '20s and '30s. These are in fact, along with Copland and Sessions, today's older masters; and very little of their music has ceased to communicate.

The 1930s witnessed an unprecedented expansion of the symphony orchestra into virtually every small town, every college and high school. According to one study there were by 1937 no fewer than 30,000 of them, all practicing classical and modern repertory and all giving public concerts. And they played American music, because Americans naturally enjoy American music until they have been taught not to. Already, moreover, there was lots of it to play and to enjoy.

So it came about that with the symphonic territory conquered, pacified, and under cultivation, restless spirits undertook a new invasion, that of the stage. Now Americans had been writing operas and getting them produced since back in the other century. Chadwick, Parker, Frederick Converse, de Koven, Victor Herbert, Henry Hadley, Charles Wakefield Cadman, and Deems Taylor had all worked for the lyric stage, but not memorably. Their operas, though history, are today no part of repertory.

7

The first opera to break new stage ground was my own *Four Saints in Three Acts*, composed to a text by Gertrude Stein in 1928, produced in '34. This was followed in 1935 by George Gershwin's *Porgy and Bess* and in 1937 by Marc Blitzstein's *The Cradle Will Rock*. In the decade's last years Gian-Carlo Menotti, an Italian trained in America, and Douglas Moore, an American schooled in France, began, with *Amelia at the Ball* and with *The Devil and Daniel Webster*, operatic careers that have extended for over thirty years and beyond our frontier. Since that time Roger Sessions, Hugo Weisgall, Gunther Schuller, Samuel Barber, and Peggy Glanville-Hicks have given us practical works in the operatic format. American opera, though subject to the inherent weakness of most opera today—which lies in its failure to coordinate serious texts with serious music—has since 1934 aspired toward making its story playable on a stage, and keeping the language of it clear to an English-speaking public. Our best works have gone that far.

Around 1930 an invention for combining sound with films had made musical planning urgent for that medium. "The industry," as Hollywood used to call itself, early employed quite competent musicians for this task, mostly German-trained, and then hamstrung them by demanding that the music remain "neutral." This effect was obtained by a casual employment of the Wagnerian *leitmotif*, by drenching the whole in rich orchestral textures, and by avoiding musical characterization, which might have caused a loss of glamour in star rôles. France and Russia were producing a livelier collaboration by using composers more up-to-date musically, such as Darius Milhaud and Arthur Honegger and Serge Prokofiev and the relatively unknown Soviet musician named Y. Stolyar who created such an imaginative musical ending for the first Russian sound-film, Nikolai Ekk's *The Road to Life*. Film "musicals," aspiring little further than to plug commercial songs, were about the same everywhere. And nowhere were real blues or jazz employed, since these styles, through their amazing power to reject impurities, were resistant to standardization.

In the United States it was the "documentary," often government subsidized, that first gave composers a chance to try out their powers. In 1936 and '37 I wrote scores for two films by

Pare Lorentz—*The Plough that Broke the Plains* and *The River* —that have become historical (for they are still widely circulated) and that influenced "the industry." Their first influence on the industry was to cause the engagement of Aaron Copland as composer for the film version of John Steinbeck's *Of Mice and Men.* This music, along with Copland's later scores for *The Red Pony* and *The Heiress,* are as close to first-class musico-dramatic workmanship as has yet been achieved in America under industry conditions. George Antheil, in those same years, labored manfully to introduce direct expressivity into film music, though without complete success. But Copland and I had proved it could be done, and Leonard Bernstein later wrote picturesque music for *On the Waterfront.* Also Gail Kubik, in *Gerald Mc-Boing-Boing,* a wartime cartoon, had neatly underlined the comedy. In 1949 I received a Pulitzer Award—still today the only one ever given to a film score—for my contribution to Robert Flaherty's *Louisiana Story.*

The 1930s likewise saw American composers take on the ballet. My own *Filling Station,* of 1937, and Copland's *Billy the Kid,* of 1938, are repertory pieces. And these were followed in the next decade by successful dance works from Schuman, Barber, Dello Joio, Bernstein, and Morton Gould. Into all of these theatre domains—the opera, the films, the dance—the break-through into viability must be credited to my work, if only on grounds of priority.

The 1930s, moreover, became our finest period in the creation and the singing of blues. They also invented a variant of jazz called swing and developed a species of partly scored jazz for bands larger than chamber-music size. A vigorous time it was, with every year new operas, films, and ballets, and with the symphony concerts constantly offering not only fresh music by new composers but also some of their finest by already maturing ones like Copland and Roy Harris, whose Third Symphony remains to this day America's most convincing product in that form.

The 1940s brought John Cage from California to New York, where he reinvigorated music's left wing, which had lost its revolutionary fervor. Before the decade was out he had also visited the new radicals in Europe and shown them possibilities they had not known regarding rhythmic structure. Later he taught them the use of random choices in writing music, a method that led them out of the unserviceable complexity that had developed with multiple-row composition, a method of writing in which not only the sequence of pitches is determined, as in classical dodecaphony, by a prechosen order, but all of music's other variables—heights, loudnesses, rests, note-lengths, methods of attack and release—are made to follow also a numerical pattern.

During this same time, the Second World War time, the European masters Hindemith, Křenek, Milhaud, and Schoenberg were teaching in America, as was also Nadia Boulanger. But none of their pupils excepting Cage, who had worked with Schoenberg, proved ready to cope on equality with the new musical energies that burst forth in Europe right after the war under the leadership of Pierre Boulez. The older Americans during this time were writing more symphonies, more ballets, more operas, reproducing their kind through teaching, expanding the repertory, exploring the fuller possibilities of the fields they had opened in the '20s and '30s.

By the end of the 1940s American composers were numerous and fecund, but essentially conservative as viewed from post-war Europe. Around 1950 a new spurt took place, and it took place everywhere. In Europe novelty took the form of electronic composition. In America it produced a new academicism, a modified dodecaphony aimed at producing within a near-atonal texture a maximum of thematic and rhythmic complexity. Elliott Carter and Roger Sessions were the leaders of this new conservatism, and their work has proved more subtle and more sophisticated than that of almost any Europeans working in similar vein. Multiple serialism has been tried very little in America, almost not at all, in fact; and our electronic production, having developed later than the European, is still small in volume, though this situation seems not likely to persist. In Europe, practically all electronic music is created in state-owned radio establishments (chiefly Paris, Cologne, and Milan) where engineers and equipment are furnished free to properly introduced composers. Hence many have tried out the medium and some have produced quite original work. Few, however, have remained long enough in the field to become specialists, excepting only the engineers themselves, several of whom in France have become composing engineers. In America there has been virtually no work done at all at the radio centers and very little private electronic composition, on account of its high costs. In the universities, on the other hand, there have long been calculating-machines; and since 1959 an R.C.A. synthesizer has been available to specially chosen students at Columbia University. It is not available, however, to outsiders; nor is in general the equipment at other universities. As a result, our composers in charge—Vladimir Ussachevsky, Otto Luening, and Milton Babbitt at Columbia, for instance—have by their very persistence, plus their salaried status, become engineer composers. Of late a cheaper instrument, the Moog synthesizer, has put electronic composition at the disposal of almost anyone; and with this new facility we may be about to see thousands of amateurs turning out electronic tapes.

At present virtually every experimental group working in the United States seems to be seated in a university, and possibly a certain scholastic timidity may be causing these composers to shun radical expressive aims. In Europe they are pretty firmly united toward creating a music of the Common Market, an idiom free from nationalistic propaganda and folkloric charm. They also seem to be in their most advanced work preoccupied with bringing to apotheosis the experiments with noise composition that were started by the Italian Futurists around 1910. And I think we may include electronic tape composition in this category.

The consistency of the European effort may well come from a conviction that the Western tonal system had by 1914 ended its evolution. This idea, I may add, is far more commonly accepted in Europe than in the United States, where believing it to be true could make our whole maturity appear as a development that occurred too late in history to be of value. Surely the European effort toward writing atonal music not for noise-making instruments but for those whose design had been perfected over centuries for avoiding tonal obfuscation has been equally a waste of effort, save possibly for proving it could be done. Furthermore, the non-tonal materials such as noise, electronically produced or not, require non-tonal methods for structuring a continuity (scales and intervals will not serve); and for this there is little available beyond an arithmetic of rhythms and durations. Whether chronometrics, calculated or random, can give psychological progress to a series of sounds that are unrelated acoustically, is a matter open to some doubt. Nevertheless, it must be tried, and thoroughly; indeed the effort is well advanced in our universities, always inclined to subsidize art that connects with engineering.

Meanwhile, certain Americans have been experimenting with another possible way out of the impasse created by the exhaustion of tonal resources, which is to learn oriental methods, in hope of producing somehow a fusion of systems that might re-energize both East and West. The Californians Henry Cowell, John Cage, and Lou Harrison have experimented with Chinese, Japanese, and Korean musical procedures, as the French composers have done with Indonesian and with East Indian. Alan Hovhaness, a Bostonian of Armenian origins, has worked with Middle East materials and a bit with Japanese. And Peggy Glanville-Hicks, Australian by birth, has made for herself out of elements from India, North Africa, and Greece a musical idiom that has proved useful in ballet, and surprisingly so for English-language opera. There is already in America a body of work influenced by Lou Harrison that represents a return to linear composition without the interference of either chords or tempered intervals, and I must say the sound of it is vigorous. It might be ever so welcome that music should turn again toward meaning, and toward the expressive delights possible through scales of different tunings. But the work I know in that direction is still experimental. And certainly no fusion of East and West has yet occurred.

What has occurred is a maturity whereby America is now a music-producing country as well as a music-consuming one. We have rich folk sources and in jazz a major folk art. We have first-class libraries, historians, pedagogues, and performers. We have a population quite expert at listening and terrifyingly addicted to it. And we enjoy the rare advantage of possessing excellent composers of all ages and all schools. No other country in the world, save France, has that. And it does give strength, whether for holding fast against the liquidation of standards or for moving forward, even though all movement may be, as it seems right now, either European-led toward European expressive goals or dominated, as in America, by engineering games.

2. American Musical Traits

Europe's grandest accomplishment in music, after those early Christian centuries when it wrenched itself away from Asia, has been to stage itself as a series of epochs. Its musical continuity therefore seems a jumpy one, just as its political history does. It is rather as if the late Roman times through Charlemagne, the Dark Ages, the medieval Renaissance, the classical Renaissance, the Protestant Reformation with its religious wars, the Baroque age with its high royal prestige, and Romanticism's revolt against exactly that, producing patriotic and libertarian revolutions— as if all these intensely highlighted moments were merely turns in a variety show of which the only unity is an unchanging geological décor. The tent remains the same, but each act brings surprise.

The art of rehearsing these changes sub rosa and then mounting them as shows, each in a freshly designed set and with appropriate music, is Europe's genius for dramatizing history. That special showmanship, moreover (plus nowadays learned program-notes about "forerunners" and "influences") almost conceals the lack of continuity. The fact remains, nevertheless, that despite those publicized researches, the entr'actes do not explain the high moments. Forgetting the jumps, lest ignorance be alleged, that seem to exist between plainsong, organum, and Renaissance polyphony, the more recent parts of history, those we can almost remember, also include great chasms. From Bach to Haydn, Handel to Mozart, Beethoven (though clearly out of Haydn) miraculously to Wagner, and from Wagner to Debussy, nothing is really explained. Each splendid kind acts merely like itself and appears to us, as it must have done to the contemporaries, profoundly of its time and place.

Now when it was suggested in the preceding chapter that Europe's major effort in today's musical modernism is to depict the new Europe, the Common Market, the hope for a Western solidarity, it was not intended to suggest that the Romantic afflatus has collapsed. It is still, in fact, the pathos content of Russian music, of much of German, and of almost all English. It was the expressive aspiration too of Schoenberg and Alban Berg and for the most part of Anton Webern. Even in America one encounters this, and not only among conservatives but also in many who view themselves as far-outs. Only recently I heard an orchestral work that involved five conductors, random entrances, electronic tapes, piano clusters, and lots of percussion, all of it making a great clatter thoroughly up-to-date. But its expressive model could only have been the symphonies of Mahler, so little of slow-feeling America and so much of tumultuous Vienna was recalled by its risings and fallings.

American music has too short a history to be considered as a series of scenes; there is scarcely enough of it even to make a narrative. I have already sought to identify it as a twentieth-century show beginning about 1910. So let us consider that show as still going on. What story it tells, if any, I do not know, being a part of it. But examined for detail, the music does betray characteristics, family traits, even hemispheric similarities by which our North American music resembles South American and Caribbean almost more than it does that of Europe.

In attempting to describe the characteristics that make American music American, I am not assuming that it is essentially different from European music. Just as North American literature is a branch of English literature, and the South American literatures are branches of Spanish and Portuguese, music in the Americas is the child of Western Europe, indeed of a musically mature Western Europe. The long evolution extending from early Christian psalmody to Handel and Bach had already produced a grammar of style and a vocabulary of feeling well before America began to speak this musical language with any ease.

The sources of American practice in harmony, counterpoint,

orchestration methods, and musical structure are therefore European, and indeed chiefly continental European. The tune content of American music, however, has tended more and more in the last fifty years to be derived from the British Isles. There had been earlier on the part of our better educated composers a tendency to imitate the contours of the German masters and of Italian opera. And there has long been some utilization for picturesque purposes of Caribbean songs and dances Franco–Spanish in origin. But since American music became adult and aware, around 1910, say, we have been less and less involved with the expressive urgencies of continental Europe and more and more with our own heritage of feeling.

This heritage has come to us mainly from England, Ireland, Scotland, and Wales. Our non-British settlers have relinquished their native poetry and tunes, preserving these in family or community use only so long as they have continued to speak the languages they spoke when they came here, which is usually just one generation. The melting-pot theory of American life is not, it would seem, a true picture. Because the English-language group has from the beginning absorbed to itself, by means of language, all the others, giving to them its ethics and customs and even going so far as to lend them its racial memories, its folklore, folkways, legends, faiths, and aspirations.

Our immigrants' eagerness for absorption is proved by their constant preoccupation with Shakers and Quakers, with Indians and cowboys, with black men from the swamps and white Protestant mountaineers. Such composers, furthermore, though many of them sons of immigrant parents, show a notable lack of yearning toward their European origins. And our blacks have followed a similar pattern. Brought to our land speaking many African languages and practicing many religions, they renounced all those, adopted us as their own, and became an English-speaking Christian people. They took on, in doing so, our hymns and our poetry. Our blacks had formerly little contact with African music and African art, or till after the 1950s with African political aspirations. They are a part of us; and our Spanish-speaking fellow-citizens in New Mexico refer to them as "Anglos."

Our Anglo-American folklore is vast, varied, and rich. The nourishment it has given to our composers is inestimable, no matter what any composer's geographical or religious origins. At the same time, however, just as some of these have adopted voluntarily the Anglo-Celtic background, almost all of our composers have in one way or another seized upon musical elements from more exotic sources.

From Africa has come to us a subtlety in the use of percussion instruments. For African ways of performing music remain in our South and in the Caribbean, though of the African tunes, not much has survived. Even our well-known tendency toward syncopated rhythm is not African. It is the Scottish snap, straight out of bagpipes by way of hymns. Polyrhythms and multiple metrics, on the other hand, are more highly developed in Africa than here; and these we have adopted from travel and from our studies in musical ethnography.

Out of China and Japan there have come, through the West Coast, the concept of polymodality and the deep satisfactions of non-tempered intervals and non-vibrato execution. On top of our Negro-inspired love of percussion in general, there has come from our Asian contacts a devotion to small, delicate drums and to all sizes of gongs. Africa and Asia meet in America not only on the percussive level, but also in the practice of teasing a tone. The ornamental slide and the blue note, the defining of true intervals by deliberately playing or singing all round them, these are as common to our blues and jazz musicians and to our back-country hymn–singers as they are characteristic of Korean and Japanese court music, which has so often appealed to composers of West Coast upbringing.

And now I am going to venture out on grounds less charted than those of musical syntax and picturesque additions. I want to find the connection between America's musical composition and her musical performing style. By 1910 the American orchestras, soloists, and schools had, with the help of European teachers, mastered the European performing tradition and been admitted to it. And if their work bore traces of a non-European accent, these were no source of pride. Every effort was made indeed to perform German, French, or Italian music as it was performed in the country of its origin.

On the other hand, young musicians here were passing their childhood in contact with a rich background of hymns and old songs, with the sophisticated art of ragtime piano playing, and with the powerfully burgeoning force of jazz all round them. And to top off this gamey nourishment, there had become available at the same time a method for digesting it.

This method had been found in the new French music, which was exciting to all, and in the just-discovered French pedagogy of composition, then being introduced at Harvard and at Columbia University. German teaching, based on Bach through Brahms and Wagner, had dealt almost wholly with Romantic feelings and with Romantic flexibilities in rhythm. Debussy, his immediate forbears and his French contemporaries, it could neither analyse nor perform convincingly. German teaching still posed as music's universal system; but the American musician, during World War I, punctured that pretense. The classical German composers were not dethroned, of course; but the German pedagogues were. And since French music could now be admired right along with German, and since the French tradition had always encouraged the absorption of exciting influences, it became possible for an educated American musician to incorporate into his musical vocabulary the non-canonical but deeply familiar musical ways of his own grass-roots. At this point, and we are now moving into the 1920s, an American accent in music was no longer a fault of taste; it was beginning to be a source of style.

Let us examine this American accent. The constant presence of dancing (both square dancing and round dancing), the metrical discipline of ragtime piano playing, the tendencies in our folk singing and our hymn singing toward a compulsive rhythm— all these elements have given us the habit of a steady beat and a remarkable ability in performance to sustain such a beat.

From the steady beat comes an appetite, if only to relieve monotony, for irregularly-spaced stress accents. The tension of free stress-patterns heard against a steady meter creates an energy that has been rare in music since Beethoven's death. And although this dynamism reaches its highest point in jazz, I find it also present in most of the American art music composed since 1920, no matter what may be the other stylistic sources of that music. In its last few years, even twelve-tone composition was showing here more interest in solving its rhythmic dilemma (for indeed it always had one) through the laying on of jazzy rhythms than through rhythmic serialization, which was the European way. For jazz can set off energy, and that we like; but a row of rhythms, an ordering of durations, is forever static.

Indeed I think you will find, if you listen carefully to American music as performed by American artists, that a very large part of what has been composed in the last forty years assumes the existence, whether or not this is overtly present at all times in the sound, of a steady continuity of eighth-notes, on top of which other metrical patterns, regular and irregular, lead an independent life.

And there are further extensions of the American way, none of which could exist if a steady beat were not constantly there. One is the large amount of syncopation present. And syncopation, as Bach and Haydn and Beethoven knew, cannot exist unless the beat is steady. Another is the frequence of the non-accelerating crescendo and of its opposite, the non-retarding diminuendo. European musicians have constantly remarked this prevalence in American performance. The phenomenon is virtually unknown in Europe except in pieces that imitate marching armies. But the American, unless some European musical concept interferes, inclines by instinct to keep his rhythm patterns independent of volume patterns.

Elliott Carter has devised a refinement in scoring which he calls "rhythmic modulation." This is a progressive changing of the basic time-beat by easy arithmetical relations in such a consistent way that lengthy accelerations and retards can be operated almost imperceptibly. The result is ever so striking, especially if thematic transformations govern the tempo changes.

The constant presence in American performance of a basic time-unit has created also a new approach to musical declamation. The possibility of executing with precision the varied durations of both vowels and consonants has made setting prose as easy as setting rhymed verse. It has facilitated, moreover, the use of phonetic distortion without loss of clarity. Indeed, distortion of the normal cadence is cardinal both to the creation of comic effects and to reproducing in grand opera the accents of passion. Curiously enough, the most extreme example of this new prosodic declamation is *The Rake's Progress* by Stravinsky, who would not have needed America to arrive at it. For the steady

19

beat is also a Russian habit. And the rhythmically independent vocal line he could have constructed after examples in Debussy's *Pelléas* and in Satie's *Socrate*. But his application of these elements to the setting of English do come out surprisingly comprehensible and almost idiomatic.

The characteristics of American music that I have tried to describe will not invariably be found applicable to the music of Chadwick or Parker or MacDowell, though they do fit the music of Charles Ives. They are present in some degree, I think, in almost everything written after 1925. And they continue to be present, though minimally, in our twelve-tone music, for all its willful subservience to European Romanticism.

Romanticism in its European sense is a period that America never passed through. It is therefore an experience of which Americans bear no group memory. Just possibly the disillusion of today's youth—based in Europe on defeat in World War II, in America on defeats in Asia, and everywhere on fear of the Doomsday Machine—may be producing quite independently of historic Romanticism new patterns of violence and of emotional regression. It may also be that even under seemingly parallel pressures the ways of Europe and America are diverging. In music, I am inclined to suspect that they are. It is not to be imagined that the American characteristics I have described wholly define American music; they merely itemize a few ways in which it differs from the music of Europe. All, of course, are superficial compared to the similarities that inevitably mark the products of a common tradition.

For all their common technical tradition, however, as of right now Europe and America are working at quite separate expressive problems. The European advanced composers are seeking to create an international speech devoid of local, national, or folkloric reference. Today's new music in Europe, whether written by French, Italian, German, or other composers, and whether performed in Paris, Milan, or the Rhineland cities, is an international idiom as abstract as the coal and steel reports from Luxembourg.

That kind of music is practiced here too, though our composers practicing it seem less determined to succeed with it than their European colleagues. Even electronic music, which one might have expected our engineering-minded young to adopt early, has been taken up only in the last ten years, though it has existed in Europe since 1945. Merely to cite names will make my point, I think. Since the death of Edgard Varèse, nobody in America is writing "advanced" music at the level of Stockhausen, Boulez, or Xenakis, not to mention six to a dozen lesser stars on the European team.

What Americans are wrestling with chiefly (and the British too) is opera—trying to make our language serviceable for serious dramatico-musical expression. I cannot predict the success or failure of this enterprise. I merely point out that American music, having become by now a musical speech notably different from European, is testing its maturity on the problem that has ever been the final test of a musical idiom, namely, can you put it on the stage?

That, I think, is what American musicians are mainly set on finding out.

3. The Ives Case

America's most remarkable native contributors to our century's music, Charles Ives and Carl Ruggles, were born in New England and grew up there. Their remarkableness comes not only from strong personalities but also from the fact that almost alone among New England composers (Henry Gilbert, 1868–1928, was another exception) they never got seriously involved with teaching. Ruggles will be our subject later; for now, let us examine his more popular contemporary.

Charles Ives started life in 1874 at Danbury, Connecticut, an upland rural county seat manufacturing felt hats. He had for father a bandmaster, a Civil War veteran who trained his son's ear and hand and who exposed him at the same time to all the musical pop-art of his day—dance tunes, sentimental songs, darnfool ditties, revival hymns, and patriotic marches. Undergraduate years at Yale, with the expert instruction of Horatio Parker, turned him into a church organist and a well-based general musician. Throughout this time his student works and other youthful pieces passed for wild, and no doubt would today (*vide* the horseplay of his Variations on "America" for organ, composed at eighteen).

Ives's music life quite early went underground, for fighting public sentiment was never his pattern. As a high-school boy he had captained the baseball team; at Yale he played varsity football and was elected to a senior society. He was completely successful at being a conventionally successful American boy. He did everything right, made good marks in school and college, offended no one, though being a musician was certainly no help to his acceptance. Wishing no part of a martyr's life, he worked in a New York insurance firm, later formed his own with a partner named Myrick, married his roommate's sister, wrote a textbook for insurance salesmen, made money, retired (effectively) at fifty-three. For a few years he had played church organs, held in fact an excellent post at New York's Central Presbyterian. But he seems to have learned quite early that reputable musicians in general viewed his compositions with such disapproval that fighting for position would have merely wasted his time. So he renounced all visible connection with music and kept his work a secret occupation known only to his wife and to a few close friends. His open life was that of a businessman, conventional, respected, impregnable to scrutiny. His secret life was that of a Romantic artist—wildly experimental, ambitious, unchanneled, undisciplined, and unafraid.

His years of most abundant outpouring were those from thirty to forty, roughly 1905 to 1915, though the full mature production covers five earlier years and three later, effectively ending at forty-four, when his health broke. After 1924, when he was fifty, he wrote one song (1925) and two accompaniments (1929) to melodies by his daughter; from 1927 he went rarely to his office and in 1930 he retired completely from business. His medical diagnosis has not been published; the weakened heart and incipient diabetes sometimes referred to seem insufficient to explain a life-change so radical and one which was maintained, with progressive deterioration of the nervous system, till the age of eighty. But the fact is clear that his mighty energies and towering determination were gone before his life as a grown man was one-third over. After that he reviewed, when able, the editing of his works, subsidized their publication, blessed younger composers with bits of money, and helped also his contemporary Ruggles, whose work he admired.

Ives never actually heard during his composing years any of his major orchestral works or choral projects. The piano sonatas, violin sonatas, works of chamber music, and songs—all of which he could no doubt hum or strum—may be accepted as more or less finished. I say more or less because quite often there are aleatory passages. But the larger orchestral and choral works— the Fourth Symphony, for example, requiring three instrumental bodies and three conductors—remained at his retirement merely plans. And if they all "come off" today more than handsomely, that is due to the loving editorial hands of Lou Harrison and Henry Cowell, among others, and to the no less loving conductor's hands of Lou Harrison, of Leonard Bernstein, and of Leopold Stokowski.

For Ives's music has attracted the admiration of discerning observers—of Mahler and Webern, of Stravinsky and Schoenberg, of Aaron Copland, John Cage, Elliott Carter, and lately of the English composer-historian Wilfrid Mellers, as well as the devotion of his pianist-editor John Kirkpatrick, who has not only performed and recorded the major piano works, including the massive "Concord" Sonata, but actually catalogued every scrap of the seemingly inexhaustible Ives manuscripts. The publication of this sonata in 1919, followed in 1924 by 114 Songs (both printed at the author's expense) marked Ives's official emergence from clandestinity and his retirement from composition. His music writing had never, of course, been entirely secret. He had occasionally shown something to a European virtuoso of the piano or violin, who would declare it hopeless; and in 1910 Gustav Mahler, then conductor of the New York Philharmonic, had proposed to play his First Symphony in Germany, a promise cancelled in 1911 by Mahler's death. But for the most part his partisans were to declare their faith far later, since access to his works and a favorable climate for admiring them were not available till after World War I.

Ives has frequently been cited by analysts for his early (so early indeed that in many cases it would seem the very first) consistent use of free dissonant counterpoint, of multiple metrics, of polychordal and polytonal harmonic textures, of percussively conceived tone-clusters and chord-clusters, and of stereophonic orchestral effects requiring several conductors. Practically all these devices, as he employed them, are describable as free, since whatever formal patterning is involved (and very often there is none) has been chosen for each expressive occasion. Ives never explored harmonic, tonal, or rhythmic simultaneities for their intrinsic complexity, as the European composers did who were to follow his example so closely in time (all unaware of him). His temporal precedence has remained therefore a historical curiosity without relation to such systematic investigations of polyharmony, polytonality, and polyrhythm as occurred in the work of Richard Strauss and Debussy, subsequently in that of Igor Stravinsky and Darius Milhaud, of Arnold Schoenberg's pupils, and of Edgard Varèse.

The popularity of Ives's music and its present wide distribution by performance and recording in America, even somewhat in Europe, are actually a response to the direct expressivity of certain works. *The Housatonic at Stockbridge,* for instance, is an impressionistic evocation, an orchestral landscape piece about a river, that even Europeans can enjoy. Longer works such as the Second (or "Concord") Piano Sonata and the Fourth Symphony, though actually structured for holding attention, are seemingly improvisational (even aleatoric) in a way that today's youth finds irresistible for effects of grandeur and chaos. And the jamborees of patriotic marches and evangelical hymns that climax *Putnam's Camp,* the Second Symphony, and many another calling forth of early memories are so deeply nostalgic for Americans that the California critic Peter Yates could sum them up as the only American music that makes him cry.

The present writer too has wept over these. He is less impressed, however, by the "Concord" Sonata, with its constant piling of Pelion on Ossa. It has been his experience that Ives's work in general, though thoroughly interesting to inspect, frequently comes out in sound less well than it looks on the page. Some of this disappointment comes from musical materials which, although intrinsically interesting for appearing to be both highly spontaneous and highly complex, seem to be only casually felt. Their extensive repetition in sequences and other structural layouts would tend to reinforce this suspicion, since real spontaneity does not repeat itself. The opening of the "Concord" Sonata is a case in point. Here is improvisational and, though busy enough, quite easy-going material that simply will not develop; it only "riffs," makes sequences. And if it gets transformed as it goes along, its successive states are as casually conceived as the first; none sticks in memory as an evolving thought.

Another sort of material, Ives's simplest, can be found in certain of the songs. These seem so aptly related to the words both by sentiment and by a naturalistic declamation (for which he had a gift) that one expects almost any of them, embellished as they so often are by an inventive accompaniment, to be a jewel. And yet they do not, will not, as we say, come off. Again there has been dilution, a casual filling-in of measures that would have needed for full intensity an unrelenting tinycraft, thought through and hand-made, such as one finds in Schubert, who was surely his model for song-writing just as Beethoven admittedly was for the larger instrumental statements. Ives's weakness is seldom in the vocal line, which is musically sensitive even when the poetry is poor, but quite regularly in the piano part, which fails to interweave, harmonically or rhythmically, with the voice. As a result it seems to be following the melody rather than providing a structure for it.

Among the rewarding songs is *Two Little Flowers,* composed in 1921 to a poem by his wife, a simple piece in the lieder style of Brahms, say, or Robert Franz. But even here the harmony can seem casual unless carried forward in performance by a rhythmic thrust.

Paracelsus, also for voice and piano, composed in 1921 to excerpts from Browning, begins with an instrumental page of the highest rhythmic and tonal complexity (actually a quotation from Ives's "Browning" Overture). According to the analysis of this work in *Charles Ives and His Music* by Henry and Sidney Cowell, it is thematically and motivically integrated to ideas expressed in the poem. Nevertheless, the music loses impetus when the poetry begins. Though the voice declaims eloquently, the piano seems to wait for it. The free rhythms in both parts support no clear trajectory, but leave to the singer all responsibility for carrying the music forward.

This unequal and ultimately ineffectual division of labor shows up most clearly in two songs of folkloric appeal—*Charlie Rutledge* of 1914–15 (on a cowboy ballad) and *General William Booth Enters Heaven* of 1914 (out of Vachel Lindsay). The words in both have a tendency to announce the music's illustrative effects rather than to comment on them, a vaudeville routine ill-suited to serious music. To invent examples: "I hear a bird," followed by a piano trill, or "His big bass drum" (boom boom) are comic effects. Only the reverse procedure can properly evoke. *Charlie Rutledge,* moreover, is over-dramatized in the voice. A deadpan cowboy lilt against a dramatic piano-part might have turned the trick. Also, Vachel Lindsay's not entirely ingenuous apotheosis of a Salvation Army leader would surely have benefited by a bit of musical irony. With the bass-drum-like boombooms and the triumphal hymn so frankly overt, the piece can become an embarrassing game of let's-play-revival-meeting.

Ives in his writings about music made a point of preferring "substance" to "manner." And indeed throughout his work, in spite of references to gospel hymns and village bands, of massive tone-clusters and rhythmic asymmetries, there is virtually no method of writing consistently enough employed to justify a charge of "mannerism." He moves from method to method eclectically, as great composers have always done, to bring out meaning; and his imitations of choiring voices and bands and bugle calls are as literal as he can make them. His ingenuities toward exemplifying ethical principles and transcendental concepts through thematic invention I find less rewarding from the simple fact that they seem self-conscious, lacking in spontaneity. Moreover, they are sometimes not quite first-class; the effect desired is easier to recall than the music itself.

In this sense, though there is no doctrinaire Romanticism of "form determined by content," neither is there any arriving at emotional or other fulfillment through strictly musical means, as in the classical *and* Romantic masters. By "substance" Ives means, I think, sincerity in the conception of musical pictures or ideas. He cannot mean the identity of a musical theme with what he hopes to express by means of it, for if he did the music would be stronger-knit around these ideas, whereas actually it tends to exist beside them like a gloss or commentary. When time shall have dissolved away his nostalgias and ethical aspirations, as they have largely done for Beethoven and for Bach and even for the descriptive leitmotifs of Wagner, what sheer musical reality will remain in Ives's larger works? Where will be the "substance" he wrote so eloquently about and desired so urgently? For all their breadth of concept and their gusto, I have no faith in them. Intentions are no guarantee of quality.

In remaining somewhat unimpressed by the Ives output in general—though there are certainly delicious moments and even perfect whole pieces, usually small, like the orchestral

Housatonic at Stockbridge and *The Unanswered Question,* possibly also the third of the "Harvest Home" chorales—the present writer has no wish to underesteem the aspiration, the constancy, and the sacrifice that Ives's musical life bears witness to. Nor to undervalue a creative achievement that posterity may prize. Actually, the man presents in music, as he did in life, two faces; on one side a man of noble thoughts, a brave and original genius, on the other a homespun Yankee tinkerer. For both are there; of that one can be sure. How they got to be there need not worry us, for every artist begins in a dichotomy. But how this could remain unresolved to the very end of his creative life might be of interest to speculate about.

Every artist's worklife has its strategy; without that there is no career. And we know from his own words that Ives, in renouncing music as a chief breadwinner, did not walk out on music. When he shortly came to renounce it as even a contributory source (through church jobs) he made that renouncement in order to save his leisure. We also know that busy as he was in business hours, and soundly successful, he still produced between the ages of twenty-four and forty-four a repertory of works larger by catalog than that of most masters. Sometimes these were corrected carefully; sometimes he threw scarcely decipherable pages over his shoulder and never looked into the piles of them. It is certain that parts of works are lost, probable that whole ones also are, and possible that others may have been destroyed by intent.

But for all his haste, he was not really careless. He labored with a fury unrelenting; he also held strongly by certain of his works and cherished prejudices violently sectarian about many other composers past and present, which he stated with wit and profanity. He valued his "Concord" Sonata so highly that after it was finished he wrote a book about it. This book, called *Essays Before a Sonata,* though it was actually written after, is less an explanation of the music than a hymn of praise to the men who were the inspiration of its four movements—Emerson, Hawthorne, Thoreau, and for comic relief the Alcotts. The greatest of these, for him, was Emerson; and there his confidence was so unquestioning that clearly for Ives the Unitarian preacher-essayist had replaced revealed religion. Would that we all could thus say, "I believe!" But the fact that Ives did have this source of faith—along with insurance, of which he also wrote a book in praise—helps us to picture the years of his complete devotion to music and to business, a devotion shared only with the domestic affections—with a wife named Harmony and an adopted daughter, neither of whom caused him any trouble or took much time.

His aspiration to be a great composer would be clear from the *Essays* if it were not equally revealed on every page of his music. And a need for working abundantly to accomplish this is proved by both the voluminousness of his production and the state of his manuscripts. This need must also have led him to a plan. For a man of his ability and known powers of organization to go all self-indulgent and careless during his twenty best years, and regarding music, which was very nearly his whole private life, is not believable. It must be that he simply decided to pour forth his inspiration at all times, finishing off in clean score only such works as demanded that and leaving the rest to be copied out in his retirement years.

Retirement from composition came earlier than he had expected, and the First World War would seem to have hastened his breakdown. His Emersonian confidence in democracy through the "over-soul," and his business-based optimism derived from an idealistic view of insurance, were shaken by Europe's suddenly revealed corruption and her suicidal holocaust, which America had joined. So that when his bodily strength, after years of overstrain, collapsed in 1918, something also happened to the brain. He may have seemed to be just physically ill, but his creative life was arrested.

It is possible to imagine this arrest as an acceptable, though unplanned, consequence of the total strategy. For Ives began immediately to behave with regard to his works as if his retirement from music had been foreseen. He initiated their publication, subsidized their performance, aided young men whose devotion to them and pity for him caused them to spend untold hours on their cataloguing, editing, and promotion. Since it was clear to all, including himself, that he would not write again, his *oeuvre* came to be treated like those of the immortal dead. So confidently, in fact, that by the time of his actual death in 1954 the congress of devoted younger men which was to take care of itemiza-

tion, description, biography, analysis, and praise had so far done
its work that the subject of this might well have been satisfied to
wind up his campaign. He had composed voluminously and without fear; later he had witnessed the well-timed issuance of his
works, their performance, publication, and recording. Not the
present high state of their fame, of course, but enough to show
that an apotheosis had begun.

There is no reproach to such a strategy, nor much probability
that the sequence of events was accidental. An artist's life is
never accidental, least of all its tragic aspects. And the tragic
aspect of Ives is neither his long and happy domestic existence
nor his short, abundant, and successful-within-his-own-time creative life. It is the fatal scars left on virtually all his music by a
divided allegiance. Business may be a less exacting mistress than
the Muse, what with staffs and partners to correct your haste.
But Ives's music does show the marks of haste, and also of
limited reflection. Dividing himself as he did, he had to run that
risk. I doubt that he knew, either young or later, how great a
risk it was. For if he had, would he have dared to make the ploy
for both God *and* Mammon?

I prefer to think he did not, that the transcendental optimist
and all-American success boy was simply trying to have everything, and at no cost save the strenuous life. Then the darker
aspects of the world, which he had avoided ever and of which
his music, all health and exuberance, shows no trace, surfaced
with the First World War; and they put the fear of God into
him. He stopped composing, became an invalid, retired from
business, and abandoned all his earnings beyond what seemed to
him a competence. One view of the bottomless pit, plus a decent
income justifiably retained for his family, plus care taken for his
music's survival, all add up to a New England story complete
with personal devil, an angry God, and a maimed production.
Less maimed perhaps than that of his pedagogical contemporaries (though among those MacDowell may well survive him),
but maimed nevertheless. For it is not teaching that cripples; no
master has ever feared that. It is gentility; not giving one's all to
art.

30

4. Ruggles

There is nothing notably genteel about Carl Ruggles. He is a bohemian rather, who up to forty earned a living out of music, then found a patron on whose kindness he has lived for over fifty years, supporting also till her death a wife passionately loved and bringing up one son. He has also been for many years a landscape painter. Music he has followed from his youth without qualms about failure, poverty, disapproval, or what-will-people-say. Wiry, salty, disrespectful, and splendidly profane, he recalls the old hero of comic strips Popeye the Sailor, never doubtful of his relation to sea or soil.

A revealing story about him is the familiar one told by Henry Cowell twenty years ago. Having gone to see him in Vermont, Cowell arrived at the former schoolhouse that was Ruggles's studio and found him at the piano, playing the same chordal agglomerate over and over, as if to pound the very life out of it. After a time Cowell shouted, "What on earth are you doing to that chord? You've been playing it for at least an hour." Ruggles shouted back, "I'm giving it the test of time."

As of today, all of Ruggles's music has withstood that test, as has the man. His oldest surviving piece—a song to piano accompaniment composed in 1919—is more than fifty years old; his latest, from 1945, is twenty-five; and he himself, as I write, is ninety-four. His works have traveled in America and in Europe; and though they have not experienced the abrasions of popularity, they have been tested microscopically by the toughest analysts without any examiner finding anywhere a flaw. Except-

31

ing perhaps himself, since he has rescored some works several times before settling on their final sound and shape.

Born in 1876 of whaling folk on Cape Cod, he learned to play the violin in Boston and had lessons in the composer's craft at Harvard. Then he got experience of the orchestra in the good way, by conducting one for eleven years. That was in Minnesota. During all this learning time he wrote no music that he cared later to preserve.

There was some work done on an opera, its subject Gerhard Hauptmann's play *The Sunken Bell*; but this was never finished, Ruggles having gained through the effort a conviction that he had no talent for the stage. His earliest work that he has allowed to survive is the song called *Toys,* composed in 1919 at the age of forty-three. Over the next twenty years he produced virtually all his surviving repertory, each piece intensely compact, impeccably inspired, exactly perfect, and exactly like all the others in its method of workmanship.

This method, of which the closest model is the music that Arnold Schoenberg composed before World War I, can be classified among musical textures as non-differentiated secundal counterpoint. By non-differentiated I mean that the voices making up this counterpoint all resemble one another in both character and general shape; they are all saying the same thing and saying it in much the same way. This manner of writing music, whether practiced by Bach or by Palestrina or by Anton Webern, for all of whom it was their usual method, produces a homogeneity highly self-contained, and more picturesque than dramatic.

By secundal counterpoint I mean that the intervals present at the nodal points of the music (say roughly at the down-beats) are predominantly seconds and sevenths. This interval content distinguishes it from the music dominated by fourths and fifths (composed chiefly between the years 1200 and 1500, we call this music quintal) and from the music colored by thirds and sixths (the tertial) that followed the quintal for four centuries. Secundal writing, compared with quintal, which is rock-like, and with tertial, which is bland, produces through continuous dissonance a grainy texture that in most of Ruggles's music is homogenized, or made to blend, by the use of closely similar timbres, such as an all-string or all-brass instrumentation. And as happens in most of Bach, the music comes out polyphonic as to line but homophonic as to sound.

In spite, however, of all its homogeneity (exterior mark of its introspective nature) music like this is never quite without objective depiction. For observing this in Ruggles, the early song *Toys* is most revealing. The words, written by Ruggles himself, are:

> *Come here, little son, and I will play with you.*
> *See, I have brought you lovely toys.*
> *Painted ships,*
> *And trains of choo-choo cars, and a wondrous balloon,*
> *that floats, and floats, and floats, way up to the stars.*

Let us omit reference, save in passing, to the fact that the father seems to have let go of the balloon before his son could lay hands on it. Also, since stars are mentioned, that the play-hour seems to be taking place out of doors on a moonless night, a most unlikely circumstance. But these are literary quibbles.

Musically the piece, for all its steadily dissonant sound-texture, is illustrative throughout.

It begins with a gesture-like call in the pianoforte accompaniment, stated both before and after the summons, "Come here, little son and I will play with you."

The phrase "painted ships" is accompanied by a rocking motion that leads to a splash.

The "choo-choo" mention is followed by rhythmic sounds, low in the register and accelerating, that clearly picture a steam-driven locomotive getting up speed.

And the "balloon that floats" not only does so in the piano part, which arpeggiates upward chromatically, but also in the vocal line, which leaps and leaps till on the word "stars" it reaches high B-natural and stays there.

Similarly, the piece for strings called *Lilacs*, though I doubt whether any description quite so specific is intended, is all of short rounded lines at the top and of long gangling tentacular root-like curves in the bass.

And *Portals*, another string piece, has high-jutting points to it that might be either Gothic arches or simply man's aspiration. The quiet moment at the end of an otherwise energetic work could represent man's humility on entering the high portals; but if the earlier part is not the noble gates themselves but merely the soul of man climbing toward them, then the ending must represent him arrived and sitting down to rest. The motto on the score tells us nothing so specific; it merely asks, "What are those of the known but to ascend and enter the unknown?"

Angels, for seven muted trumpets and trombones, is quietly ecstatic from beginning to end, and the angels are not individualized. They are clearly a group, a choir perhaps. I do not even know whether they are singing; they may be merely standing close together and giving off light, as in the engravings of William Blake. Whatever is happening, they are doing it or being it together, for the instruments all pause together, breathe together, start up again together, as in a hymn. Whether this close order depicts a harmony of angels or merely one man singing about them in seven real parts is not important; it could be both. But in any case, the music's sentence structure, always clear in Ruggles, is nowhere more marked than in this work, where ecstasy is communicated through a series of statements about it, each with a beginning, a middle, and a tapered ending, and all separated from one another like formal periods.

The Sun Treader and *Organum,* both scored for large orchestra rather than for a small blended ensemble, achieve homogenization of sound through the constant doubling of strings by wind instruments. And this device, so dangerous in general to the achievement of variety, is here not monotonous, but eloquent rather, as if one speaker were carrying us along on winged oratory. The Ruggles counterpoint is there too, constantly chromatic, flowing, airily spaced but also compact and dissonant, and speaking, for all its rhythmic diversity, as with a single voice. This may be the voice of the sun treader, or it may be a picture of his actions; it matters little. What matters is that the piece go on. It lasts eighteen minutes (long for Ruggles) without any let-up of intensity. *Organum* is longish too, but less choreographic, more songful. Both are full of their message, which is apocalyptic, and yet systematically, intensely self-contained.

The way that Ruggles has of making his music always come out in non-symmetrical prose sentences—a planned spontaneity, one might call it—is not really in opposition to his preoccupation with ecstasy. For that ecstasy in the expression, that unrelenting luminosity of interval and sound, is needful for producing the quality that was his over-all intent and which he calls "the sublime." Now what does he mean, what does anybody mean, by "the sublime"? I should say that this word, when applied to a work of art, can only mean that the work expresses and hence tends to provoke a state of ecstasy so free from both skin sensuality and cerebral excitement, also so uniformly sustained, that the ecstasy can be thought of as sublimated into the kind of experience known as "mystical." Ruggles, in fact, once said as much, that "in all works there should be the quality we call mysticism. All the great composers have it."

The titles of his works and their explanatory mottos mostly tend to evoke, if not a mystical experience, at least the familiar cast and décor of religious visions—*Men and Mountains, Men and Angels, The Sun Treader, Vox Clamans in Deserto, Organum,* or, quite vaguely for once, just *Evocations.* These subjects, save for the presence of angels and for a voice from the wilderness, are not nearly so close to Christian mysticism as they are to pantheism, to a spiritual identification with nature such as can be called forth in almost any New Englander by the presence of lilacs, or of mountains measurable by the size of man.

But it is not the subjects of his ecstasy that create sublimity. Many a witness has gone dizzy looking at beauty. With Ruggles it is with the need for sublimity that dizziness ends and hard work begins. For there is no sublimity without perfection; and for Ruggles there is no perfection until every singing, soaring line, every subtle rhythm and prose period, every interval and every chord has received from his own laborious hands the test of time. There must be no gigantic proportions, no ornamental figurations, no garrulous runnings-on, no dramatization, no jokes, no undue sweetness, no invoking of music's history, no folksy charm, no edifying sentiments, no erotic frictions, no cerebral cadenzas, no brilliance, no show-off, and no modesty. There is nothing in his music but perfectly flexible melodies all perfectly placed so as to sound harmonious together, and along with these a consistently dissonant interval-texture, and a subtly irregular rhythm that avoids lilt.

The auditory beauty of Ruggles's music is unique. It actually sounds better than the early Schoenberg pieces, *Verklärte Nacht* and *Erwartung*, that are perhaps its model, almost I should say its only model. It sounds better because it is more carefully made. Its layout is more airy; no pitch gets in any other's way; the rhythm is more alive; it never treads water, only sun. It is by very hard work and all alone that this perfection has been attained. And it is through perfection, moreover, the intensely functioning refinement of every musical grain and chunk, every element of shape and planning, that a high energy potential has been both produced and held in check, like a dynamo with its complex insulation. And it is this powerful energy, straining to leap a blue-white arc toward any listener, that constitutes, I think, what Ruggles means by sublimity. It is no wonder that out of a ninety-year lifetime there remain fewer than a dozen pieces. Intensities like that cannot be improvised.

Wilfrid Mellers, comparing Ruggles to Arnold Schoenberg, has written in his book of praise to America, *Music in a New-Found Land,* that "both were amateur painters who, in their visual work, sought the expressionistic moment of vision. Both, in their music still more than in their painting, found that the disintegrated fragments of the psyche could be reintegrated only by a mystical act. Schoenberg, as a Viennese Jew, had an ancient religion and the spirit of Beethoven to help him; Ruggles had only the American wilderness and the austerities of Puritan New England. For this reason he sought freedom—from tonal bondage, from the harmonic straight-jacket, from conventionalized repetitions, from anything that sullied the immediacy and purity of existence—even more remorselessly than Schoenberg."

Ruggles's dilemma, of course, has been the perpetual dilemma of American composers. On one side lie genius and inspiration, on the other an almost complete lack of usable history. We have access to the European masters, to Bach and Mozart and Beethoven and Debussy, but only through their music; we cannot remember them nor reconstruct what they were thinking about; and what we *can* remember, through our documents and our forebears, is so different from anything Europe knows or ever knew that both to the European listener and to the American, naïf or learned, every inspiration is a scandal. A Frenchman or an Austrian of gifts can be fitted early into his country's immortality machine—nurtured, warmed for ripening, brought to market. An American of talent is from the beginning discouraged (or over-encouraged), bullied by family-life and by school-teachers, overworked, undertrained, sterilized by isolation or, worse, taken over by publicity, by the celebrity machine.

American composers have tried several solutions. One has been to fake a history; that is to say, to adopt some accepted European method of working and to hide behind it so effectively that the ignorant are impressed and the intellectuals immobilized. Horatio Parker, Edward MacDowell, and Walter Piston did this. And their inspiration, discolored by its own shield, lost personality and some of its meaning; but these men did write music of distinction that has not died.

Another way of facing the awful truth is to face it squarely— to discard the concept of distinction, to use any and all materials that come to hand and to use them in any context whatsoever. Walt Whitman did this in poetry, Charles Ives in music, also Henry Cowell in his early years. And though they mostly could not make their art support them, they produced in quantity and their inspirations were not deformed. By sacrificing the ideals of perfection and distinction, as well as all hope of professional encouragement—Ives actually for twenty years hiding away (and wisely, I think) from the danger of professional persecution—they achieved in their work an enormous authenticity.

Ruggles faced the dilemma in still another way, which was to slowly construct for himself a method for testing the strengths of musical materials and a system of building with them so complex, so at every point aware of tensile strengths and weaknesses, that by this seemingly neutral application of psychological and acoustic laws, works were constructed that are not only highly personal in content but that seem capable of resisting wear and time. Poe is a somewhat parallel case in letters. In music Elliott Carter is surely one. And in all three cases—Ruggles, Carter, and Poe—not only has authentic inspiration survived, but beauty and distinction have not been sacrificed. Such artists may wear their integrity like a chip on the shoulder, but it is real. Ambition, "that last infirmity," though it may torment their sleep, has been kept from their work. With Ruggles and Carter the output has been small; but no compromise has taken place, nor has any hindrance occurred to the artist's full ripening.

Good music, reputable and palatable, has been composed in all three of the circumstances I describe—by copying Europe, by working without rule, or by constructing a method—and I fancy that all three ways for getting around the American dilemma will continue to be used. For there is still no "spirit of Beethoven" here, either walking beside you down the street as he does in Vienna, or buried nearby in any of our graveyards. It will be some time before one of our young musicians, feeling the call to speak to man of God, to God of man, or of man to men, will find his feelings channeled by understanding or his consecration accepted. Everything is set here to educate him, to brainwash him, and to reward him with success; nothing is prepared to help him become a great man, to carry out his inspiration, or to fulfill his blessedness.

For inspiration, as we can learn from all great work, comes only out of self-containment. And style, that touchstone of authenticity, comes only from authentic inspiration. What is style? Carrying-power, I say; nothing more. At least, carrying-power is style's direct result. From carrying-power come distinction and fame, recognition while one is still alive. And from them all—from inspiration, style, and distinction, provided the inspiration be authentic, the carrying-power through style very strong, and the distinction of personality visible to all—from all these comes immortality.

Now both Ives and Ruggles have through their music achieved a modicum of that. To Ives has come also, of late, popularity. The music of Ruggles, far more recondite, is also more intensely conceived and more splendidly perfected. Ives belongs (though he is grander, of course) with the homely tinkerers like the eighteenth-century tanner William Billings, and also with the roughneck poets of his own time Carl Sandburg and Vachel Lindsay. But for all of Ives's rude monumentality and his fine careless raptures—welcome indeed in a country vowed to a freedom that its artists have rarely practiced—he falls short, I think, of Whitman's total commitment, as he does also of Emerson's high ethical integrity. Ruggles, judged by any of these criteria, comes out first-class. Europe, where he has been played more than here, has never caviled at such an estimate; nor has his music, under use or after analysis, revealed any major flaw. Standing up as it does to contemporary tests, including public indifference, how can one doubt that it will also stand the test of time?

5. Varèse

From 1914 to 1918 music shone in Europe with a dim light, so low indeed that with most theatres and concert halls shut down, orchestras surviving on a precarious personnel, publication largely arrested, and patronage diverted to war works, young composers with careers to make (once exempt from military duties) looked longingly toward life in the Americas. Thus it came about that in 1916 New York fell heir to the French-trained Swiss Ernest Bloch, to the French harpist-composer Carlos Salzedo (though he had served earlier at the Metropolitan Opera), and to the Italo-Burgundian, schooled in Paris and Berlin, Edgard Varèse. It was shortly too that Carl Ruggles, who in 1917 had lost his Minnesota orchestra through the internment of all his German-citizen players, arrived in the metropolis, teaming up a few years later with Salzedo and Varèse for giving concerts of advanced music. The International Composers' Guild, which they formed in 1921, lasted till 1927, when it was supplanted by a rival group, The League of Composers. Meanwhile in 1922 Varèse had already formed a similar society in Berlin with the aid of his friend and teacher Feruccio Busoni, along with affiliated groups in Moscow through Arthur Lourié, and in Italy through Alfredo Casella.

Born 1883 in Paris, faubourg du Temple, child of a North-Italian engineer and a Burgundian peasant mother, Varèse passed his first two decades at Le Villars in the Maconais with his maternal grandfather, with whom he was happy, and in Turin with his father, who discouraged his musical tastes. Lessons in harmony and counterpoint were nevertheless at last allowed from Giovanni Bolzoni, director of the Turin Conservatoire, and orchestral experience acquired at the opera house there by playing in the percussion section.

By twenty Varèse had scotched all plans for making an engineer of him (though a taste for science was to dominate his life and music) and got himself off to Paris for further training. This took place for two years at the Schola Cantorum (under Vincent d'Indy and Albert Roussel), where he resisted preformulated methods of composing but where he acquired nevertheless a skill in counterpoint and a delight in all the music that had preceded Bach. He supported himself at this time as a musical copyist and librarian's assistant. Moving to the Conservatoire National as a student of Charles-Marie Widor, he attracted also the favorable notice of Jules Massenet; and these strong patrons procured for him two years later a municipal award of money, the *Première Bourse artistique de la ville de Paris*. In the meantime, and very early, he had formed friendships among the avant-garde—with Pablo Picasso, Sar Péladan, Max Jacob, Erik Satie, Amadeo Modigliani, and Guillaume Apollinaire. He knew Lenin too; he had founded a people's chorus; and he was planning an orchestral work of vast scope for one hundred twenty players. At twenty-five, in 1908, he met Debussy. He also moved in that year to Berlin, where he came to know Busoni, Richard Strauss, Gustav Mahler, the conductor Karl Muck, the writers Hugo von Hofmannsthal and Romain Rolland. He also founded a *Symphonischer Chor,* and he collaborated in two productions with Max Reinhardt. To Debussy in Paris he mailed as a gift Schoenberg's *Fünf Orchesterstücke*.

From his beginnings Varèse had enjoyed support from the high placed as well as among the musically advanced. At twenty-seven, in 1910, his orchestral work *Bourgogne* was performed in Berlin through the influence of Richard Strauss by the Blüthner Orchestra under Josef Stransky. Varèse said later of its effect on both press and public: "I became a sort of diabolical Parsifal on a Quest, not for the Holy Grail, but for the bomb that would explode the musical world and allow all sounds to come rushing into it through the resulting breach, sounds which at that time —and sometimes still today—were called noises."

By the time he returned to Paris in 1913 Varèse had formulated clearly his yearning after a music in which pitches would not be bound to the tempered scale nor harmony to any thoroughbass. If Schoenberg had already, as it was said, "freed the dissonance" from harmonic control, Varèse was for the rest of his life to labor at "freeing sound" from any control at all save that of the conscious designer. He did not hold, however, with *The Art of Noise*, celebrated manifesto by the Italian Futurist Luigi Russolo. "Why," he asked, "do you merely reproduce the vibrations of our daily life only in their superficial and distressing aspects?" And he was later to denounce the twelve-tone method of Schoenberg and his pupils as a "doctrinaire" or "establishment-type" modernism.

In 1914 he conducted concerts in Prague that included Debussy's *Le Martyre de Saint Sébastien*. In 1915 he introduced Jean Cocteau to Picasso, was mobilized for war, received a medical discharge, and left for the United States, arriving in New York on the 15th December. All his music had in the meantime disappeared, part of it lost in a Berlin fire, the rest abandoned in Paris. In America he knew only Karl Muck, conductor of the Boston Symphony Orchestra; his fortune amounted to ninety dollars.

As before, he copied music; and as before, he conducted orchestras and choruses. In 1917, with America mobilizing for war, he led a mammoth performance of the Berlioz "Requiem" Mass at New York's Hippodrome. In 1918 he gave concerts in Cincinnati. In that year too he married Louise Norton, poet and translator of French poetry. And he met Carlos Salzedo. The next year he organized the New Symphony Orchestra, of which the first concert received such abuse in the press that his conductorship was dropped in favor of Arthur Bodansky. In 1919 he also began, at thirty-six, a wholly new composer's life. It was as if all Europe, its history and its training and its valued friendships among both classical and modernistic artists, were merely a prelude to America. His first piece composed in the new and now definitive residence he called, in the plural, *Amériques*, meaning, in both the historical and the personal sense, discoveries. Completed in 1921, this work for huge orchestral forces was not heard till 1926, when Leopold Stokowski conducted it in Philadelphia.

Meanwhile, with Salzedo he had organized the International

Composers' Guild and begun giving concerts. They played the new Europeans, naturally, but also Ruggles and Ives and Henry Cowell and Dane Rudyar. And Varèse, with his new-found freedom and his Burgundian's insistence, continued to produce music that for all its authenticity and its novelty in a time which sought out both, never failed to shock. In 1921 he produced *Offrandes,* for voice with orchestra; in 1924 *Octandre.* In 1923 his *Hyperprism* set off New York's first European-sized *scandale,* the next year a similar one in London, where Eugene Goossens gave it for the B.B.C. In 1925 Stokowski conducted *Intégrales* in New York and in 1927 *Arcana,* the second of Varèse's American works for huge orchestra.

Beginning in 1928 Edgard and his wife Louise lived for five years in Paris, where in 1931 he wrote *Ionization,* his first work (and possibly anyone's in the West) composed for an orchestra of percussion instruments. This work, not given till two years later in New York, was the only product of his sojourn in France. Actually, except for a handful of musical friendships revived, his stay there was more remarkable for its literary and visual-arts associations than for musical successes, though most of his earlier works (excepting *Ionization* and *Hyperprism* but including the massive *Arcana* and *Amériques*) were performed in Paris during that time. The American conductor Nicholas Slonimsky was particularly zealous in his favor; and the Paris musician-critics— Florent Schmitt, Paul Le Flem, Emile Vuillermoz, Fred Goldbeck, and Boris de Schloezer—were deeply impressed by his music. But the neoclassical group led by Honegger and Milhaud, backed up by Stravinsky and Jean Cocteau, withheld their support. One composer-pupil, André Jolivet, seems to have been his entire French harvest of direct influence.

Among the visual artists Varèse was always welcome. Sculptors in particular—Giacometti, Zadkine, Calder, Marcel Duchamp—approved his broad aesthetic vistas, as did the painters Paule Thévenin, Amédée Ozenfants, Diego Rivera, and Joan Miró. His metaphysical horizons at this time were dominated by the sixteenth-century alchemist-physician Paracelsus, whose astro-mathematical speculations had also stimulated Charles Ives. As early as 1928 Varèse had presented to the Cuban Alejo Carpentier and to the French poet Robert Desnos, a libretto theme to be entitled *L'Astronome*; and a year later the novelist Jean Giono was at work on *Espace*, another Varèse idea. *L'Astronome,* incomplete, was next offered in 1932 or '33, to Antonin Artaud, who never really worked on it. Nor indeed was it ever to bear music. *Espace* likewise failed of completion, though an *étude* for *Espace* (for choir, two pianos, and percussion) was performed in New York, 1947. *Ecuatorial,* another work of large poetic horizons did, however, come out of this Paris time, to be completed in New York and presented there in 1934. The text was a Spanish version by the Guatemalan poet Miguel Angel Asturias of a Mayan incantation "vast and noble," according to Varèse's biographer Fernand Ouélette, "which rolls forth in the same accents as David's Psalms." He also compares the work to Satie's *Socrate* for its musical austerity and starkness. The scoring is for a choir of bass voices, with trumpets, trombones, piano, organ, percussion, and two *ondes Martenot* (an electronic instrument).

Though preoccupied by electronics, of which the musical possibilities had been little developed, Varèse wrote one more work for a classical instrument, the flute solo of 1936 *Density 21.5.* This much admired short piece he composed for Georges Barrère's platinum instrument; and its title identifies that metal, though this is now listed in the scientific tables, I believe, as of density 21.45. In 1941 he wrote to Professor Léon Théremine: "I no longer wish to compose for the old instruments played by men, and I am handicapped by a lack of adequate electrical instruments for which I conceive my music." He did not write any music, in fact, between 1936 and 1950, when he began *Déserts* (to be finished in 1954) for orchestra and two tracks of "organized sounds" on magnetic tape, the latter indicated as not indispensable to a performance.

One does not know whether Varèse's long silence was due to his having worked out the precious vein of composition opened in 1919 but by 1934 virtually exhausted, to ill health, which he did suffer somewhat in his middle years, to an emotional depression which throughout the 1930s and the time of World War II had certainly produced in his mind black thoughts and a tragic view of life, or to a need for electronic instruments not yet perfected. A lack of public acceptance for his work may also have contributed. The League of Composers, for example, gave him no support in New York, viewing him perhaps as a rival from the days of the International Composers' Guild. But Varèse was not one to be stopped in his tracks, especially in view of the high regard in which his work was held by musicians of radical stripe. The fact remains, however, that he did cease to compose and even to seek performances, save for bringing out in 1947 the studies for *Espace*. As early as 1932 he had requested from the Bell Telephone Laboratories a niche for sharing acoustical experiments, and financial aid from the Guggenheim Foundation for continuing them. He was not successful.

When *Déserts* was completed in Paris and performed there in 1954 Varèse was already seventy-one. The next year he composed a tape, *The Procession at Vergès,* for inclusion in the Thomas Bouchard film *Around and About Joan Miró.* In 1958 he composed an independent tape work, *Le Poème électronique,* involving two hundred forty small speakers arranged for spacial travelings of sound on the ceiling of Le Corbusier's pavilion at the Brussels International and Universal Exposition, built for the fair by the Philips electrical enterprises and destroyed shortly afterwards. The fact that during the performances cinematic images were projected on the tent-like ceiling does not mean, as many visitors thought, that there was a relation of any kind between the film and the music beyond their beginning and ending together. Actually neither Le Corbusier nor Varèse knew in advance what the other had prepared. Two vocal works engaged his last years—*Nocturnal* (for soprano, choir, and orchestra, 1961) on a text from Anaïs Nin's *The House of Incest,* and the unfinished *Nuit,* also on a text from the same book. He died in 1965 at eighty-two.

Varèse's music leans toward mystico-poetic and mystico-mathematical titles. Never did he explain its relation to these, but certainly they corresponded to some thought or region of thought by which he was inspired. The music itself, moreover, is resistant to analysis, even when there is a verbal text. Such resistance, especially in the early decades of a composition's life, is a mark of quality. Further, Varèse himself was a musician of classical training and he enjoyed many sophisticated friendships, musical and artistic. There is no possibility of taking him for a *naïf* or for a primitive, though there is every reason to recognize in him an extreme romantic spirit, tempestuous, determined, and demonic. That spirit worked for the most part as it had been trained to work, through classical instruments and toward a personalized expressivity. His structural and syntactic freedoms were those of a European who had known both Satie and Debussy, as well as Busoni's acoustical speculations, and who started out in America at thirty-three with the principal works of these masters already behind him.

Debussy's concept of the chord as an acoustical agglomerate expressive in itself but leading nowhere, and of melody as an eclectic choice of pitches bound only to expression, with rhythm, counterpoint, and instrumental investiture serving also the expression, while form, which serves them all, remains nevertheless so free that it can be invented for each piece—all this remains as basic to the music of Varèse as it is to that of Debussy. Where it reaches beyond Debussy is in treating complexes of orchestral sound with the independence that Debussy reserved for the chord. Varèse builds directly with orchestral colors and orchestral agglomerates, diminishing the roles of harmony and melody to a minimum, and developing counterpoint through the super-position and interpenetration of these sound-blocks, rhythm aiding the acoustical clarity by means of a sizable percussion group constantly counterposed, even in chamber-sized ensembles, to the tonal instruments.

The result is very different in sound from the music of Debussy, which is static (like painting or like frieze-sculpture). In Debussy one thing happens at a time, as when an artist draws, until all the needed strokes are there, at which point the piece is finished. With Varèse several things are going on, each moved by its own rhythmic dynamism and all together making a complex of sonorities so rich and so active that one does not dare define it as mere noise; and yet it is not exactly music either. Not at least in the standard sense of pitch-patterns tuned to a common fundamental. Free it is, as French music ever is when at its best, eloquent with the raucous voice of the great Romantics, and wholly thought out, thought through, conceived after no image save its author's sensibility, and entirely indited by hand. It sells no method, cures no ill, refuses truck with all establishments. For sure it is the child of Claude Debussy.

"Music in the pure state," it has been called, and "tornadoes of sonorities." Also "a nightmare dreamed by giants." For even the smallest of his chamber-groupings manages somehow to turn on a great racket, especially when electric sirens become involved. Curiously, no sonic boom, no over-charged loudspeaker is allowed to mar the electronic works. *Le Poème électronique* is for the larger part of its time miraculously delicate, a chamber piece of ravishing quietness, and though played on that most blatant of all sound-sources, an ensemble of loudspeakers (thankfully each one tiny), a work of rare delicacy. One wishes Varèse could have lived to make more like it, for all the opposition of the Philips Company, which Le Corbusier fought off for him, and for all the complexities of almost microscopic wiring that it took two months for the engineers to bring into tune and timing.

Varèse in his later years was the recipient of many honors and awards, including membership in the Swedish Academy, a "Nobel Prize," his friends said, "without the money." On the occasion of his death a tribute by the present writer was pronounced before the American Academy of Arts and Letters, of which he had been also a member. The conclusion of that tribute reads as follows:

> From *Amériques* of 1919 to the *Poème électronique* of 1957 he worked with timbre alone, with kinds of sound, great chunks of them, organizing these into a polyphony comparable perhaps to the intersecting polyhedrons that are the shapes of modern architecture. Nevertheless, these pieces are not static like a building, nor even like the music of Debussy; they move forward, airborne. What moves them forward? Rhythms, I think, rhythms counterpointed to create tension and release energy. There are also, in the timbre contrasts and the loudness patterns, designs for producing anxiety and relief, just as there are in tonal music. And these designs create psychological form, though the music is not overtly planned for drama.
>
> It seems to hang together not from themes and their restatements but from tiny cells or motives

which agglomerate like crystals. As Varèse himself described this phenomenon, "In spite of their limited variety of internal structure, the external forms of crystals are almost limitless." To have produced with so cool a concept of artistic creation music of such warm sonorous interest and such urgent continuity makes of Varèse, and I think there is no way round this, the most original composer of the last half-century and one of the most powerfully communicative.

6. Aaron Copland

Julia Smith's book on Aaron Copland refers to him on its first page as "this simple and great man in our midst." And indeed from his youth Copland has so appeared. Having known him as friend and colleague for nigh on to fifty years, I too can attest that his demeanor is sober, cheerful, considerate, his approach direct and at the same time tactful. I have never seen him lose his temper or explode. His physical appearance has not radically changed since 1921; nor have the loose-hung suits and unpressed neckties, the abstemious habits and seemly ways which by their very simplicity add up to a princely grace.

Considering the irritability of most musicians, Copland's diplomat-façade might well be thought to conceal a host of plots and poutings, were it not so obviously his nature to be good-humored and an ancient principle with him not to quarrel. When he came home from Paris at twenty-four, his study time with Nadia Boulanger completed, and began to be a successful young composer, it is said that he determined then to make no unnecessary enemies. It is as if he could see already coming into existence an organized body of modernistic American composers with himself at the head of it, taking over the art and leading it by easy stages to higher ground, with himself still at the head of it, long its unquestioned leader, later its president emeritus.

This consecrated professionalism was Copland's first gift to American music; it had not been there before. Varèse and Ruggles, though consecrated artists, showed only a selective solidarity with their colleagues. Ives had been a drop-out from professionalism altogether. And the earlier professionals, the lot of them, had all been individual operators. Copland was the very first, I think, to view his contemporaries as a sort of peace corps whose assignment in history was to pacify the warring tribes and to create in this still primitive wilderness an up-to-date American music.

His first move in that direction in 1924 was to take over de facto the direction of the League of Composers. This gave him a New York power enclave; and his classes at the New School for Social Research, held from 1927 to 1937, were soon to give him a forum. He also wrote in magazines, listing about every three years the available modernistic young and offering them his blessing. Also from the beginning, he had established a Boston beachhead, where the new conductor Serge Koussevitzky, taking over from Walter Damrosch Copland's Symphony for Organ and Orchestra, 1925, thereafter performed a new work by him every year till well into the 1930s.

Copland had in New York from 1928 to 1931, in addition to his access to the League of Composers, his own contemporary series, shared with Roger Sessions and called the Copland-Sessions Concerts. At these he played both American and European new works, attracted attention, distributed patronage, informed the public. His collaboration with Sessions, the first in a series of similar teamings-up, marks a second stage of his organizational work. Having by that time solidified his own position, he could enlarge his American music project by calling on, one after another, personalities comparable to his own for weight and influence.

After the Sessions concerts ended in 1931, Copland shared briefly with Roy Harris, just returned then from his studies with Boulanger, an influence centered chiefly in Boston, where Koussevitzky was launching Harris with the same steadfast persistence he had used for Copland. A close association with Walter Piston began in 1935, when Copland took over for a year the latter's composition class at Harvard. In 1937 with Marc Blitzstein, Lehman Engel, and myself, the four of us founded the Arrow Music Press, a cooperative publishing facility, and with several dozen others the American Composers' Alliance, a society for licensing the performance of "serious" music, a need at that time not being met by existing societies.

Aaron Copland

During the mid-1930s there were five composers—Copland, Sessions, Harris, Piston, and myself—whom Copland viewed as the strongest of his generation both as creators and as allies for combat. And all were to serve under his leadership as a sort of commando unit for penetrating one after another the reactionary strongholds. Their public acknowledgment as co-leaders of American music took place in 1935 at the New School through five concerts, one devoted to each composer's work, all presented as Copland's choice for contemporary excellence in America.

Two foreign composers—Carlos Chavez, during the 1930s conductor of the Orquesta Sinfónica de México and an official of the Fine Arts Ministry, and Benjamin Britten, England's most accomplished composer since Elgar—were to benefit from Copland's friendship, as he from theirs. But his American general staff did not participate in these alliances. Nor have they shared in Copland's influence over our two remarkable composer–conductors Leonard Bernstein and Lukas Foss, though as recognized composers they have all been played by these leaders. In general Copland's foreign affairs and post-war domestic alliances, as well as his worldwide conducting tours of the 1960s, seem more specifically aimed at broadening the distribution of his own music than at sharing the wealth. And this no doubt because his commando comrades had all become successful independently, while the post-war young, having placed their hopes in a newer kind of music (Elliott Carter, Boulez, Cage, the complexity gambit, and the serial-to-noise-to-electronics gambit), have not been able to muster up the personal loyalties needed for calling on his organizational experience.

I have dwelt on Copland as a colleague, a career man, and a mobilizer, because I consider his contribution in those domains to be no less remarkable than that of his music. This music has been analyzed in books by Julia Smith and by Arthur Berger. All its major items are in print and most are recorded. It comprises piano music, chamber works, orchestral works, and ballets, all of high personal flavor and expert workmanship. Less striking, I think, are the vocal works—consisting of two operas, several sets of songs, an oratorio, and a handful of short choral pieces. Among these the choral works are possibly the happiest, because of their animated rhythmic vein. And five Hollywood films made under first-class directors (three, I think, were by Lewis Milestone) on first-class themes (two from John Steinbeck, one from Thornton Wilder, one from Lillian Hellman, one from Henry James) are imaginative and distinguished in their use of music.

Julia Smith has discerned three stylistic periods in Copland's work. His first period, from age twenty-four (in 1924) to age twenty-nine, includes but one non-programmatic, non-local-color work, the Symphony for Organ and Orchestra, composed for Nadia Boulanger to play in America. I found this work at that time deeply moving, even to tears, for its way of saying things profoundly of our generation. The rest of that production time—*Music for the Theatre,* the Concerto for Piano and Orchestra, the necrophiliac ballet *Grogh,* the *Symphonic Ode,* the trio *Vitebsk* (study on a Jewish theme), and divers smaller pieces —is largely preoccupied with evocation, as in *Grogh* and *Vitebsk,* or with superficial Americana, characterized by the rhythmic displacements that many in those days took for "jazz" but that were actually, as in George Gershwin's vastly successful *Rhapsody in Blue,* less a derivate from communal improvising, which real jazz is, than from commercial popular music. No wonder the effort to compose concert jazz came to be abandoned, by Copland and by others.

Its last appearance in Copland's work is in the otherwise nobly rhetorical *Symphonic Ode* of 1929, which led directly into the Piano Variations, high point of his second period, which in turn initiated a series of non-programmatic works that was to continue for the rest of his productive life. The *Vitebsk* trio, in spite of its allusions to Jewish cantilation, can on account of its tight musical structure be listed, I think, among Copland's abstract works. And so can the orchestral *Statements* of 1933–34, so firmly structured are these mood pictures. Of more strictly musical stock are the Short Symphony of 1932–33, later transcribed as a Sextet for Piano, Clarinet, and Strings, the Piano Sonata (1941), the Sonata for Violin and Piano (1943), the Piano Quartet (1950), the Piano Fantasy, and the Nonet for Strings (these last from the 1960s). One could include perhaps the Third Symphony (1946) on grounds of solid form, but I tend to consider it, on account of its incorporation of a resplendent *Fan-*

fare for the Common Man (from 1942), one of Copland's patriotic works, along with *A Canticle of Freedom* and the popular *A
Lincoln Portrait*.

The initiation of a third period, or kind of writing, followed
that of the second by less than five years; and it too has continued throughout his life. This embodied his wish to enjoy large
audiences not specifically musical, and for that purpose it was
necessary to speak simply. Its major triumphs are three ballets
—*Billy the Kid* (1938), *Rodeo* (1942), and *Appalachian Spring*
(1944)—all of them solid repertory pieces impeccable in their
uses of Americana and vigorous for dancing.

Actually the dance has always been for Copland a major inspiration, largely as an excitement of conflicting rhythms, con-
trasted with slow incantations virtually motionless. As early as
1925 the unproduced ballet *Grogh* had been transformed into
the prize-winning *Dance Symphony*. And his jazz experiments
of the later 1920s were closer to dancing than to blues. In 1934
he composed for Ruth Page and the Chicago Grand Opera Company a ballet, or dance drama, entitled *Hear Ye! Hear Ye!*, satiriz-
ing a murder trial and based largely on night-club music styles.
It was not a success, and with it Copland said good-by to cor-
rupt musical sources, as well as to all attempts at being funny.

Actually his return to ballet and his entry into other forms of
show business had been somewhat prepared that same year by
the production on Broadway of my opera *Four Saints in Three
Acts*. Its willful harmonic simplicities and elaborately-fitted-to-
the-text vocal line had excited him; and he had exclaimed then,
"I didn't know one could write an opera." He was to write one
himself with Edwin Denby three years later, *The Second Hurricane*, designed for high-school use. But my opera had set off trains
of powder in both our lives. In 1936 it led me into composing a
symphonic background for *The Plough that Broke the Plains*, a
documentary film by Pare Lorentz, in which I employed cowboy
songs, war ditties, and other folk-style tunes. Again the effect on
Copland was electric; as a self-conscious modernist, he had not
thought that one could do that either. Shortly after this, Lincoln
Kirstein proposed to commission from Copland a work for his
Ballet Caravan (the parent troupe of today's New York City
Ballet), an offer which Copland declined, no doubt still unsure

53

of himself after the failure of *Hear Ye! Hear Ye!*. I, on the other hand, with a brasher bravery, did accept such a commission and produced in 1937 *Filling Station,* another work based on Americana.

At this point Copland reversed his renunciation and returned to his earliest love, the dance, this time by my way of cowboy songs, producing in 1938 for Ballet Caravan *Billy the Kid,* a masterpiece of a dance score and a masterpiece of novel choreographic genre, the ballet "Western." Copland's *Rodeo,* of 1942, made for Agnes de Mille and the Ballet Russe de Monte Carlo, is another "Western." And *Appalachian Spring* (for Martha Graham, 1944) is a pastoral about nineteenth-century Shakers. All make much of Americana, the hymn lore of the latter piece having as its direct source my uses of old Southern material of that same kind in *The River,* of 1937, another documentary film by Pare Lorentz.

If I seem to make needless point of my influence on Copland, it is less from vanity than for explaining his spectacular invasion, at thirty-eight, of ballet and films, and less successfully of the opera. His love for the dance was no doubt inborn, and an acquaintance with the theatre had been developed through long friendship with the stage director Harold Clurman. But his previous ballet experiments had come to naught, and his essays in writing incidental music for plays had not led him toward many discoveries. He yearned, however, for a large public; the social-service ideals of the 1930s and the musical successes of Dmitri Shostakovich having created in him a strong desire to break away from the over-intellectualized and constricting modernism of his Paris training. To do this without loss of intellectual status was of course the problem. Stravinsky's neoclassical turn toward conservatism, initiated in 1918, had offered guidance to the postwar School of Paris and to all those still-young Americans, by the 1930s quite numerous and influential, who through Nadia Boulanger had come under its power.

But they had all preserved a correct façade of dissonance; and this surfacing, applied to every species of contemporary music, was making for monotony and for inflexibility in theatre situations. The time was over when composers—Debussy, for instance, Alban Berg, Richard Strauss—could comb literature for themes suited to their particular powers. On the contrary, themes appropriate to a time of social protest and of trade-union triumphs seemed just then far more urgent, especially to Copland, surrounded as he was by left-wing enthusiasts. He wanted populist themes and populist materials and a music style capable of stating these vividly. My music offered one approach to simplification; and my employment of folk-style tunes was, as Copland was to write me later about *The River,* "a lesson in how to treat Americana."

A simplified harmonic palette was being experimented with everywhere, of course; and a music "of the people," clearly an ideal of the time, was one that seemed far nobler then than the country-club-oriented so-called "jazz" that many had dallied with in the 1920s. And thus it happened that my vocabulary was, in the main, the language Copland adopted and refined for his ballet *Billy the Kid* and for his first film *Of Mice and Men.* The German operas of Kurt Weill, which were known to him, performed no such service, though they were all-important to Marc Blitzstein, whose *The Cradle Will Rock* was produced in 1937. Shostakovitch's rising career and some Russian film music may have also been in Copland's mind. But his break-through into successful ballet composition, into expressive film-scoring, and into, for both, the most distinguished populist music style yet created in America did follow in every case very shortly after my experiments in those directions. We were closely associated at the time and discussed these matters at length.

Copland's high-school opera *The Second Hurricane* (to a text by Edwin Denby), produced in 1937, followed Blitzstein's lead into a city-style harmonic simplicity, rather than to my country-style one. It contains delicious verse and a dozen lovely tunes, but it has never traveled far. Nearly twenty years later he wrote another opera, *The Tender Land,* again a pastoral involving Americana-style songs and dances; but that also failed in spite of resonant choruses and vigorous dance passages. When he moved from ballet to films (*Of Mice and Men,* 1939; *Our Town,* 1940) he carried with him no such baggage of vocal ineptitude; nor was he obliged to use the dance for animation. His powers of landscape evocation in pastoral vein and his slow, static, nearly motionless suspense-like moods were useful for psychological spell-casting; and a struggle-type counterpoint, suggestive of medieval organum with rhythmic displacements—taken over from his non-programmatic works—gives dramatic intensity, as in the boy-fights-eagle passage toward the end of *The Red Pony.* For a man so theatre-conscious and so gifted both for lyrical expansion and for objective depiction to be so clearly out of his water on the lyric stage is surprising. The choral passages in his operas are the happiest, for in these he can mobilize four parts or more to produce the same polyrhythmic excitements that are the essence of his dance works, as indeed they often are of his abstract, or "absolute," music. But for vocal solos and recitatives none of that is appropriate; and his dramatic movement tends in consequence to lose impetus, to stop in its tracks. There is no grave fault in his prosodic declamation, which is on the whole clear, though here and there, as in the Emily Dickinson songs, the solo line may be a little jumpy and the vocal ranges strained. His melody in general, however, his harmony, and his musical form are those of a master. What is wrong? My answer is that just as with Stravinsky, also by nature a dance man muscle-oriented, and even with Beethoven, whose work is so powerfully rhythmicized, the vocal writing, however interesting intrinsically, neglects to support the play's dramatic line.

A strange and urgent matter is this line. And its pacing in spoken plays is not identical with the pacing required for a musical version of the same play. Mozart, with his inborn sense of the theatre is virtually infallible on a stage; and so is Wagner, even when in *Das Rheingold* and in *Parsifal* the dramatico-musical thread may unwind so slowly that it seems almost about to break. But it never does break, and as a result each act or separate scene develops as one continuous open-ended form. Composers whose music requires rhythmic exactitudes work better with the dance or in the closed concert forms. Composers conditioned to producing mood units also tend to be ill at ease about dramatic progress and to treat the story as a series of moments for static contemplation, like Stations of the Cross. On the other hand, operas constructed as a sequence of "numbers" (Mozart to Gershwin) do not of necessity lack dramatic animation. Even the musical dramas of Monteverdi, the *opere serie* of Handel and Rameau and Gluck, can move forward as drama through their closed-form *arie* da capo and their oratorio-style choruses. I suspect it is their naturalistic recitatives that carry them from set-piece to set-piece toward a finale where a priest in full robes or some deus ex machina, in any case a bass voice singing *not* in da capo form, releases the dénouement.

The basic need of any ballet or film score is an appropriate accompaniment for the dance narrative, for the photographed landscape, or for the mimed action. Opera demands of music a more controlling rein, for its function there is not to accompany a dramatic action but to *animate* it—to pace it, drive it, wrestle with it, and in the end to dominate. For that Copland lacks the continuing dynamism. His schooling in the concert forms (in the sonata with Rubin Goldmark, in the variation with Boulanger), the rhythmic and percussive nature of his musical thought, its instrumental predominance, the intervalic viscosity of his textures—all of motionless fourths and seconds, as in medieval organum, plus tenths, so beautiful when finally heard but so slow to register—have created a musical vocabulary strong, shining, and unquestionably of our century.

My favorite among the concert works, the most highly personal, the most condensed, and the most clearly indispensable to music, it seems to me, is the *Piano Variations* of 1930. The Short Symphony in its sextet form and the Nonet also remain handsome under usage. The Piano Quartet, though structurally imaginative, suffers from a tone-row in which two whole-tone scales just barely skirt monotony. The Piano Sonata, the Violin Sonata, and the Piano Fantasy have failed on every hearing to hold my mind. And the charming Concerto for Clarinet (1948) with strings, harp, and piano, is essentially "light" music long ago retired to the status of an admirable ballet by Jerome Robbins, *The Pied Piper*.

Suites from the three great repertory ballets, nuggets from films and operas, one overture, divers mood-bits and occasional pieces, and the rollicking *El Salón México*, constitute a high-level contribution to light music that may well be, along with Copland's standardization of the American professional composer, also at high level, his most valued legacy. Certainly these works are among America's most beloved. Nevertheless, the non-programmatic works, though not rivals to twentieth-century European masterworks, have long served American composers as models of procedure and as storehouses of precious device, all of it ready to be picked right off the shelf.

"It's the best we've got, you know," said Leonard Bernstein. And surely this is true of Copland's music as a whole. Ruggles's is more carefully made, but there is not enough of it. Ives's, of which there is probably far too much for quality, has, along with its slapdash euphoria, a grander gusto. Varèse, an intellectually sophisticated European, achieved within a limited production the highest originality flights of any. Among Copland's own contemporaries few can approach him for both volume and diversity. Roy Harris has five early chamber works and one memorable symphony, his Third, but he has written little of equal value since 1940. Piston is the author of neoclassical symphonies and chamber pieces that by their fine workmanship may well arrive at repertory status when revived in a later period; for now, they seem a shade scholastic. Sessions, I should say, has for all his impressive complexity and high seriousness, not one work that is convincing throughout. And I shall probably be remembered, if at all, for my operas.

But the Copland catalog has good stuff under every heading, including that of opera. He has never turned out bad work, nor worked without an idea, an inspiration. His stance is that not only of a professional but also of an artist—responsible, prepared, giving of his best. And if that best is also the best we have, there is every reason to be thankful for its straightforward employment of high gifts. Also, of course, for what is the result of exactly that, "this simple and great man in our midst."

7. Looking Backward

The 1930s in America had been characterized by an unexpected expansion of the symphony orchestra. In full depression times, with seemingly no money anywhere, the boom occurred. Schools found ways to buy instruments and scores, communities hired players and conductors, the Works Progress Administration organized unemployed musicians into concert-giving groups often comparable to the dozen or more established orchestras that had long been the glory of our great cities. And all this, where not strictly amateur, under union conditions. Till in 1937, according to *America's Symphony Orchestras* by Grant and Hettinger, there were no fewer than thirty thousand ensembles practicing symphonic repertory and performing it in public.

By the end of the decade, with a war on in Europe and prosperity back, the WPA groups came to be disbanded. But the popularity of symphonic exercise had become so firmly established in our schools and in our communities that the number of orchestras went on growing. And in spite of war, and the enforced absence of many from cultural pursuits, by 1945, according to a report of the National Music League, there were forty-five thousand orchestras.

Already in the late 1930s, with the orchestral expansion established and successful, it had become known to managers and educators that another boom was building up, an excitement about opera. Indeed if the war, with its constant shiftings of troops and factories and personnel, had not interrupted that enthusiasm, the founding of opera workshops that characterized the late '40s and '50s might well have got started a decade earlier.

The Saturday afternoon broadcasts of the Metropolitan Opera certainly had a great deal to do with spreading this interest, though they could not have started it. For from the early 1930s, when they began, these broadcasts were already popular, rating in the polls twice as high as the Sunday programs of the New York Philharmonic and right up in the range of the commercial entertainers.

The orchestra boom had found American composers ready for distribution. Ever since the 1890s they had been writing symphonic works that were structurally coherent, clear in thought, and neatly orchestrated. An American orchestral repertory existed, and there were American composers ready to add to it at a drop of the slightest hint about performance.

The opera boom, even though delayed by a decade, had no such library at hand. Not that there were no American operas. There were many. And a dozen of these had been produced at the Metropolitan and Chicago opera houses—skillfully built works by Parker, Chadwick, Charles Wakefield Cadman, Henry Hadley, Reginald de Koven, Victor Herbert, and Deems Taylor. But nobody wanted to hear them again. The thirst was for new works, along with the European nineteenth-century ones. And the new composers, those whose music sounded like the twentieth century—Copland and Roger Sessions and Roy Harris— were turning out to be either inept at vocal writing or lacking a sense of the stage. Our earlier opera composers had written gracefully enough for voice and sometimes dramatically. But their music, like their librettos, lacked modernity appeal. Reviewing at this point three decades, let us remember that that of 1910 to 1920 had continued the successful career of Horatio Parker—which included two operas, one produced at the Metropolitan—and the unsuccessful career—particularly regarding opera, toward which he had made serious efforts—of George W. Chadwick. The other chief conservatives—Hadley, Converse, Mason, Hill—were pursuing a quiet path. And MacDowell, the most striking of them all, had been dead since 1908.

A modernist trend, barely visible before 1919 regarding Ives, shortly about to become so regarding Ruggles, earlier showy as all get-out with Leo Ornstein, and serio-comic with Henry Cowell in California, this trend had become a movement after the arrival from Europe around 1916 of Ernest Bloch, Carlos Salzedo, and Edgard Varèse. It was in fact this very turning away from an academicized Romanticism, redolent of nineteenth-century Central Europe or of impressionist France, and toward a radically non-academic, even subversive, up-to-dateness that was to give American music a new confidence, backed up by a French turn in the pedagogy of composition (at Harvard and Columbia) and by the invigoration of our low-life ambience through blues and jazz.

Actually it was the gradual fulfilling in America of radical promises already achieved in Europe which gave the "advanced" tone to our music life of the 1920s, with its modern music societies and across-the-Atlantic exchanges of scores and artists. But the modern masters—and everybody knew who they were: Debussy (dead), Ravel, Schoenberg, Stravinsky—were pre-war products. And the young ones—in Europe Milhaud, Honegger, Berg, Webern, Prokofiev; in America Sessions, Copland, Piston, Cowell, along with the Paris-based Virgil Thomson and George Antheil—were not ready to give out a new line. So the old-line Romantics—in Europe Richard Strauss, Rachmaninoff, Dohnanyi; in America the standard academics, plus Deems Taylor and the young Howard Hanson—went right on as if the twentieth century did not exist. At the same time Ruggles and Varèse moved forward from their already advanced positions, and Ives proceeded slowly with the editing and publishing of his works.

The 1920s, with their open power-struggles between modernists and conservatives and even among the modernists themselves, were an active and quarrelsome time. The decade ended with a clear victory for modernism and with the consolidation of a modernist establishment powerful not only in its own concert-giving societies, where it operated to make or break careers, but in the universities as well. Also in the orchestras, where Stokowski, Koussevitzky, and Frederick Stock (following the examples of Karl Muck, Walter Damrosch, Pierre Monteux) backed the leaders of the modernist establishment and even did some testing on their own.

Copland's bare and clangorous Piano Variations, of 1930, closed off the radical decade and initiated a new one, in which young America was to take a new line, at once neo-Romantic and formalistic. The best of Roy Harris's richly meditative chamber music and his eloquent Third Symphony led the way. Sessions and Piston during these years did more teaching than composing; their full maturity was not to arrive till in the 1940s. But the successes of a still younger generation—Samuel Barber and William Schuman, both born in 1910—enriched the time with chamber and orchestral works warmly felt and expertly composed. And if Sessions and Copland themselves represented a certain retreat from radical modernism, based in both cases on Stravinsky's neoclassic example, Barber and Schuman and the slow-ripening Piston were to embody in their works an even more conservative approach to musical form. They did not follow the easy-going sequence-routines of Rachmaninoff and Hanson, directly adopted from Wagner. And they avoided also free linear expansion as practiced by Harris (though there is a bit of this in Schuman) as well as the elaborately prepared asymmetries of Copland and Stravinsky (not to speak of Schoenberg's codified language of the heart) for the classical proportions of Haydn, Mozart, Schubert, and Brahms. Old wine in old bottles seems to have been their aim. And the content varies from Barber's voice-like rounded contours through the jumpy themes and jazzy metrics of Schuman (not so far as might be thought from Stravinsky via Gershwin) to the sophisticated and hermetic way that Piston expresses private meanings by developing analytically, much as Bartók was doing, materials based on intervalic contradictions.

In Sessions's work of the period intervalic contradiction was also explored but rather for the purpose, or so it has long appeared to me, of calling to our attention, by seeming to deny, a Romantic afflatus that aspired toward nineteenth-century Vienna. In this sense his music was the least contemporary of all, unless one counts the wish to reproduce monumental Romanticism in a high dissonance saturation as characteristic of modern times. Which of course it is. Even Brahms's need for serving earlier masters—Handel, Mozart, and middle-period Beethoven—was after all not very different.

In the long run American music has suffered little from the weightlifters and the muscle-bound. We have no match here for the heavy strainings of a Reger, a Pfitzner, a Scriabin, a d'Indy; nor anything that resembles the non-stop outpourings of an Anton Rubinstein, a Bruckner, a Gustav Mahler, an Albéric Magnard. There is a bit of all these, of course, in Charles Ives. And in Sessions, as in Elliott Carter, there is a special kind of (perhaps American) painful delivery, both of them learned men who seem determined to use all they know in every piece. In Ruggles, on the other hand, slow worker though he was, no comparable strain is felt; merely his need for producing at no matter how much trouble, a homogeneous texture capable of expressing musical thought without digression.

America's problem has from the beginning lain largely in her composers' lack of a plain and unfussy mastery. They are taught so elaborately and mature so late! Moreover, the suspect nature here of anything suggesting distinction is a heavy cross for an artist to bear. Composers of natural gifts we have in plenty, along with a few who once have seemed to be about to establish a firm fecundity comparable to that of Europe's great men. But the hope more often than not has petered out.

Certainly such hope was strong in the 1930s, and not only for concert music but for opera. My own *Four Saints*, produced in 1934; George Gershwin's *Porgy and Bess*, in 1935; Menotti's *Amelia al Ballo*, of 1936; Marc Blitzstein's political-tract *singspiel* of 1937, *The Cradle Will Rock*; Aaron Copland's *The Second Hurricane* of the same year; Douglas Moore's *The Devil and Daniel Webster*, of 1938—all these seemed at the time to be lively, contemporary in feeling, and promising of more to come. Menotti, Moore, and I have indeed composed more operas, and with continuing success, artistically speaking. In the 1950s, Carlisle Floyd composed to his own text a *Susannah* which, though orchestrally inept, was both verbally and vocally first-class. His subsequent works have not been up to the first, though his *Of Mice and Men* may have again, in 1970, hit the jackpot. Samuel Barber's *Vanessa* and *Antony and Cleopatra* impress me as standard Metropolitan operas, and no remarkable improvement on those of Deems Taylor from the 1920s or on Howard Hanson's *Merry Mount*, produced at the Met in 1934. Robert Ward's *The Crucible* (1961), the best so far of the Ford Foundation commissions, is a solid but not quite first-class play by Arthur Miller set to solid but not quite first-class music. Hugo

Weisgall's *Six Characters in Search of an Author,* produced in 1959, adds to Pirandello's already complex dramatic fantasy a musical viscosity of doubtful service to the script. Three recent operas also merit mention—*Montezuma* by Roger Sessions, produced in West Berlin 1964, *The Visitation* by Gunther Schuller, produced in Hamburg 1968, and *Mourning Becomes Electra* (on the Eugene O'Neill play) by Martin David Levy, produced at the Metropolitan in 1967. I cannot see that any of these mightily Germanic works has added stature to American opera, though all of course are musically professional.

An effort is worth noting here on the part of American musicians to compose short operas of a comedy so broad that one might almost call them comic strips. Menotti's *The Telephone* is surely the most effective of these. But Leonard Bernstein's *Trouble in Tahiti* has also had a merited currency. And I, for one, find Lukas Foss's *The Jumping Frog of Calaveras County* definitely entertaining. Even the usually sentiment-inspired Douglas Moore has written what he calls a "soap opera" entitled *Gallantry,* a charming parody in lyric vein. And George Kleinsinger's *Archie and Mehitabel,* about a cat and a cockroach, though it may be a bit commercial of tone, exploits a humor that is not childish.

This sort of writing, when practiced on a witty book by a composer clearly sophisticated, can be as fluffy as a joke by Ronald Firbank. In heavier hands it tends toward a collegiate coarseness. On the whole I find the tendency possibly useful for propelling the American composer toward light textures and toward an awareness of style, since humor demands stylistic tension far more than tragedy does. Humor can also be a protection against the fragility of sentiments, can even enclose them like a capsule, for easy swallowing. Many more operas than these have been written and produced in the last thirty years. I have tried limiting my mention to works having real distinction and some liveliness. Others too may evince these qualities; I have not heard them all. I have merely wished, after commenting on the 1930s, to review certain outgrowths of that decade's achievement.

These outgrowths have provided in symphonic music virtually no new names, certainly no major ones. In chamber music we have Elliott Carter, a whopping one, and Ross Lee Finney, an authentic one. In opera, apart from one short work by Carlisle Floyd, we have for novelty only the strange case of the Argentinian Alberto Ginastera, whose *Bomarzo* and *Don Rodrigo* productions, heavily subsidized from political sources (largely Rockefeller, I believe), created some stir. Bearing unquestionably some novelty, both musical and aesthetic, these works seem to have achieved also at the New York City Opera an all-time high for musical complexity in the repertory circumstance. That complexity may be illusory, as may well be also their musical quality, though this last I hesitate to believe, considering their composer's known excellence in concert works. An overweening effort to knock out all competitors seems to me the more likely supposition.

In music teaching there has been nothing new of note, since our chief pedagogical establishments training composers all bear the stamp of the older generation. The Eastman School of Music in Rochester, New York is the creation of Howard Hanson; and today's Juilliard School of Music in New York City bears witness still to the administrative wisdom and the firmness of William Schuman, from 1945 to 1962 its president. Walter Piston at Harvard and Roger Sessions at Princeton and at the University of California in Berkeley gave solid training to composers as different in manner as the stage-oriented Leonard Bernstein, the abstract-and-electronic Milton Babbitt, and the dissonantly introspective Andrew Imbrie. Also Copland and Harris have advised composing students fruitfully; and powerful stimulators they were, both of them, though neither is a drillmaster. Actually the only novel addition to America's teaching resources in the last thirty-five years has been Arnold Schoenberg, who, arriving as a refugee in 1934, within two years became an enormous pedagogical presence. Oscar Levant worked under him; Lou Harrison and John Cage were definitely formed by him; also strongly influenced was Leon Kirchner.

Cage and Harrison might be considered heirs of the 1930s, since their work in percussion dates from toward the end of that time. I prefer, however, since both were living then on the West Coast and were still under thirty, to view their subsequent careers, along with those of Carter and Babbitt and the new far-outs, as belonging to a later development. This development, though many of its origins lie on the West Coast, is today far closer in touch with post-war Europe than the now elderly commando unit or the Barber-Menotti-Schuman generation, which had followed so closely, not exactly in our steps, but on our heels.

Succeeding developments will need all they can muster of energy and fresh ways to match those of the 1930s. For that was surely in American music the definitive decade. After 1910 everything led up to it, and after 1940 everything was different. The survival today of Copland's commando and their continued creation of viable works, each in his own style, is evidence both of their individual strength and of that of the time in which they ripened. For their music—along with that of Ives, Ruggles, and Varèse—is what anybody anywhere means by American music. Virtually everything that took place here after 1940, except for the isolated grand achievements of Carter and Cage, is more of same. And if not that, as with electronics and musical "happenings," it has turned to Europe for guidance—to Stockhausen, to Luciano Berio, and to Boulez.

The effort to create both for home consumption and for export a national school of composition has nevertheless succeeded, even though that success has not yet put the United States in a position of leadership in music comparable to that which we enjoy in literature. For if our elderly composers are easily the match for what Europe can offer today in the same age-bracket, our experimental groups are by international standards a shade provincial.

All music today, I fear, is resting on its laurels. And if Europe, both Central and Western, remembers the years from 1890 to 1914 as a Golden Age and the post-World War I as a Silver Epoch, America, even its youth-fringe, looks back nostalgically to the ebullient 1930s, that dramatic and frightening decade which began with economic disaster and ended in a worldwide war.

8. Cage and the Collage
of Noises

In 1967 John Cage, working at the University of Illinois in Urbana with the engineer-composer Lejaren Hiller, began to plan, design, and move toward the final realization in sound (with visual admixtures) of a work lasting four-and-a-half hours and involving a very large number of mechanical devices controlled by engineers, along with seven harpsichords played by hand. Nearly two years later this work, entitled *HPSCHD* (a six-letter version, suited to computer programming, of the word *harpsichord*) was produced on May 16, 1969 in the university's Assembly Hall, seating eighteen thousand people.

By this time the work had come to include as sources of sound not only the keyboard instruments of its title (which Cage pronounces *harpsichord*) but also fifty-two tape machines, fifty-nine power amplifiers, fifty-nine loudspeakers and two hundred eight computer-generated tapes. The visual contributions to this performance employed sixty-four slide-projectors showing sixty-four hundred slides and eight moving-picture projectors using forty cinematographic films, probably silent in view of the general auditory complexities just mentioned.

Richard Kostelanetz, reviewing the event for *The New York Times,* reported further that "flashing on the outside under-walls of the huge double-saucer Assembly Hall . . . were an endless number of slides from 52 projectors" (a part of the sixty-four?). Inside "in the middle of the circular sports arena were suspended several parallel sheets of semi-transparent material, each 100 by 400 feet; and from both sides were projected numerous films and slides whose collaged imagery passed through several sheets. Running around a circular ceiling was a continuous 340-foot screen, and from a hidden point inside were projected slides with imagery as various as outer-space scenes, pages of Mozart music, computer instructions, and non-representational blotches. Beams of light were aimed across the undulated interior roof. In several upper locations mirrored balls were spinning, reflecting dots of light in all directions. . . . The audience," he adds, "milled about the floor while hundreds took seats in the bleachers."

The auditory continuity he describes as "an atonal and structural chaos . . . continually in flux." However, "fading in and out through the mix were snatches of harpsichord music that sounded . . . like Mozart; . . . these came from the seven instrumentalists visible on platforms in the center of the Assembly Hall." The sound appealed to him as in general "rather mellow, except for occasional blasts of ear-piercing feed-back that became more frequent toward the end."

Mr. Kostelanetz identifies the aesthetic species to which this this work belongs as "that peculiarly contemporary art, the kinetic environment, or an artistically activated enclosed space." Actually this "artistically activated" space is not very different from the Wagnerian *gesamtkunstwerk*, or music drama (also a mixed-media affair), except for its very modern emphasis on the mechanics of show business. Wagner took these for granted, preferring to use them less as glamour items than for underlining myths and morals. In both cases, I think, the production of ecstasy was the aim; and in both cases surely music (or sound, in any case) was the main merchandise. For Wagner's music is clearly what has survived best out of his whole splendid effort to create a new kind of tragedy. And as for the Cage-Hiller *HPSCHD*, it was already on sale as a musical recording, completely shorn of its visual incidents and compacted down to twenty-one minutes of playing-time, when the great mixed show of it all was put on in Urbana.

In 1937, thirty years before this work was started, Cage had proclaimed his credo regarding the future of music: "I believe that the use of noise to make music will continue and increase until we reach a music produced through the aid of electrical instruments which will make available for musical purposes any and all sounds that can be heard." The composer, in these prophesied times, will not limit himself to instruments or concepts based on the overtone series but "will be faced with the entire field of sound." And new methods for composing with this vast vocabulary, he also stated, were already beginning to be developed, methods which were free and forever to remain free (I quote) "from the concept of a fundamental tone."

The idea of making compositions out of noise, that is to say of sounds not responsible to a common fundamental, had been in the air ever since the Futurist painter Luigi Russolo in 1913 praised as sources for an "art of noises" "booms, thunderclaps, explosions, clashes, splashes, and roars." Busoni too saw music as moving toward the machine. And Varèse was dreaming of electrical help by 1920 certainly. Also George Antheil, Leo Ornstein, and Darius Milhaud had very early composed passages for nontonal percussion. Cage, however, when he began to compose in 1933, was virtually alone in following out the Futurist noise principle as a career. Others had worked occasionally in that vein, but none other seemed really to believe in it as a destiny or to be able to perfect for its mastery devices for giving it style, structure, and variety. Cage's own music over the last thirty years, though not entirely free of interrelated pitches, has nevertheless followed a straighter line in its evolution toward an art of collage based on non-musical sounds than that of any other artist of his time. He seems to have known by instinct everything to avoid that might turn him aside from his goal and everything that could be of use toward achieving it. Precious little service, naturally, was to be expected out of music's classical models.

The ultimate aim was to produce a homogenized chaos that would carry no program, no plot, no reminders of the history of beauty, and no personal statement. Nowadays, of course, we can recognize in such an ideal the whole effort of pop art. But I do not think that pop art's obvious jokes and facile sentiments were a major motive. I think Cage wanted, had always wanted, to save music from itself by removing its narcotic qualities and its personalized pretentiousness, as well as all identifiable structure and rhetoric. In this regard his aim has been close to that of Erik

Satie, whose music he adores. But its consistent pursuit presents a story so utterly American, even West Coast American, that this Frenchman from Normandy with a Scottish mother, though he might well have delighted in Cage's salt-sprayed humor, would have lacked sympathy, I suspect, for his doctrinaire determination.

John Cage is a Californian born in Los Angeles in 1912, whose father had come there from Tennessee. A lanky red-head with white skin that freckles, a constant walker, a woodsman, and a tinkerer, he has all the tough qualities of the traditional mountaineer submissive to no authorities academic or federal. He had good lessons in piano playing and in composition, the latter from Arnold Schoenberg among others. Teaching during the late 1930s at the Cornish School in Seattle, he made friendships in the Northwest that stimulated his take-off as a composer toward East Asian art principles. The painter Morris Graves, the composer Lou Harrison, and the dancer Merce Cunningham all came into his life at this time; and so did the young Russian woman from Alaska whom he married.

He also conducted percussion concerts and composed percussion works. His *Construction in Metal*, of 1939, for bells, thunder-sheets, gongs, anvils, automobile brake-drums and similar metallic objects, is organized rhythmically after the Indian *tala,* in which the whole has as many parts as each section has small parts; and in Cage these parts, large and small, are related to each other in lengths of time as square and square root. In 1938 he also began to "prepare" pianos by inserting coins, bits of rubber or wood, bolts, and other small objects between the strings at nodal points, producing a gamut of delicate twangs, pings, and thuds that constitutes for each piece its vocabulary.

At this time, and for the next decade, Cage's music continued to be organized for phraseology and length after the square-and-square-root principle. Its melodic structure, if one may use this term for music so far removed from modes and scales, is expressive, in the Indian manner, of "permanent" emotions (heroic, erotic, and so forth) though in some cases he does not hesitate, as in *Amores* (1943), to describe things personally experienced, in this case a lovers' triangle. But his melody remains aware of Schoenberg's teaching about tetrachordal structure, and it also

Cage and the Collage of Noises

observes a serial integrity. Since music without a thoroughbass can seek no structure from harmony, and since Cage's orientalizing proclivities inclined his expression toward "permanent" emotions, as opposed to those which by their progress and change might suggest a beginning, a middle, and an ending, he had available to him no structural method save what he could invent through rhythm.

Now rhythm, being the free, the spontaneous, the uncontrolled element in Schoenberg's music and in that of his Viennese companion-pupils Berg and Webern, appealed strongly to Cage's inventive mind as a domain offering possibly a chance for innovation. The Schoenberg school had made few serious attempts to solve problems of structure; they had remained hung up, as we say, on their twelve-tone row, which by abolishing the consonance-dissonance antithesis had relieved them of an age-old problem in harmony. The fact that in doing so it had also abolished the scalar hierarchies, previously the source of all harmony-based form, led them to substitute for harmonic structure an interior cohesion achieved through canonic applications of the twelve-tone row, but not to any original efforts at all regarding organic form. Rhythm they never considered for this role, since rhythm, in the European tradition, had long before been judged a contributory element, not a basic one like melody or harmony. And besides, the Germanic practice, in which they had all grown up, had lost its rhythmic vitality after Beethoven's death, and no longer distinguished with any rigor between rhythms of length and rhythms of stress, as Beethoven and his predecessors had done to so remarkable a result.

What the Schoenberg school actually used as a substitute for structure was the evocation of certain kinds of emotional drama familiar to them from the Romantic masters. This is why their music, though radical in its interval relations, is on the inside just good old Vienna. Even Italians like Luigi Dallapiccola and Frenchmen like Pierre Boulez, who took up the twelve-tone method after World War II, being not attached atavistically to Vienna, could not hold their works together without a libretto. Their best ones are operas, oratorios, cantatas. And their only substitute for organic structure was the *sérialisme intégral* actually achieved by Boulez in a few works, a complete organization

71

into rows of all the variables—of tones, lengths, heights, timbres, loudnesses, and methods of instrumental attack. The result was so complex to compose, to play, and above all to follow that little effort was made to continue the practice.

The experiment had its effect on Cage, all the same, almost the only direct musical influence one can find since his early lessons with Cowell and Schoenberg and his percussion-orchestra experiments with Lou Harrison. For Cage, like everybody else, was deeply impressed by Pierre Boulez, both the music and the mentality of the man. Knowing well that twelve-tone music lacked both rhythm and structure, Cage had early aspired in his works for percussion groups and for prepared piano to supply both. Whether he had ever thought to serialize the rhythmic element I do not know; he may have considered his *tala* structure more effective. But he was impressed by the Boulez achievement in total control, and Boulez in return was not without respect for Cage's forcefulness.

At this point—we are now in the late 1940s—Cage sailed off toward the conquest of Europe. But Europe by this time was in the hands of its own youth-centered power group. Boulez in France, Karlheinz Stockhausen in Germany, a henchman or so in Belgium and Italy, were beginning to be a tight little club. They ran a modernist festival at Donaueschingen and a concert series in Paris, dispensed patronage and commissions through the German radio, and influenced publishers. Cage, always pushing, assumed his right to parity in the European councils. He can be overbearing, I know, and maybe was. I do not know what confrontations occurred; but he came back chastened, retired to his backwoods modern cabin up-country from Nyack, became a searcher after mushrooms, found solace in Zen Buddhism.

By 1951 he had come up with another novelty, one that was to sweep through Europe, the Americas, and Japan without bringing him any personal credit. I refer to the aleatory method of composition, in which the variables so strictly controlled by Boulez through serial procedures were subjected, all of them, to games of chance. We may suppose, I think, that between a numerically integrated work of sound and one showing arrangements and orders that reflect only hazard, there is not of necessity much recognizable difference. A similar degree of complexity is bound to be present, provided the variable elements are sufficiently numerous and the game of chance used to control them sufficiently complex to avoid the monotony of a "run." If John Cage was not the first aleatory composer, he may still have been the first to hit upon the aleatory idea. It fits with his modest but perfectly real mathematical understanding, with his addiction to things oriental (in this case to the Chinese *I Ching, Book of Changes,* where he found the dice-game he still uses), with the Zen Buddhist principle that nothing really has to make sense (since opposites can be viewed as identical), and above all with his need at that particular time for a novelty.

According to Gilbert Chase in *America's Music,* Cage first started using chance in connection with thematic invention for getting from one note to the next. Then at each small structural division chance was also used to determine whether the tempo should be changed. This was in a work for prepared piano called *Music of Changes.* But inevitably, with chance involved in the tempo changes, hence in the overall timings, "it was not possible," says Cage, "to know the total time-length until the final chance operation, the last toss of coins affecting the rate of tempo, had been made." And since the work's length could not be decided in advance, the square-and-square-root structural proportions could not be used. Therefore structure, for the first time in Cage's experience of it, became as indeterminate an element in composition as texture, both shape and meaning disappeared, and composition became in Cage's words "an activity characterized by process and essentially purposeless." He has not yet fully explained, however, just how in choosing by chance his musical materials he arrives at the ones to be processed through the dice-game, though there is no question of his "inventing" these materials. He does not; he "finds" them through objective, impersonal procedures.

And so it came about that after Schoenberg had dissolved all harmonic tensions by assuming dissonance and consonance to be the same, and Boulez had through his *sérialisme intégral* removed seemingly all freedom, all elements of choice from composition beyond the original selection of materials themselves and their initial order of appearance, Cage had now made music completely free, or "indeterminate," an achievement he was especially pleased with because it eliminated from any piece both the history of music and the personality of the composer. And such personal elements as were in danger of governing the choice of materials he has endeavored to obviate by treating imperfections in the paper and similar accidents as real notes. His subsequent elaborations of indeterminacy for working with electronic tape, though ingenious, are merely developments of the aleatory or impersonal principle. And thus we arrive with *HPSCHD*, the harpsichord piece of 1969, at an effect of total chaos, completely homogenized save for occasional shrieks of feed-back.

Let me trace again the surprisingly straight line of Cage's growth in artistry. His father, for whom he had deep respect, was an inventor; not a rich one, for he lacked business sense, but a fecund one. And his inventor's view of novelty as all-important has been John's view of music ever since I first knew him at thirty, in 1943. He prizes innovation above all other qualities—a weighting of the values which gives to all of his judgments an authoritarian, almost a commercial aspect, as of a one-way tunnel leading only to the gadget-fair.

He has, I know, felt warmly toward certain works and composers, especially toward Satie; but he has never really accepted for his own all of music, as the greater masters living and dead have done. Stravinsky's distrust of Wagner, almost anybody's suspicion of Brahms, or Schoenberg's utter impatience about Kurt Weill—aside from such minor irritations, generally composers have considered the history of music as leading up to them. But Cage has no such view. He thinks of himself, on the contrary, as music's corrective, as a prophet denouncing the whole of Renaissance and post-Renaissance Europe, with its incorrigible respect for beauty and distinction, and dissolving all that in an ocean of electronic availabilities. Electronic because those are what is around these days. He knows the sound of any loudspeaker, through which all this must come, to be essentially ugly (he has said so), and he probably knows that the presence of Mozart in *HPSCHD* gives to that work a neoclassical aspect definitely embarrassing. But the enormity of his transgression in both cases humanizes after all the overweening ambition. It is

not the first time that an artist has fancied himself as destroying
the past, and then found himself using it.

Actually Cage is less a destroyer than a typical California crea-
tor. Like many another West Coast artist—Gertrude Stein, for
example—he selects his materials casually and then with great
care arranges them into patterns of hidden symmetry. The difference between such artists and their European counterparts
lies not in occult balances, which have been standard in Europe
ever since Japan was revealed to them in the 1850s, but in the
casual choice of materials. That Europe will have none of. From
Bach and Mozart through Debussy and Stravinsky to Boulez
and Berio and Xenakis, just as from Chaucer through Byron to
Proust and Joyce, or from Giotto through Picasso, forms themselves, the words, the colors, the sounds, the scales, the melodies
are ever precious, the psychic themes adventurous and terrible.
Their treatment may be comical or tragic, sometimes both; but
the matter must be noble no matter how ingenious the design.

Cage would say of all that, "just more post-Renaissance imitation of nature." He believes, or pretends to believe, that the artist,
instead of copying nature's forms, should follow her ways of behavior. As to what these ways are, unless he believes them to be
really without pattern, I cannot imagine. A man as well read as
he must know that neither biological forms nor crystal shapes
are matters of chance, also that animals and plants are as ruth-
less about seizing food and holding a place in the sun as any
European artist ever was.

The truth is that Cage's mind is narrow. Were it broader his
remarks might carry less weight. And his music might not exist
at all. For with him the original gift, the musical ear, is not a
remarkable one. Neither did he ever quite master the classical
elements, harmony and counterpoint—a failure that has led
him at times into faulty harmonic analysis. His skill at rhythmic
analysis and rhythmic construction is very great, one of the finest
I have known. And his literary facility is considerable. One book,
called *Silence,* contains most of the best among his writings on
musical aesthetics. *A Week from Monday* is a joke-book, the
clownings of a professional celebrity who has admired Gertrude
Stein and played chess with Marcel Duchamp. *Notations* is a

collection of reproduced musical manuscripts from 261 composers, some laid out in staves and measures, many in the mechanical-drawing style or the multitudinous chicken tracks that are the individual shorthands, no two alike, of today's musical inventors. The aim of this vastly revealing book, with its gamut of personalities and handwritings, was to raise money through the publication and eventual direct sale of these gift manuscripts for the benefit of a foundation through which Cage aids musicians, dancers, and other artists congenial to his tastes. In *Virgil Thomson: His Life and Music* (the biographical part is by Kathleen O'Donnell Hoover) my works, every scrap of them up to 1959, have all been analyzed with care and described, as often as not, with love. There is some frankly expressed petulance too, and a sincere regret that my career has not followed an undeviating modernism. The catalogue of my music—complete, detailed, and accurate—is a bibliographic triumph. For Cage is at all times a precision worker.

He is also a major musical force and a leader among us. This leadership is not merely a matter of position and of precept; it is also kept up by mammoth shows like *HPSCHD* and the one produced in 1966 at New York's 69th Regiment Armory and entitled modestly Variation VII. Nobody else among the far-outs can lay hands on so much expense-money or has the persistence to carry through such detailed projects in score-planning and in electronic manipulation. Nobody, perhaps, except Iannis Xenakis, who works by a mathematics of probabilities. All this assiduity at the service of music's physical aggrandizement I find more admirable for pains taken than for its ability to hold my attention. Lasting for twenty-one minutes or four and more hours, the Cage works have some intrinsic interest and much charm, but after a few minutes very little urgency. They do not seem to have been designed for holding attention, and generally speaking they do not hold it. Constructed not for having a beginning, a middle, and an ending but for being all middle, all ambience, all media-massage, they turn out easy to taste and quick to satisfy.

A lack of urgency has been characteristic of Cage's music from the beginning. The instrumental sounds, whether altered or normal, are charming at the outset and agreeably varied from one piece to another, even in such delicate gradings of variety as from one piano preparation to another. But whenever I have played his recorded works for students I have found that no matter what their length they exhaust themselves in about two minutes, say four at most. By that time we have all got the sound of it and made some guess at the "permanent" emotion expressed. And there is no need for going on with it, since we know that it will not be going any deeper into an emotion already depicted as static. Nor will it be following nature's way by developing an organic structure. For if the mind that created it, though powerful and sometimes original, is nevertheless a narrow one, the music itself, for all its jollity, liveliness, and good humor, is emotionally shallow.

It is at its best, I think, when accompanying Merce Cunningham's dance spectacles. These could as well, I fancy, do without music at all, so delicious are they to watch. And Cage's music for them is never an intrusion, but just right—cheerful, thin, up-to-the-minute in style. The last of his big machines I have listened to (I avoid those that employ amplification) is the Concert for Piano and Orchestra of 1958. This, heard live, is all of precious materials, since its sounds come from classical instruments, themselves the product of evolution and of careful manufacture. And though the composer has tried hard to remove their dignity—playing trombones without their bells, putting one tuba's bell inside another's, sawing away at a viola placed across the knees for greater purchase—the fact remains that even treated rudely these instruments give a more elegant sound than electric buzzers and automobile brake-bands, or even than tom-toms and temple-blocks. As for the spectacle of David Tudor crawling around among the pedals of his pianoforte in order to knock on the sounding-board from below, that too was diverting to watch, though the knocking was not loud enough to be funny. All in all the visual show added so much to the whole that when, again for students, I played the recording of this piece (made in the hall itself at Cage's twenty-fifth-anniversary concert), we were all disappointed, I think, at its puny and inconsequential sound.

In the long run non-classical sound-sources, especially the synthetic ones, are as great a hazard to music as industrially processed foods can be to gastronomy (not to speak of nutrition).

And Cage's compositions, in the days when he used to play or conduct them *live*, were far more agreeable to the ear than the electronically generated ones which dominate his later production. Even those earlier ones conceived for direct audition are less likely nowadays to turn up in the concert hall than they are in the form of recordings. So that the whole of his repertory (saving the famous *4'33"* of silence) tends to be sicklied over with the monochrome of transmitted sound. And this is a misfortune for us all, since much of his work is inspired by the joy of cooking up a piece out of fresh sounds.

The trouble with loudspeakers is as follows. Their transmission of familiar music performed on familiar instruments can be highly resembling, even deceptively so, provided the acoustical size of the original combo is appropriate to that of the room in which it is being heard. This life-likeness diminishes with large amplification or diminution, as with an opera or symphony cut down to bedroom size or a harpsichord solo piped into a theatre. Now any resemblances to an original, as with photography, for example, depend for their vivacity on the receptor's acquaintance with the original or with its kind. Faults of transmission can therefore be forgiven in return for the delights of recognition. But when the source is unfamiliar no comparison is at hand. How can we know what a sound electronically designed would resemble if we heard it pure? We cannot, of course, since it does not exist until transmitted. A flavor of the canned is built into it.

And what is this canned taste? In music it is a diminution of the parasitic noises that condition every instrument's timbre, the scratching of resin on a fiddle string, the thump of a piano-key hitting bottom, the clatter of a flute's finger-mechanism, a slight excess of breath-intake, the buzzing of a reed. I know that these things get picked up too, often in exaggerated form, so exaggerated in fact that they are on the whole better kept out of a recording. But the effort to do this does neutralize a bit the timbre of any instrument or voice. Just as oil painting done by artificial light tends to lose frankness of color and to wear a slight veil, so does any musical sound transmitted by loudspeaker lose some of its delight for the ear. And when that sound is one for which no compensatory acquaintance exists with any original, a

Charles Ives, whether we knew it or not the father
of us all, here no longer young, not yet old.

War March, "They Are There," by Charles Ives,
composer's 1917 manuscript of page 3.

Ives's *War March*, page 3 of Lou Harrison's 1942
edited transcript, containing also one measure
from his reconstitution of the missing page 4.

Charles Tomlinson Griffes,
a genius, died at thirty-five.

Edgard Varèse, our Italo-Burgundian cyclone,
and Heitor Villa-Lobos, Brazil's perpetually
active volcano, in their middle forties, Paris 1929.

Above: Ira and George Gershwin, 1937, two years
after *Porgy and Bess*. George was to die that same year.
Below: Carl Ruggles, completely deaf and very old, went
right on "being one being living." (*Bill & Gwen Sloan*)

Top: George Gershwin's neat piano hands.
Left: Roger Huntington Sessions, no end
impressive at not far from seventy.
(*Bill & Gwen Sloan*) Right: Roy Harris,
in youth squarely a charmer, in middle age
a business man, later prone to anger,
at all ages clearly a "star."
(*Bill & Gwen Sloan*)

Ernest Bloch with the cellist Alexander Barjansky, to whom *Schelomo* had been dedicated in 1917, photographed some twenty-five years later.

Left: Carlos Chavez, Mexico's major master. Right: Roque Cordero, Panama's finest. (*Southern Music Publishers*)

Left: Henry Cowell, the variety of whose sources and composing methods was probably the broadest of our time. (*Sidney Cowell*)
Right: Domingo Santa Cruz, Chile's effective organizer of both pedagogy and performance, for twenty years too its chief composer.

George Antheil. Violence and a boyish cheerfulness gave style to his early music.

Left: Randall Thompson, songful instrumentally, mellifluous chorally, in a drawing by John Canaday, art critic of *The New York Times*. Right: Wallingford Riegger, a pixie and a Marxist, vastly expert instrumentally (*Bill & Gwen Sloan*)

Aaron Copland, Virgil Thomson, Nadia Boulanger, and Walter Piston at the Museum of Modern Art, 5 April 1962, after playing in a concert of music by some of her former pupils.

Virgil Thomson, Leonard Bernstein, Walter Piston, William Schuman, and Aaron Copland, who composed fanfares to open the five centenary exhibitions held at New York's Metropolitan Museum of Art in 1969 and 1970, photographed at Philharmonic Hall. (*Bruce Davidson, Magnum*)

Paul Bowles, folklorist, traveler, novelist,
also a good composer. (*Dennis Stock, Magnum*)

Ross Lee Finney, in whose chamber music complexity
does not hinder sweetness. (*Christopher R. Carey*)

Peggy Glanville-Hicks has written operas
in collaboration with Robert Graves
and Lawrence Durrell, also after
Thomas Mann. (*Bill & Gwen Sloan*)

Marc Blitzstein in London 1945, where for the U.S.
Air Force he wrote *The Airborne* (words and music).

drawing by
FERNANDO GAMBOA

Left: Silvestre Revueltas of Mexico,
the most original composer
Latin America has produced.

Right: Alberto Ginastera, Argentinian of melodic and formal excellence,
has lately hit the jackpot with melodramatic operas of super-elaborate
orchestration. (*Beth Bergman, Courtesy of Boosey & Hawkes*)

Elliott Carter writes complex chamber music utterly brilliant
for virtuoso players utterly expert. (*Bill & Gwen Sloan*)

whole range of musical creation (that of today's far-outs, for instance) gets drowned in a sea of similarity.

Many of America's far-outs (old masters Foss, Babbitt, and Luening among them) have endeavored to liven up the deadness of speaker-transmission by combining tape-music with that of a live orchestra. Even Varèse, in *Deserts,* tried it once. John Cage, so far, has seemingly abstained from this apologetic stance. For even in *HPSCHD,* with all that went on together in that monster auditorium, I judge there is little likelihood of the seven harpsichords' not having also undergone amplification.

The gramophone, as a preserver of standard music, pop or classical, has ever been an instrument of culture, because the record collectors complete their listening experiences through attendance at musical occasions. This was demonstrated in the early 1940s at Columbia University's Institute of Social Research. Radio, it was also determined there, led culturally nowhere, since persons whose musical experience began with that medium rarely proceeded to make acquaintance with the real thing. Considering today's immersion of everybody everywhere in transmitted sound, and especially of the young in high amplification, there seems little chance that any music not transmitted and amplified will long survive outside its present classical habitats—which is to say, opera houses, concert halls, conservatoires, studios, and certain low dives where jazz is played, maybe too in mountaineer heights far from Nashville, and a few churches. Unless, of course, the young, today so hooked on amplification, should suddenly say to rock itself, "Good-by."

But for now the troubled waves are like a sea; and whether the youths and maidens gather three hundred thousand strong in fields near Woodstock, New York just to be together while rock artists, even amplified, cannot combat the distances; or whether they mill around inside an auditorium built for a mere eighteen thousand souls while a thoroughly prepared electronic happening (accompanied by visuals and swirling lights) is served up, along with allusions to Mozart, under the highest academic auspices and the authorship of two famous masters, is all the same, so far as I can see, though Woodstock, by report, was much more fun.

79

Both, however, are thoroughly contemporary in feeling. And either or both may mean, like any children's crusade, that we have come to the end of that line. Also that the Viet-Nam war, by ending, might change all sorts of things. Could it send John Cage back to making music, turn him aside from the messianic hope of giving birth to a new age? Destroying the past is a losing game; the past cannot be destroyed; it merely wears out. And moving into a higher age by playing with mechanical toys is a child's game. New ages in art come slowly, silently, unsuspected. And publicity can bring only death to a real messiah. My instinct is to believe that whatever may be valid for the future of music as an art (and *as* an art is the only way I can conceive it) must be taking place underground. Today's prophetic ones, I truly believe, either lie hidden, or else stand around so innocently that none can see them. Otherwise someone would for certain betray them, and the price-controlling powers would shoot them down. I cannot see today's mass-conscious celebrities as anything but a danger to art, whatever in their youthful years they may have left behind for us that is authentic and fine.

Music has its fashion industry and its novelty trade. And John Cage, as a composer, seems today's leader in novelty-fashions, at least for America. From modest musical beginnings, through ambition, perseverance, and brains, he has built up a mastery over modern materials, their choice, their cutting and piecing, their sewing into garments of any length and for many occasions. And he has exploited that mastery, at first as a one-man shop, later as an enterprise employing many helpers, always as a business internationally reputable, and essentially a novelty business. None other on that level, or in America, is so sound. Rivalries, if any, will come from Europe, from that same post-Renaissance Europe he has so long despised and feared. Boulez, for the moment, is not a danger, being chiefly occupied with conducting. But Stockhausen has novelty ideas. And Xenakis, with a higher mathematical training (for that is a requisite now in musical engineering), might well be about to take over the intellectual leadership.

European far-outs are a team and a cartel, as Cage learned more than twenty years ago. No American composer knows any such solidarity. The best substitutes we can mobilize are foundation support, ever capricious; a university position, where every-body is underpaid, over-verbalized, and paralyzed by fear of the students; or a celebrity situation, in which one can have anything, but only so long as the distribution industry permits and the press finds one diverting. In the contrary eventuality artistic death, with burial in an unmarked grave, comes quickly, for unlike Europe, we have no immortality machine.

Perhaps John Cage, with his inventor's ingenuity, should try building us one. And I don't mean the kind that destroys itself, such as the artist Jean Tinguely used to construct. Nor yet the kind that Cage has so often assembled of late years, designed to destroy, with luck, the history of music. I mean something that might relieve today's composers from the awful chore of follow-ing "nature's ways" and give them building-blocks again for constructing musical houses that might, by standing up alone, tempt us to walk in and out of them.

But Cage's aim with music, like Samson's in the pagan temple, has long been clearly destructive. Can he really pull the whole thing down around him? You never know. He might just! And in that way himself reach immortality. But his would be no standard immortality of structured works and humane thoughts. It would be more like a current event, "Sorcerer's apprentice sets off H-bomb in Lincoln Center."

It could happen, though. For Cage, like Samson, is a strong one; and he has helpers. They admire what he does and, what is far more dangerous, believe what he says. The young, more-over, seem to be yearning nowadays after a messiah. And a musical one might be the likeliest for them to follow. Indeed, Cage's rigid schedule of beliefs and prophecies, his monorail mind and his turbine-engined, irreversible locomotive of a career all make it easy for the young to view him as a motorized and amplified pied piper calling out, "Get on board-a little children; there's room for a million more."

9. Let Us Now Praise Famous Men

The fact that certain European composers methodologically of the left—Stockhausen, Berio, Xenakis—have been engaged to work in America has not made their creations a part of American music any more than the much longer residence here, including citizenship, of Stravinsky, Schoenberg, Hindemith, and Křenek gave to their music a recognizably American cast. A European formation in music is seemingly ineradicable. And so indeed is the lack of one. The cases of Roger Sessions, Roy Harris, Walter Piston, Elliott Carter, Arthur Berger, and Ross Lee Finney, like Edward Burlingame Hill and John Alden Carpenter before them, are significant in this regard. No amount of European overlay, though it may have masked their essential Americanism, has deceived anyone into mistaking them for Europeans.

Similarly, the Cage progeny belong clearly with the American left, whether their work be hand-made or electronically processed. Two early pupils, Morton Feldman and Christian Wolff, have made music of great delicacy and sweetness; others, Gordon Mumma, for instance, and the Japanese Toshi Ichiyanagi, are harder to distinguish from Cage himself. And Earle Brown, in his youth an associate of Cage, has composed music that travels the modernist circuits of Europe, its expressive content being sufficiently American (largely through rhythmic animation) and its workmanship sufficiently European (serial enough) to make it welcome. It is stylish music in any country and most agreeable, being light of texture, steely, and without fragility.

Everywhere, it seems to me, the music of today, for all its internationalist aims and methodology, reflects its origins—French, Germanic, Italian, Spanish—no less than did that of the last century. And in this Tower of Babel the American voice becomes more and more distinct as the volume of our work augments. Naturally also it becomes louder as the university establishments mobilize larger and larger foundation grants, as well as larger and larger locales for its display.

A university rather than a conservatoire background has characterized American music for nearly a century now. But formerly this university music was related to the humanities. Of late it has taken its tone, and even some of its budget, from the engineering sciences, specifically from electronic studies and from the use of computers. Our musical modernism is no part of any government-sponsored radio and television set-up, as it is in Europe, because America has no such set-up. But we do have rich universities scientifically oriented, and masses of youth handy with a slide-rule.

Also we love free-wheeling. Most of American humor, all of our pop-art, the literary traditions of Walt Whitman, Mark Twain, and Gertrude Stein, whole regions of American life, including the sacred jam-session, derive from the gusto of improvisation. Combine the delights of indeterminacy with the adventure of a dice-game, and you can see how Cage's Americans, complete with foundation funds and university blessings, have come to resemble very little their colleagues of Europe and Asia, in spite of the fact that tapes and loudspeakers sound very much alike all round the world.

So too have the more conventional composers—those who still work with tunings related to a fundamental—come unstuck from their European counterparts. Certainly we have had our quota of Schoenberg followers and of Stravinsky imitators, but so has Europe. The monumental music of Roger Sessions, on the other hand, seems to yearn toward all of Europe, rather than toward just one stylistic sector of it. In the long run I take it to be dominated, like the music of Vincent d'Indy, by an emulation of Beethoven. And if in its pursuit of excellence it occasionally stumbles over its own coils, it is nevertheless work of a high viscosity, a stubborn obscurity, and some grandeur. It is impressive, moreover, not only by weight but by volume, running to eight symphonies and three operas, in addition to concertos and chamber works. It has no parallel in Central Europe, England, or Scandinavia. Even Olivier Messiaen in France and Alberto Ginastera from Argentina are less hermetic. Only Carlos Chavez, in Mexico, writes music of comparable density.

Less weighty than the music of Sessions, that of Ross Lee Finney—dodecaphonic and serial in late years—runs higher in the charm of sheer sound, with no loss of complexity interest, especially his chamber works for strings. Though Germanic in its origins, for translucency it resembles the music of the Frenchman Henri Dutilleux.

The music of Elliott Carter, less abundant than these, and achieving its highest intensity in the chamber combinations, is more complex of texture than either Sessions or Finney and at the same time easier to follow. I am not sure how this miracle comes about; but I fancy some of it is due to the composer's dramatizing instincts and imaginative ear, his ability to couch a complex thought in pleasing sounds. In any case, his Piano Sonata of 1945, his two String Quartets, and his Double Concerto for piano and harpsichord each accompanied by its own chamber group, are works of such striking originality that they have achieved a European success even in these times, when Europe seems to be viewing all our music with severity.

That severity may be due to the fact that our music is not quite like theirs any more. When it was, they could be more tolerant of it. And when it was not, but clearly no rival, as in Gershwin's irresistible *Rhapsody in Blue* or his sweet-singing opera *Porgy and Bess*, they could admire it without stint. When Cage threatened both their modernist assumptions and the hegemony of their rising power-group, he was removed—complimented yes, but firmly excluded from its patronage. Perhaps, like Gershwin, Carter is no danger to Europe from the plain fact that nobody there is even aspiring to write tonal music of that intricacy or of that intrinsic interest. With nobody to feel rivalry, everyone is free to admire. In any case, Carter's chamber works do get round internationally; virtually all find them distinguished and beautiful.

Roy Harris's works, I am sorry to say, do not travel so widely or so well. One can find priceless items among the early chamber works, and there is one remarkable symphony. These alone will preserve his fame. But his later music, though more expert, even in America tends to be less remembered.

Lou Harrison's music resembles nothing written in Europe today. Thirty years ago he wrote symphonies for percussion that could remind one of Java and Siam. Subtly sensuous and never tiring to the ear, they are among our most cherishable properties. In the last decade Harrison's Asian interests have moved to Korea, where he mastered the classical Chinese court music. He has composed in this style for its classical instruments, including the jade gong; and an adaptation of its rhetoric to European textures (not an imitation) has given him vocal works and a film score, *Nuptial,* of surprising and powerful simplicity. Between these two periods of Asian allegiance, he wrote serial pieces (as any pupil of Schoenberg might have done) and a body of work, choral, orchestral, and other, based on historic European tunings *not* tempered (which no other Schoenberg pupil did do).

One such work, a monodic opera entitled *Rapunzel's Daughter* (after William Morris), won a prize in Rome when it was sung there in 1954 by Leontyne Price. The varieties of instrumental tuning for which he has composed include Greek ones and Elizabethan ones, as well as Korean. A work commissioned by the Louisville Orchestra requires for its correct intonation, if I remember rightly, fourteen especially-built flutes. In a work for full orchestra, entitled Symphony on G, just intervals and their commas are employed to rich effect. It is a work of sustained eloquence and high Romantic afflatus, belonging in no way to our university tradition of symphonic writing.

Obviously so accomplished and so varied a production, especially when carried out from so far-off a center as San Francisco, has no resemblance to the stylistically constricted and professionally combative careers that hold attention in the East. But Lou Harrison is a great man (*une grande nature,* the French would say) with a remarkable ear, a composer both authentic and highly original as well as (thank heaven) abundant.

Henry Cowell's music since his death in 1965 has somewhat faded in program frequency. But there is so much of it in all forms and for all occasions that it is bound to remain with us a goodly while. There are more than twenty works in symphonic form alone. He has written for many instruments and under many ethnic influences, including those of the Iranians, the Icelandics, the East Indians, the Japanese, and our own Southern mountaineers. His *New Music* edition, published quarterly from 1927, brought numerous modern composers into print. His book of 1930, *New Musical Resources,* is a classic. *Charles Ives and His Music* (written with his wife Sidney Cowell) is the definitive work on this composer. His analyses of new music published regularly in *The Musical Quarterly* and other professional journals are authoritative and useful. His classes at Columbia University and at the New School for Social Research were ever a source of enlightenment to students. Few musicians indeed have left so deeply their mark on music's life—West Coast, East Coast, Latin America, and Asia—as this modest and indefatigable Californian.

His music is not complex, but it sings. It is not highly polished, but it has structure. It is not strikingly ambitious either, but it has presence. And never is it bogus or vulgar or stupid or falsely inspired. Cowell too was a great man, by his active mind and his ethical behavior, as well as by his high-standard musical abundance.

William Schuman and Samuel Barber are composers of sound repute. The former I cherish for his ballets, especially *Undertow.* The latter has contributed valuably to our vocal repertory in *Knoxville: Summer of 1915* for soprano and orchestra and in his *Hermit Songs,* remarkably to piano literature with a sonata and a concerto that are repertory works. His Adagio for Strings is world-famous. Schuman has no such international status, but his music can be listened to. Both composers are classical as to form, with Schuman regularly observing a high dissonance texture, Barber following a more Romantic taste in harmony. Schuman has also served as president of the Juilliard School of Music and later of Lincoln Center for the Performing Arts, where administrative efficiency does not seem to have hindered his development as a composer of strongly individual gesture. With all our composers of the establishment—Copland, Sessions, Harris, Carter, Finney, Mennin, even the songful Barber—the rhythmic drive is powerful. They are masters, moreover, of the concert forms—the closed forms—but distinctly uncomfortable in the open-ended continuities of opera, which Douglas Moore and Lou Harrison have handled with greater freedom.

Ned Rorem, after eight years of residence in Paris, has aspired to produce in English a vocal repertory comparable to that of Francis Poulenc. There are also Rorem orchestral works of some brilliance—particularly *Eagles* and *Lions*—and a handful of chamber works—*Lovers,* for instance, and Eleven Pieces for Eleven Players—which, if not quite Carter or Copland, are pleasing to hear. And there are operas, all of them so far unsuccessful. Nor do his choral works, of which there are many, seem to me infallible. Certainly it is in the solo songs, of which there are literally hundreds, that Rorem makes his bid for consideration beside the creators of German and French lieder.

Consideration in this company one can grant him for his taste in the choice of poems and for grace in the melodic line. But no such intensity is present as in the German masters from Schubert through Wolf and Mahler or in the French from Duparc and Fauré through Poulenc. In fact no such intensity exists anywhere in English song (nor does it in Italian, for that matter, nor in Spanish, only a little in the Russian and the Scandinavian). Even the Elizabethans and Purcell, for all their sweetness and their wit, are like the Italians of those same times, more dainty than deep, more decorative for the line of a mood than emotionally penetrating. English-language poetry, sung, has never achieved psychology or drama as we know these qualities through the German and the French.

Consequently Rorem's effort, no less than that of Barber, of Douglas Moore, of Ernst Bacon, David Diamond, William Flanagan, the great Copland himself, and of Ives in concert songs, remains nobler for its persistently setting out on what may well be a hopeless errand than for any world's record achieved. When Poulenc, as a friend, discouraged his vocal efforts and praised the orchestral, Rorem sincerely believed him to be jealous. What can one say of so impregnable a stance? Nothing except that the English art-song is not yet a major form, and that even Benjamin Britten, with all his great gifts, has come nearer to depth in French song—to Rimbaud's *Illuminations*—than he has in English. For devotional texts Britten is ideal; but for cracking the nut of English lyric poetry, he is just another hopeful; and so is Rorem. So are we all indeed. For English opera there may be some precedent—in Britten, in Douglas Moore, in my own work. But for lieder in English I know of no model, excepting the patter songs of Gilbert and Sullivan, which are perfect. And I seriously doubt that Poulenc, Ravel, Debussy, Fauré have any more to offer an American of today than Schubert, Schumann, Brahms, Wolf, Mahler. Or for that matter, the Elizabethans and Purcell. Let us all try very hard to write English songs; by all means let us try. But I have yet to see a break-through in the matter, something as radically alive and different from its predecessors as Schubert's flexible and flowing songs are from the stiff layouts of Mozart and Beethoven. Actually Theodore Chanler's songs, though few in number, are probably the best we have. And those of William Flanagan have a soaring intensity all unusual to the English language.

Returning to the advanced composers, I have a great devotion to the music of Kenneth Gaburo, which I find utterly delicious for sound, whether vocal or instrumental, directly heard or processed. Like the music of Lou Harrison and of Elliott Carter—though it resembles neither, being more far-out in both methods and materials—I find that it most remarkably comes to life, as if the tired old tempered scale, so hopelessly out of tune when classical harmony is not there to refresh it, had been forgotten and the ear consulted again about making music. Its sentiments, moreover, seem direct and manly, never borrowed. I admire this music for its integrity, and I delight in it.

There are other American composers whose music is precious to me—Ben Weber, Stefan Wolpe, Colin McPhee, Arthur Berger, Leon Kirchner, Irving Fine, Chou Wen-chung, and Henry Brant. The operas of Carlisle Floyd and Peggy Glanville-Hicks, of Jack Beeson, Avery Claflin, and Robert Ward have undeniable quality. And there have been four brilliant composers of Russian birth— Alexander Tcherepnin, Nicolai Berezowsky, Nicolai Lopatnikoff, and Nicolas Nabokov, all of whom have written their finest as Americans.

American is something a musician need not be ashamed to be. Painting was the first humane art to develop here, beginning in the eighteenth century and flourishing in constant touch with England. American letters have a sound nineteenth-century history, and a still stronger one in the twentieth, where they have come to overshadow the parent stem. Music has been the last to ripen, and its story seems to me altogether of this century. That is why I have written these essays. I do not believe any art's history to be one of continuous evolution or steady growth. Music's active epochs are short—from Haydn through Schubert barely fifty years, for instance. And the American maturity I write about may already be over, giving place to a time of noise and its casual arrangement.

I have written elsewhere that I expected the latter half of this century to witness the consolidation of our century's innovations into an amalgamated twentieth-century style. Something like this took place during the last quarter of the eighteenth; and I think it has taken place in our time, since World War II. Everybody successful or establishment-minded writes music now, diatonic or chromatic, with a thickish overlay of dissonance, and since 1950 with a decreasing dependence on serial continuities. Everybody orchestrates brilliantly; everyone has his tune characteristics, his devices harmonic or arithmetical for holding a piece together. Structure and form, nevertheless, remain a problem; organic form does, in any case. With harmony itself become so weak, so little urgent, arithmetical symmetries and the use of librettos have become the main resources.

And exactly as in the late eighteenth century, one composer's work is very much like another's. The chief question now seems: is it music or noise? Both are subject to compositional arrangement, of course, but by different acoustical procedures. Although the performance of the human ear in auditory perception and of the brain in auditory memory are only beginning to be investigated, it is clear already that the future of composition with noise, like that of music itself, will be influenced by the knowledge of how we hear and how certain sounds come to be pleasing or not; hence how arrangements of sound can communicate emotional patterns of anxiety and relief. For these indeed are what give continuity in all the time-arts.

Myself I see no hindrance to the survival of both noise-art and music. Photography did not kill oil painting; on the contrary, it set off in landscape painting a development known as impressionism which invigorated all painting. Similarly, the gramophone and the radio, far from killing off music, have contributed to their distribution, changed their sociology, and corrected their aesthetics.

So I am not worried. Let the boys have fun. Let us all have fun. Let Europe survive. Let America exist. Indeed I am convinced that in music it already does exist. At least that.

10. The Operas of Virgil Thomson

BY VICTOR FELL YELLIN

Virgil Thomson's main contribution to American music is his blending of the musical elements of melody, harmony, and rhythm into a musical style proper to American speech. Earlier composers such as Stephen Foster, George W. Chadwick, and Charles Ives, and certainly contemporaries such as Marc Blitzstein and George Gershwin have captured aspects of the American cadence. But only Thomson's music provides a consistent, uniform, and therefore classic model of American musical speech unencumbered by stylistic mannerisms or personal eccentricities. Thomson not only created a style for himself, but also a serviceable procedure that other composers may use without imitating Thomson's particular gestures or falling into avantgardism. Too early to say here but history may confirm that Thomson's innovation for American opera compares with that of the original composers of opera in Florence, Peri and Caccini, with Schütz in seventeenth-century Germany, Lully in France, and the Elizabethan composers in England, all of whom laid down basic models for correct musical declamation.

Rather than writing a primer on American musical declamation and drama (which, considering his way with words, he should also do) Thomson has composed three operas: *Four Saints in Three Acts*, *The Mother of Us All*, and *Lord Byron*.

To call Thomson's musical declamation something new needs a historical note. Largely untouched by European trends, America's music, composed and folk, popular and serious, until the end of the eighteenth century was mainly vocal. Its hymns and ballads presented a remarkably homogeneous blend of words and music. If not always indicated by notation, then at least in performance, the stresses and cadence of the language were reflected in melody.

But along with political independence from England came cultural allegiance to the rest of Europe. People and ideas arriving from across the water in the late 1700s made East Coast urbanized citizens self-conscious about their two centuries of isolation. In music the old-fashioned itinerant singing-masters were replaced by newly arrived professionals. As if suddenly aware for the first time of original sin, Americans strove to cover up the nakedness of their angular melodies, incisive prosody, and plain harmonies; and the old hymns were "corrected." Societies were formed devoted to the European masters, to the elevation of taste, and incidentally, as in Philadelphia, so as not to eschew the practical side, to aid indigent musicians. Under the sway of the welcomed cultural imports the first composer of a grand opera, William Henry Fry, music critic of the *New York Tribune,* enunciated his philosophy for American musical prosody:

> [The composer] must also treat the English language with reference to the peculiarities necessary to effective stage declamation, and to the genius of melody as a universal dialect, which claims, indeed, supremacy over words; and as the ordinary structure of English verse ill coincides with such requisites, an amount of eccentric lyrical labors is necessary, that must deter dramatic writers from the undertaking, unless a proper estimate be set upon this required mastery of the language, rendering it flexible to the musical touch, and malleable for all the forms into which composition requires it to be beaten.

Assuming that music or at least melody was a "universal" language and that this language found its highest expression in Italian opera, Fry understandably had to conclude that if natural English prosody did not fit Italian melody, it would have to be altered. From Fry's day till the arrival on the scene a century later of his successor as music critic of the *New York Herald-Tribune,* American composers with few exceptions, when they attempted opera, followed Fry's dictum. To be sure the "universal" language changed from Italian to German to French, as in turn each became musically fashionable, but the attitude of composers remained the same. One need only glance through John Knowles Paine's *Azara* (1901) or Arthur Nevin's *Poia* (1910) to verify their deafness to American speech accents. The accompanying translated text is more appropriate to the melodic line than the English to which the music was composed.

Even without Fry's fundamental error, progress towards a true American opera was inhibited by an age-old suspicion of the theatre that lingered in puritanical minds. One of America's earliest opera houses was called the Boston Museum, another the Howard Street Athenaeum in attempts to assuage the guilt of society patrons. As late as 1900 Thomas Whitney Surette, a most influential music educator, branded opera as sin. And when American composers attempted to compete in the operatic field, more often than not their works were denied performance by the foreign-dominated companies or sabotaged by singers who had never learned to vocalize English. George Chadwick first considered writing in Italian his opera about Italian immigrants, *The Padrone,* but later changed his mind only to have this American verismo opera rejected for the Metropolitan by Giulio Gatti-Casazza, its Italian director.

After such a history few composers could be expected to waste their time on opera. And so things remained until, by one of those fortuitous confluences of history Virgil Thomson, working in Paris, convinced his older friend Gertrude Stein to write a libretto for him.

With *Four Saints in Three Acts* (Hartford 1934) and *The Mother of Us All* (New York 1947), both composed to Stein texts, Thomson reoriented serious American opera toward the fundamentals governing American sung speech by divorcing opera from the imitation of foreign language, from a preoccupation with nineteenth-century dramaturgy, and from the affectation of grandiose symphonic gestures. With a no-nonsense approach, a taste for simplicity, and an assurance derived from roots going back to a less self-conscious America, Thomson began his solution of the

American opera problem. Because details of the collaboration and of subsequent activities which resulted in the productions of these operas have already been published in *Virgil Thomson: His Life and Music* by Kathleen Hoover and John Cage, and in Thomson's own memoirs, *Virgil Thomson,* I shall restrict my comments to the works themselves.

Maurice Grosser, the scenarist, has described *Four Saints in Three Acts* as:

> both an opera and a choreographic spectacle. Imaginary but characteristic incidents from the lives of the saints constitute its action. Its scene is laid in sixteenth-century Spain. Its principal characters are Saint Teresa of Avila, Saint Ignatius Loyola, and their respective confidants, Saint Settlement and Saint Chavez—both of these last without historical prototypes. These are the four saints referred to in the title. Other characters are a Compère and Commère, a small chorus of named saints —Saint Pilar, Saint Ferdinand and others—and a larger chorus of unnamed saints. Saint Teresa, for reasons of musical convenience, is represented by two singers dressed exactly alike. This device of the composer has no hidden significance and is not anywhere indicated in the poet's text, though Miss Stein found it thoroughly acceptable. The Compère and Commère, who speak to the audience and to each other about the progress of the opera, have also, as characters, been introduced by the composer.

Natural prosody, or the rhythm of language, is the key to the understanding of Thomson's operas. His method of composition, with minor exceptions, is based on the textual stanza, phrase, word, and syllable. The first two of these suggest to him melodic line, harmonic progression, dynamic thrust, and sonority; the last two, shape and rhythmic pattern:

> With the text on my piano's music rack, I would sing and play, improvising melody to fit the words and harmony for underpinning them with shape.

From this method, at once simple and direct, evolved a vocal line and accompaniment unfettered by musical preconceptions, abstract stylistic formulations either conservative or modern—

with one exception. While traditional opera, in which the libretto's dramatic inevitability as well as its logical syntax permitted composers a wide latitude in their choice of musical procedures, themselves often discontinuous, Stein's fanciful cubistic text, so it seemed to Thomson, called for a disciplined music so inevitable in its unfolding that the music supplied the continuity missing or merely implicit in the text. It is this dramatic and expressive quotient of opera we receive, indeed, from opera in a foreign tongue; a feeling of structure and logic even though we do not understand the words.

Thomson's improvised response to the text runs the gamut from undifferentiated speech through rhythmic speech, Anglican chant on one note (without specific rhythm indicated), rhythmic chant on one note, cadenced recitative, and arias based on tuneful melody.

Though seemingly simple, American speech rhythms are as complex as English spelling. Most previous composers who instinctively reacted against rhythmic complexities inconsistent with the relative rhythmic simplicity of European musical patterns they felt sacrosanct, bent the language to fit the music. How many times has the natural syncopation of a bisyllabic word such as *many* (♪♩·) been transformed into its opposite (♩·♪) just to fit a rhythmic cliché? For example:

Here, I believe, is one of the secrets of Thomson's idiom. As the text presents in seemingly random fashion highly varied rhythmic patterns, these are captured in progressive stages of musical stylization, from actual speech dependent upon the performer's or director's sense of declamation to the controlled rhythmic and metric patterns of the composer. Thus an unending set of rhythmic variants unfolds as the opera progresses. Aided by Stein's outpouring of these rhythms, Thomson weaves their permutations into a musical fabric that is ever-changing in detail yet yields a piece of musical whole cloth.

Not all the rhythms are, however, subservient to the text. In songs like St. Teresa's:

a dance-tune rhythm is dominant; now with syncopation, now without, depending on the metrical lining-out of the tune rather than on the speech stress. And it is these periodic excursions into dance rhythms that balance speech rhythms, avoiding thus the dreaded tedium of conventional recitative.

Another way in which the composer subordinates text rhythms to the music is illustrated in the following:

Here the monosyllabic sequence provides no clue to a musical solution. Thomson thereupon constructs a chorale which he propels forward by means of off-beat percussive ejaculations of the text.

Thomsonian melodies derive not only from the rhetoric of the text but also from traditional musical sources. Arias sung by St. Teresa, "Not April Fool's day a pleasure," and by St. Ignatius, "Pigeons on the grass alas," illustrate this approach.

Where is the Thomson innovation then? Many American (and English) composers had either parodied or rejected the long-evolved operatic style loosely identifiable by the term *bel canto*. Others, who accepted such traditional European procedures, imitated even the smallest melodic-rhythmic details of foreign language prosody. By retaining the overall structure and vocal method of traditional European opera, yet at the same time eschewing its specifics and capturing as his own the flow and pattern of American-English speech, Thomson has created a formula that combines the strength of a cosmopolitan tradition with the authenticity of a work of art linguistically conditioned.

The Mother of Us All has many of the characteristics of a second child. Both the offspring's growing pains and parental anxiety seem to have decreased, and any casual observer could feel less tension in the household in 1946 when the two artists again worked together. Just as this last completed text by Gertrude Stein (who died in July of that year) communicates most directly the story of American life from the Federal period to World War I, so the music seems to have become more abstract. Yet the balance of words and music, that is text as a plastic material to be shaped by music, is maintained.

Because both operas were written by the same team it is interesting to compare and contrast *The Mother of Us All* with its predecessor. Unlike the libretto for *Four Saints in Three Acts*, *The Mother of Us All* tells a story and radiates ideas rather than portraying the emotion of religious ecstasy. The subject matter has much to do with the change of emphasis. Susan B. Anthony, as the Mother, like most of our American saints, was a very practical person whose success in the cause of woman suffrage was due more to efficient uses of power than to the manipulation of any mass sense of guilt. Moreover, the picture-album pageantry of the American experience during the last century and a half, unified by the sometimes anachronistic juxtaposition of American personalities, historical, anecdotal, and fantastical, has a nationalistic immediacy not present in *Four Saints in Three Acts,* which addresses itself to our more cosmopolitan side. It is this cross-reference to the musical and historical life of Anglo-Saxon America before the coming of age of other ethnic groups that has always made *The Mother of Us All* more meaningful viscerally and intellectually to Cambridge, Minneapolis, or Los Angeles than to Manhattan audiences.

Actually, the two works have much in common. The Compère and Commère of *Four Saints* become in *The Mother* the genial interlocutors Virgil T. and Gertrude S.; St. Ignatius becomes Daniel Webster; St. Teresa I, Susan B. Anthony; St. Teresa II, Ann. Other saints are transformed into both actual and mythical personages: John Adams, Indiana Elliot, Thaddeus Stevens, Angel More, Donald Gallup, and Ulysses S. Grant. The choruses of both operas are, in effect, ensembles of sacred or secular personalities. There is even one literal quotation. "When this you see remember me," an autograph-book jingle, appears twice in *Four Saints,* first (a) at the end of "St. Ignatius's vision of the last judgment" in Act III sung by St. Teresa II in a minor-mode version of the opera's opening phrase: (b) "To know to know to love her so," and later, in Act IV, (c) sung by full chorus to the same tune. The identical text, this time set to a new melodic phrase (d), appears in the opening bars of *The Mother* sung by Susan B. Anthony.

98

Chorus I
To know to know to love her so.—

Full Chorus
When this you see re-mem-ber me.

Susan B. Anthony
When this you see re-mem-ber me,

Because the scenario of *The Mother* is more or less explicit in the Stein text, a more logical relationship between this text and the dramatic-musical form can be found than in *Four Saints*, where the music alone provides structure. Greater textual logic seems to afford the composer greater latitude, and one notices the freer use of abstract musical procedures. In the first scene of Act I (Prologue), musical sonorities change with cinematic abruptness as they connect butt end to butt end to produce an effect for the audience of different points of view or visual emphasis on a virtually static stage. Each sonority is in a different key. In some cases the fast-moving dialogue is counterpointed against a repeating chord-progression that changes only at a precise dramatic moment. These cadence-like repetitions underline a new kind of recitative with a high quotient of melodic interest.

Extensive quotations from the speeches, letters, and literary works of its historical characters has also had the effect of making the rhetoric and vocabulary of *The Mother* more complex than that of *Four Saints* in so far as it reflects nineteenth-century prose style. Mirrored in Thomson's vocal lines, this prosodic richness and variety give a certain luxuriance to the melodic contours of *The Mother*. Memorable is such a line as Daniel Webster's:

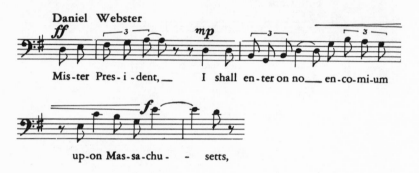

Susan B. Anthony's language, even though direct, is rich in rhythmic pattern and melodic inflection:

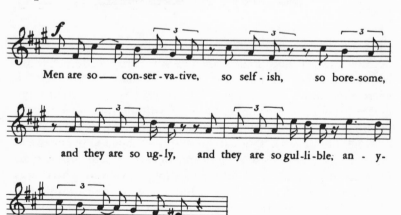

Other differences between *The Mother* and *Four Saints* have to do with Thomson's continuing studies in chromatic and dissonant sonorities rooted in parallel triads. The Prelude to Act I, scene four, is a particularly succinct example:

It is a miniature landscape with falling snow. In contrast to the sunny snow of *Four Saints* made bright by "sound[ing] them with the thirds and that," the calm of the frigid night scene is created by two slow-moving series of parallel triads (in invertible counterpoint), each series with its own clearly defined tune and sonority, celesta or woodwinds. Bitonal dissonance *sans* counterpoint accompanies quarreling or unwelcome interruptions. In Act I, scene three Jenny Reefer, a comical feminist, sings her bugle-call melody:

Jenny Reefer

U - lys - ses S. Grant was not the most earn - est

nor the most no - ble of men,

A make-believe tension is here produced by sharply attacked chords in two keys one half-step distant: $\frac{C}{D}$-$\frac{G}{F\sharp}$. Echoing Miss Reefer's intervention is the ruckus started by the cantankerous brother of Indiana Elliot during his sister's wedding (scene five). Here dramatic tension is prolonged by a staggering number of literal repetitions (twenty-eight) of the same bitonal progression. As other characters react to the unwelcome disturbance, the same dissonant relationship is maintained on different pitch levels and is not resolved until Ulysses S. Grant himself appears to restore peace, and the wedding waltz resumes in the uncontradicted tonality of F-sharp major. Later, the same bitonal combination abruptly sours the ceremonies before the unveiling of Susan B. Anthony's statue in the Congressional Hall when Indiana Elliot speaks testily about marriage.

The Operas of Virgil Thomson

Along with literal quotations of text are musical quotations of tunes, though not as many as the listener might think. John Cage found no less than "thirty-eight references to nursery tunes" in *Four Saints.* Evidence for his statistic seems to be based more on the text than on the music. Such lines as:

One two three four five six seven all good children go to heaven.

and many other phrases from children's games give to their melodic settings the semblance of nursery tunes. Similarly, in *The Mother,* the wedding hymn, the "carpet-sweeper" music, Daniel Webster's Sousa-march-like aria, Act II, scene three (a), his tender farewell to Angel More, (b) and the introductory march of Act II, scene three, all sound like quotations of American tunes. In reality they are not; that they seem so is a tribute to Thomson's fluency and testimony to his deep roots in the soil of American music. Unlike other composers whose "American" style seems to be the result of research, Thomson's musical syntax as well as his melodic sense can be traced to non-academic influences going back with his ancestors to colonial times.

A notable harmonic formula permeating much of the composer's music, especially his vocal works, involves parallel thirds in the upper parts accompanied by parallel fifths in the male voices:

Reminiscent of eighteenth-century Anglo-American tunesmith's disregard of "correct" voice-leading, this blending of rugged with sweet sonorities is as much as any other single fingerprint a Thomson hallmark.

Of course, there are literal musical quotations whose raison d'être varies from the obvious to the obscure. Missing from the RCA-Victor recording, although present in the vocal score of *Four Saints*, is the quotation from "America," both words and music:

Chorus I: My country 'tis of thee
              Sweet land of liberty
              Of thee I sing.

St. Settlement: Saint Teresa something like that.

More difficult to explain is the use of "London Bridge is falling down" in *The Mother* as the setting for "Daniel was my father's name." Other material in *The Mother* is borrowed from the composer himself, as for example the waltzes in Act I, scene five, derived from his 1945 documentary film *Tuesday in November*.

Comparisons among compositions by the same composer seem always to uncover similarities that may be considered self-quotation. Such a relationship is clearly heard between the Maestoso chorus from *Four Saints,* Act III: "With be there all their time" (a), and Susan B. Anthony's: "If I believe that I am right," in *The Mother,* Act I, scene four. (b), Moreover the anacrucis rhythm:

or a slight variation is to be found as the rhythmic skeleton for the wedding hymn of *The Mother,* Act I, scene five, (c) a short orchestral passage from *Four Saints,* Act III, (d) or the tempo di tango, also in Act III, (e) and St. Teresa's: "Begin to trace," Act IV (f) whose melodic contour foreshadows the wedding hymn from the other opera.

In general, Thomson's design for opera falls somewhere between the format in which closed musical forms are linked together by spoken dialogue or recitative, and music drama where the entire act is unified by orchestral interludes and by the development of musical motives of inherent or environmental dramatic significance. His structures, while following dramatic function, are tempered by an unerring sense of musical logic. When, for instance, the tedium of unabated vocal sound threatens the sonorous equilibrium, voices and text are suppressed and a soothing orchestral symphony created, as in *Four Saints*. And despite the fact that the operas are memorable for their unending succession of melodies, motives do recur, though by no means in the Wagnerian manner but rather as mnemonic devices that underpin the structure by unexpectedly recalling earlier scenes.

As mentioned above in another context, in *Four Saints* the melody of "To know to know to love her so" returns in the minor mode as "When this you see remember me," sung by St. Teresa II. The orchestra's intermezzo preceding the prologue to Act IV presents as well a minor-mode version of the "To know" theme which is then recapitulated almost identically in Act IV by full chorus. *The Mother* exhibits both development and repetition of thematic material, as in the wedding scene, Act I, scene five, where the hymn introduces the scene, is sung as an aria by Susan B. Anthony, serves the ensuing dialogue, provides background music for the ceremony, and is restated triumphantly at the end. The wedding hymn also recurs at the end of the opera, Act II scene three, when the statue of Susan B. Anthony answers Indiana Elliot's declaration about marriage, and later for Susan B. Anthony's penultimate phrase:

> Life is strife, I was a martyr all my life not to what I won but to what was done.

Orchestration plays a large role in creating atmosphere and dramatic viability in both operas. All too often, in praising Thomson's linguistic sensitivity, writers have ignored his ear for orchestral sonorities. But certainly a good ear is not limited to one kind of sound. It is not only his melodic-rhythmic lines and their harmonic underpinning, but also his blending and separation of the qualitative aspect of sound generally referred to as orchestral timbre that accounts for the effectiveness of his operas.

Thomson's orchestration is all the more important because of the special nature of his other musical materials. On the one hand, over-orchestration, the excessive application of layers of instrumental sonority, would not be appropriate to an operatic style that emphasizes text, melody, and singing. On the other hand, since orchestration is one of the most significant factors determining genre in musical theatre, the composer cannot rely merely on the accuracy of his text-setting, melodic interest, or tonal design, leaving sonority to chance or to arrangers, as some composers are wont to do. However, because Thomson operas are essentially vocal and expressive of human values, the function of his orchestra is primarily to support the singers and only secondarily to participate in the drama.

The orchestra provides the time-continuum as well as the ambience in which the action occurs. It comes then as no surprise that there is a minimum of figuration, ornamentation, or instrumental combinations calculated to create effects not specifically germane to characterization or the dramatic situation. When a special sonority is demanded as in the "Snow" or "Cold Weather" preludes of *The Mother,* Thomson's ingenuity is cogently demonstrated. For it is only through the separation of each of the three simultaneous tonal lines by means of distinct instrumental sonorities—celesta, woodwinds (one flute, two clarinets), and English horn solo—that the independence of each tonality is achieved and the counterpoint, so essential to the expressiveness of the scene, made manifest. The success of these thirty-two measures no doubt prompted Thomson to incorporate them into the overture to the opera, and later to use them as a model in such works as *The Seine at Night, Louisiana Story, Wheat Field at Noon,* and the *Missa Pro Defunctis.*

Like other composers equally fluent in both theatre and concert music, Thomson often leaves the abstraction and elaboration of musical ideas originally conceived for the stage to concert works, where his composer's drive to "research" a musical hypothesis has more room for expansion.

With the opera *Lord Byron* Thomson breaks new ground. Its libretto by Jack Larson, a departure from the idiosyncratic Stein texts, challenges a composer whose previous operatic successes are so closely linked to her originality. *Lord Byron* is a challenge also because of its subject matter, which vies with transatlantic composers of English opera on their home ground. Though heard only in a rehearsed audition, this writer feels *Byron* will prove both Thomson's operatic prowess independent of a Stein text and his position as the leading composer of opera in English, no matter what the hemisphere. The journey from musical cosmopolitanism to national awareness and back to a blending of the two in *Byron* prepared him for the task of bringing together all his talents in musical characterization, explication of text, and the expression of emotion, to recreate one of Europe's least understood celebrities in contemporary terms.

One is also aware, in *Byron,* of Thomson's many settings of English poetry from the Elizabethans to Blake and Whitman, where his feeling for the language has proved to be universal rather than merely American, and where he seems to have made his own the tradition of the older English vocal masters. Two excerpts from *Lord Byron* that recall these roots are Thomas

The Operas of Virgil Thomson

Moore's aria in Act I, a poetic tribute to the dead Byron set to the tune of Moore's own "Believe me if all those endearing young charms," and the "Kisses" trio-madrigal of Act III, with its sportive play on sibilants and its tragic undertone.

In the closing paragraphs of his autobiography, 1966, the composer mentioned two urgencies, one for music, one for himself:

> Of what, then, here and now, is music needful? A genius of the lyric stage, I say, a composer who will give stature to the operatic and poetic theater . . .

and later, referring to *Lord Byron:*

> At the moment, a libretto in verse has been completed for him; and putting it to music seems vastly urgent.

History alone will tell what Thomson's position will be when time shall have erased barriers to objective evaluation. But it is this writer's conviction that in the three operas *Four Saints in Three Acts, The Mother of Us All,* and *Lord Byron* (and no doubt more, for the Thomsons are a long-lived race), he has established a new kind of opera in English which transcends nationalism, nineteenth-century dramaturgy, and twentieth-century stylistic dogmas. And what is equally important, he has accomplished this without resorting to private or metaphysical visions that might obscure his aim. His discoveries, like most significant discoveries, are fundamental and simple, and thus capable of elaboration by others without compromising individual style or innate expressivity.

This assessment may seem extremely partisan, especially in view of the current ascendancy of music based on numerology or on electronic sound, both of these usages superficially polar to Thomson's aesthetic. Yet so long as imagination with craftsmanship is valued, so long as the voice remains the unique instrument which alone communicates both passion and intellect, and so long as simplicity is judged superior to prolixity, the Thomson operas will survive, artistic gems in themselves and models of excellence.

11. Music in Latin America

BY GILBERT CHASE

The music life of Latin America is rather like twins, brought up in the same family but by no means identical in personality. The Spanish-speaking countries are one thing, Portuguese Brazil another. In Brazil where the predominant influence goes back to African sources and bears a rich harvest of popular and folkloric music, musical nationalism is a strong tradition; and over it all looms the heroic figure of Heitor Villa-Lobos, born in 1887 but whose work only became well known after 1920. His early works —songs, choruses, operas, pieces for piano, for guitar, for small orchestra—offer a preview of the immense and varied production that was to follow, totaling over seven hundred numbers. Most prophetic of these is the popular *Brazilian Suite* (1908–12) for guitar, a pairing of European and Brazilian elements such as he later brought to fruition in the *Bachianas Brasileiras*. What will I believe endure of his immense output are the *Chôros,* the *Bachianas,* the Nonetto, perhaps many of the small piano pieces based on, or alluding to, typical Brazilian themes; perhaps also *Momoprecoce* for piano and orchestra (1929). Villa-Lobos was certainly the first composer of Latin America to achieve universal fame as a modernist. He could in fact be called its first modernist and its last traditionalist.

Early obsessed with a type of urban popular music called *chôro,* Villa-Lobos adopted the term to his own uses as a symbol for the spirit of Brazil. The ultimate result was the sixteen

Above: Photographed at Thomson's apartment
c. 1950: Virgil Thomson, Gian-Carlo Menotti,
William Schuman; (standing) Samuel Barber
and Aaron Copland. (*John Stewart*)
Left: Nicolas Nabokov, lyrical, eloquent,
orchestrally rich, essentially of
the theatre and long successful in
ballet. (*Berko, Aspen, Colo.*)

Left: Jack Beeson as The Young Husband in his TV opera *My Heart's in the Highlands*, 1970. (*Morris Warman*) Right: Gunther Schuller, horn-player, jazz expert, opera composer, and a serious music educator.

Irving Fine who died at forty-eight. His music was both sweet and strong. (*Harold Shapero*)

Left: Carlisle Floyd, a sound composer of operas, usually to
his own librettos. (*Evon Streetman, Courtesy of Boosey & Hawkes*)
Right: Ulysses Kay writes music abundantly and with grace.

Douglas Moore in his studio at Cutchogue, Long Island. (*Charles H. Meredith*)

Virgil Thomson, William Flanagan, and Ned Rorem, all striking as song composers.

Solo for Piano (Concert for Piano and Orchestra), page 30

Above: John Cage today. "I believe that the use of noise to make music
will continue and increase." [Cage, 1937] (*James Klosty*) Below: A page
of John Cage's manuscript from his Concert for Piano and Orchestra.

David Diamond has written communicatively
in all the concert forms. (*Ciro*)

Right: Howard Hanson, straightforward in every work. Left: Ben Weber.
The sound of it all is "musical," the feeling in it far from shallow. (*Bill & Gwen Sloan*)

Above: Leon Kirchner's music for chamber groups is technically high-class and expressively effective. (*Pach Bros., N.Y.*) Top right: Henry Brant, our most brilliant (by far) orchestrator, does not stoop to electronics for his effects, uses real instruments throughout. (*Bill & Gwen Sloan*) Bottom right: Arthur Berger's music, though it seems to seek complexity, achieves direct expression. (*Naomi Savage*)

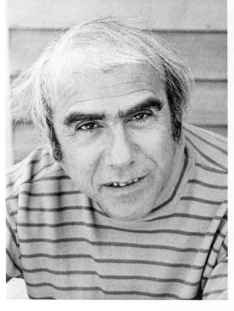

Left: Earle Brown, whose music, though far-out as to sound and structure, is transparent and generally light as air. (*BMI Archives*) Right: Kenneth Gaburo, among our far-outs, has the finest ear. (*James Campbell*)

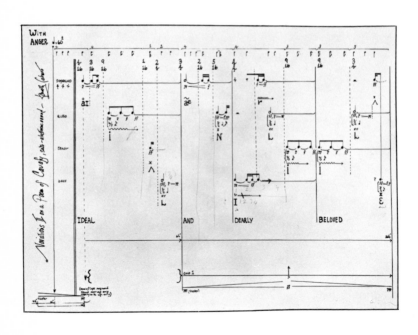

Variations II on a Poem of Cavafy by Kenneth Gaburo.
First page of composer's manuscript.

LUKAS FOSS, *Fragments of Archilochos*

Left: Lukas Foss does everything well.
Right: From Lukas Foss's
Fragments of Archilochos, 1966.
Page 11 of the composer's manuscript.

Harry Partch, who builds his own instruments and
tunes to a 43-tone octave. (*Bill & Gwen Sloan*)

Peter Mennin, William Bergsma, and Norman Dello Joio. (*Ben Greenhaus*)

A page of manuscript by Milton Babbitt from his
String Quartet No. 4—clean, lean, and not inelegant.

Mario Davidowsky, Milton Babbitt, Vladimir Ussachevsky, and Otto Luening
with composer students Pril Smily Delson and Alice Shields at the
Columbia-Princeton Electronic Music Center, 1970. (*Vernon L. Smith, Scope*)

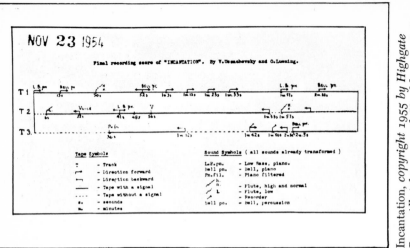

This original score of *Incantation* by Vladimir Ussachevsky and Otto Luening for an electronic tape-recording was refused for registration by the U.S. Copyright Office, since it contained no standard musical notation.

Gerhard Samuel, conductor, with Lou Harrison, a composer ever sweet in sound, enormous for variety. (*Vestal*)

chôros, composed from 1921 to '29, for various combinations ranging from solo guitar to large orchestra with chorus. The acknowledged masterpiece of this series, *Chôros No. 10* (1926), epitomizes his unique synthesis of Brazilian elements. It is scored for large orchestra (including Afro-Brazilian percussion instruments) and mixed chorus, which sings the words of a popular song called *Rasga o coração* (Rend My Heart) as well as certain strongly accented Indian-sounding words (such as Jakatá Kamarajá). The first part, entirely instrumental, evokes the Brazilian tropical forest with its imitations of birds and shrill jungle sounds. The chorus enters with the Indian-sounding words, later to be combined with *Rasga o coração* in a rhythmic counterpoint while the orchestra continues the obsessive rhythm of a *macumba* (Afro-Brazilian ritual dance), voices and instruments uniting at the climax in one of the most tremendous-sounding chords of the century.

Typical of Villa-Lobos is his instrumental treatment of the human voice. Mixed voices are used instrumentally, for example, in one of his most characteristic works, the Nonetto of 1923 (subtitled "A Rapid Impression of All Brazil"), in the *Quatuor* of 1921 ("Impressions of Worldly Life"), and most consistently in the *Bachianas Brasileiras No. 9,* written for an "orchestra of voices."

The *Bachianas Brasileiras,* a series of nine works composed from 1930 to 1948, bring together several peculiarly personal ideas and predilections. At an early age he had conceived a profound love for the music of Johann Sebastian Bach. Having lost his father at the age of eleven, Villa-Lobos shortly left home and for several years led a vagabond life, playing the cello and the guitar in theatres or nightclubs and traveling through much of Brazil's hinterland, absorbing en route much popular lore. His formal musical training lasted only a few months; the rest he acquired by experience and by studying the works of the masters, especially Debussy, Dukas, Rimsky-Korsakov, and Stravinsky. Since it was Bach among the older masters who exemplified for him the supreme ideal of Western musical art, he imagined a sort of confrontation between the universal spirit of Bach, with its sublime permanency, and the volatile, ethnically varied, sensually exciting, and sentimentally indulgent popular music of Brazil. Perhaps it is not too fanciful to say that J. S. Bach became a sublimated father-image for Villa-Lobos.

So he set out in the *Bachianas Brasileiras* to establish a dialogue between Bach and Brazil, symbolized in the double titles that he gave to the movements of each work. In No. 7 for orchestra, we have first Prelude (Ponteio), second Gigue (Quadrilha caipira), third Toccata (Desafio), fourth Fugue (Conversa), where the composer has matched the Baroque form with a corresponding type of Brazilian popular music. In the most famous of the Bachianas—No. 5 for soprano and eight violoncellos—the contrasting pairs are Aria (Cantilena) and Dance (Martelo), the first section combining the formality of a Bach aria with the passionate lyrical expression of a Brazilian sentimental song-type called *modinha*.

Villa-Lobos's vast production includes twelve symphonies, seventeen string quartets, forty works for voice with orchestra, over twenty for solo instruments with orchestra, nearly a hundred other orchestral works, seven operas, and a quantity of pieces large and small for solo instruments, especially piano and guitar.

Insofar as Villa-Lobos may be said to have a successor this would be Claudio Santoro (born 1919), who has passed successively through the phases of serialism, nationalism, populism, socialist realism, universalism, and avantgardism. Having adopted the twelve-tone method in 1940, he abandoned this when a scholarship from the French Government enabled him in 1948 to study in Paris with Nadia Boulanger. The most representative works of his nationalist phase are the Fourth and Fifth Symphonies, the First Piano Concerto, and the Third String Quartet. His Sixth and Seventh Symphonies are penetrated by a dynamic-dramatic emotionalism of the post-Romantic tradition with a semi-barbaric exuberant tinge, for Santoro, who comes from the shores of the Amazon, has the tropics in his blood. Since 1967 he has lived in West Berlin, composing chiefly electronic and aleatoric music.

Chronologically considered the careers of the three leading Latin American composers of the twentieth century—Heitor Villa-Lobos, Carlos Chávez, and Alberto Ginastera—represent overlapping generations, covering between them in their working years the entire temporal span since 1910. Villa-Lobos composed his earliest juvenilia the same year that Carlos Chávez was born in Mexico City, 1899. Chávez in turn began to write his first acknowledged compositions in 1918, two years after the birth of Ginastera in Buenos Aires. In the 1930s all three were riding the crest of the nationalist movement. For Chávez this involved a commitment to the ideology of the Mexican Revolution of 1910 to 1920 which during the next decades was to develop a comprehensive program for the cultural, political, social, and economic renovation of Mexico. On the cultural side much importance was given to the affirmation of traditional Mexican (especially Indian) values and to cooperative projects in the arts. Chávez gave the first public concert of his music in 1921, the same year that he was commissioned by the government to write a ballet on an indigenous subject. The result was *The New Fire* based on an Aztec ceremony signifying a renewal of the ancient Mexican "century" and symbolizing a new gift of life from the gods. Chávez turned again to Aztec mythology for his second ballet, *The Four Suns* (1926–30); he turned to the contemporary world however in his next, *Horse Power* (1926–27), which evokes the contrast between the easy-going life of the tropics and the dynamism of industrial progress (the finale is a Dance of Men and Machines). Sets and costumes for this ballet were designed by Diego Rivera, and it was produced in Philadelphia in 1932 under the direction of Leopold Stokowski with choreography by Catherine Littlefield. In the concert version of the score entitled *H.P.: Dance Symphony* a delightfully unexpected touch is the use in Scene II of a tango rhythm to express the seductive sensuality of the tropical sirens who surround the ship.

These ballet scores, though strong in musical and scenic invention, turned out weak in popular appeal. As a result Chávez undertook to write music for the masses with such works as *Llamadas (Calls): A Proletarian Symphony* for orchestra and mixed chorus (based on the history of the Revolution), and the *Republican Overture,* a brash and brassy arrangement of Mexican popular tunes. By 1935 Chávez had achieved prominence not only as a composer but also as conductor of the National Symphony Orchestra of Mexico (founded in 1928), and his stated aim in writing the *Republican Overture* was to provide orchestral music for the common listener. He also brought the best of the classical and contemporary repertory to Mexican audiences during his twenty years as conductor of this group.

But Chávez was by no means exclusively nationalist. Along with works of national character he was simultaneously composing in an advanced contemporary international idiom, from the *Polygons* for piano (1923) to the Concerto for Four Horns and Orchestra (1937-38). At the height of his populist period he wrote the powerful *Symphony of Antigone* (1933) evoking the Greek tragedy; and even the *Indian Symphony* (1935-36) is less a "nationalist" work than a formal synthesis of indigenous musical elements, thematic and rhythmic. The Concerto for Piano and Orchestra (1938-40) and the Toccata for Percussion Instruments (1942), while embodying Mexican elements, mark his definite commitment to the international (or "universalist") ideal that prevails in later works such as the Third, Fourth, Fifth, and Sixth Symphonies, the String Quartets, and the Piano Sonatas.

Chávez and his countryman Silvestre Revueltas (1899-1940) were the first Latin American composers to be strongly influenced by their contacts with the United States. Chávez spent many years in this country and for a time was identified with the "Americanist" movement represented by Aaron Copland and Virgil Thomson. Revueltas after studying violin and piano at the Chicago Musical College was for several years active in the United States as violinist and conductor. He was a smaller-scale Mexican Villa-Lobos—independent, always rebelling against authority, disrespectful of the establishment, and deeply committed to the popular traditions of his native land. He wrote a series of symphonic poems evoking various aspects of Mexico: *Cuauhnahuac, Colorines, Janitzio, Caminos,* all notable for their vivid coloring, their rhythmic vitality, and their striking use of Mexican themes. The work that stands out among them all is the *Homage to García Lorca* for small orchestra (1935), in which traditional Mexican dance-rhythms are combined with dissonant textures to make an exciting and moving piece. Revueltas's sense of humor is revealed in the Ivesian *8 x Radio* for eight instruments which plays with typical Mexican tunes and thumbs its nose at the purveyors of a more pompous nationalism.

In Domingo Santa Cruz of Chile (born 1899) we find a composer of the same generation as Chávez and Revueltas taking a dominant role in his country's musical affairs but with aims and results far different from those of his Mexican contemporaries. Santa Cruz is an enemy of nationalism as an artistic principle; he will have nothing to do with gauchos, peasants, or Indians. Thoroughly pedagogic and a traditionalist he is all for Bach, Beethoven, and Brahms; his ideal is the closest simulacrum of the European classical tradition that Chile can achieve. His own music blends the Baroque, the classical, and the Romantic elements, seasoning these with touches of impressionism and expressionism. He has composed four symphonies, three *Dramatic Preludes* for orchestra, several string quartets, five *Tragic Poems* for piano, and a number of large vocal works, such as the *Cantata for the Rivers of Chile* for mixed chorus and orchestra. The latter does not contradict his anti-nationalist stance since it focuses on geography, not ethnic variation.

In contrast to Chile the nationalist movement has predominated in Argentina during the entire first half of this century. And on the international scene no one can rival Alberto Ginastera, born in 1916. After plunging into musical nationalism at the tender age of eighteen he identified himself wholeheartedly with the *gauchesco* tradition in such works as the ballet *Estancia* (1941) depicting scenes of Argentine rural life; the Argentine Dances for piano (1937); the Five Argentine Popular Songs (1943); the *Pampeana No. 3* for orchestra (1954), subtitled "Symphonic Pastorale"; and his Overture to *The Creole Faust* (1943), based on a celebrated narrative poem that tells about a gaucho who comes to sell hides in Buenos Aires where he wanders into the Teatro Colón during a performance of Gounod's *Faust*, his naive impressions providing both humor and pathos.

Other works of this period strive for a sublimated nationalism, embodying Argentine melodic and rhythmic traits in a recondite rather than overt manner. In the Variaciones Concertantes for chamber orchestra (1953), one of his finest scores, the composer claims to have achieved "an Argentine atmosphere through the employment of original thematic and rhythmic elements." A close analysis would probably support this claim, but the listener is none the wiser as he enjoys the beautifully expressive and superbly orchestrated variations each featuring a particular instrument or group of instruments.

By the mid-1950s Ginastera was ready to say farewell to nationalism. Clearly signalled in the Second String Quartet (1958), the evidence is confirmed in subsequent works such as the Piano Concerto (1961) and the Violin Concerto (1963). The immensely effective *Cantata for Magic America* (1960), for dramatic soprano and fifty-three percussion instruments, projects a pan-American rather than a nationalistic vision. The works of this period reveal an imperious will to assimilate the advanced techniques of contemporary composition into a personal synthesis.

Ginastera's major achievement in the 1960s are his two operas, *Don Rodrigo* (1964) and *Bomarzo* (1967), the former commissioned by the municipality of Buenos Aires and produced at the Teatro Colón before earning further acclaim at the New York City Opera. *Bomarzo*—based on the life of an eccentric Italian nobleman of the sitxeenth century whose neuroses are sensationally documented—was commissioned by the Opera Society of Washington, D.C. where it received its world premiere in May 1967. Its success became a triumph when it entered the repertory of the New York City Opera the following year. Not since the Brazilian Carlos Gomes triumphed at La Scala, Milan in 1870 with *Il Guarany* has a Latin American composer made such an impression on the international operatic scene. Ginastera proved that grand opera could still be viable by combining those same ingredients that made it successful in the first place including sex and violent death (the former causing *Bomarzo* to be banned in Buenos Aires). Updated as it is with Freudian fantasies and with most of the favored techniques of contemporary composition—including both serial and aleatoric devices—*Bomarzo* will doubtless rank among the few successful operas of the 1960s.

Latin American composition at the beginning of the 1970s seems to have pushed musical nationalism into the distant background, the new generation being entirely identified with international mobility. Musicians are less dependent now on local inspirations than on international training centers of which the foremost is the Latin American Center for Advanced Musical Studies in Buenos Aires, sponsored by the Instituto Torcuato di Tella and directed by Alberto Ginastera. Prominent composers and musicologists are invited each year as visiting professors and lecturers, and the Center is equipped with an electronic studio. Also young composers from even the least developed countries of Latin America have an opportunity to benefit in Buenos Aires from the intense concert activity and from contact with leading musical personalities.

Among the earliest of the avant-garde groups was that founded in Buenos Aires in 1937 by Juan Carlos Paz, a composer who early opposed the nationalist movement with twelve-tone compositions. Avant-garde musical activity has even spread to some smaller cities—Córdoba, Argentina, for example organized in 1966 a festival of experimental music in connection with the Third American Art Biennial. Among its organizers was Horacio Vaggione, head of the Experimental Music Center of the University of Córdoba and one of the most interesting of the younger Argentine composers. Similar centers have developed in such places as Santiago (Chile), São Paulo (Brazil), and Caracas (Venezuela).

The seventies should be a vigorous decade for Latin American music. Going native is no longer the fashion, but anyone who feels a nostalgia for the familiar rhythms and for the sound of bongos and maracas can still find music that exploits the appeal of local color.

106 American Composers

ANTHEIL, GEORGE born Trenton, New Jersey 8 July 1900; pupil of Constantin von Sternberg and Ernest Bloch; married Elizabeth Markus 1925; one son. As piano recitalist in Germany 1921–23 created scandals through the violence of his works and piano playing (*Sonate Sauvage, Airplane Sonata*); similarly in Paris 1923–33, where he enjoyed the friendship of Ezra Pound, James Joyce, Sylvia Beach and gave concerts with Virgil Thomson. Under the influence of Stravinsky's *Rite of Spring* he composed in 1924, to a scenario by Fernand Léger, *Ballet méchanique,* originally planned for sixteen mechanical pianos and percussion. In 1926 this was performed in Paris mechanically and in New York by hand. Its New York failure turned Antheil toward opera: *Transatlantic,* Frankfurt 1930; *Helen Retires* (book by John Erskine), New York 1934. From 1936 he worked in Hollywood, composing for films, writing also ballets, operas, and symphonies. His work after *Ballet méchanique,* though disappointing as modernism, is increasingly professional. He published two books on glandular criminology (1930 and 1937), a military prophecy *The Shape of the War to Come,* 1940, and an autobiography *Bad Boy of Music,* 1945. He died in New York 1959.

Though Antheil's career suffered from overweening ambition, his music has many qualities of excellence. Almost any work has delicious moments along with pompous ones. As a result, his music, though not strongly current in repertory, does not die. Pieces of it are constantly being revived.

AUSTIN, LARRY born Duncan, Oklahoma 1930; A.B. North Texas State University 1951, M.S. 1952, additional graduate work University of California, Berkeley 1955–58; studied composition with Darius Milhaud, Andrew Imbrie, Seymour Shifrin, Violet Archer, and Gerhardt Dorn; married Edna Navarro 31 October 1953; seven children. Since 1958 he has taught at the University of California, Davis. In 1964 he received a grant for a year in Rome. In 1963 he organized the New Music Ensemble, which performed contemporary music that included group improvisation. He was co-director of the first Festival of Live Electronic Music at Mills College (Oakland) and the University of California, Davis 1967. Much of his recent work has employed electronic sound, color television, computer programming, mixed media in general. A lecturer and a conductor Austin is also the editor of *Source* magazine. His published works include: Piano Variations, *A Broken Consort, The Maze, Changes* for trombone and tape, *Current* for clarinet and piano, Piano Set, *Bass,* and Improvisations for orchestra and jazz soloists (performed by Leonard Bernstein and the New York Philharmonic in 1964). Other works: *Homecoming,* a cantata for soprano and jazz quintet, 1959; Fantasy on a Theme by Berg for jazz band, 1960; *Triptych* for chorus and string quartet, 1961; *Collage,* 1963; *Continuum for a Number of Instruments,* 1964; *Quartet in Open Style,* 1964; *Catharsis,* 1965; *Roma,* 1965; *Open Style* for orchestra and piano soloist, 1965. More recent works: *Duet Amphitryon* taped electronic music, 1967; *Brass* for amplified, modified brass instruments, slides, and film, 1967; *Accidents,* 1967; *Cyclotron Stew* for cyclotron with tape montage, 1967; and *The Magicians* for children, tapes, black light, and films.

Austin's music, without being remarkable for its far-outness or radically inventive, belongs with the new left. It reflects an ambitious and industrious temperament oriented toward the facile and the comic, even when the forces deployed are of monumental proportions.

BABBITT, MILTON born Philadelphia 10 May 1916; A.B. New York University 1935; M.F.A. Princeton 1942, where he studied with Roger Sessions; married Sylvia Miller 27 December 1939; one daughter. Taught music at Princeton from 1938 (mathematics 1943–45); at Salzburg Seminar 1952; also at Berkshire Music Center and Internationaler Ferienkurse, Darmstadt; presently member editorial board *Perspectives of New Music* and a co-director of the Columbia-Princeton Electronic Music Center. Has received the Joseph Bearns prize, a Guggenheim fellowship, a National Institute of Arts and Letters award, and twice an award of the New York Music Critics' Circle; member National Institute of Arts and Letters.

Compositions include: Music for the Mass, 1940; Three Compositions for Piano, 1947; Composition for Four Instruments, 1948; Composition for Twelve Instruments, 1948; Composition for Viola and Piano, 1950; String Trio, 1951; Woodwind Octet, 1953; String Quartet No. 2, 1954; *All Set* for eight instruments, 1957; *Relata II*, 1968; String Quartet No. 3, 1969; Composition for Synthesizer, 1961; *Correspondences* for string orchestra and synthetic tape, 1969; also works for solo voice with instruments, with synthesized accompaniment, and with synthesized accompaniment plus another voice recorded.

Babbitt's music has the clarity of distilled water and just possibly the sterility. Certainly it leaves in the listener no appreciable deposit of emotion. It is more like an athletic experience, exhilarating, tonic, helps you to breathe. Not the electronic works, which I find gummy and airless, but those for classical instruments, which represent a high degree of both abstraction and distinction. The natural elegance which pervades all his work is most strongly present when the textures are thin.

BARBER, SAMUEL born West Chester, Pennsylvania 9 March 1910; studied piano with Isabella Vengerova and composition with Rosario Scalero at Curtis Institute of Music, Philadelphia; was graduated 1932, Mus.Doc. (honorary) 1945. He received the Prix de Rome 1935; Pulitzer Prize for Music 1935 and 1936; Guggenheim fellowship 1945; New York Music Critics' award 1946; member National Institute of Arts and Letters. His compositions: Serenade for string quartet, 1929; *Dover Beach* for voice and string quartet, 1931; Sonata for Cello and Piano, 1932; Overture to *The School for Scandal*, 1932; *Music for a Scene from Shelley*, 1933; *The Virgin Martyrs* (choral) 1935; Symphony in One Movement, 1936; String Quartet in B minor, 1936; Adagio for Strings, 1936; *Essay for Orchestra*, 1937; Symphony No. 1, 1937; Concerto for Violin and Orchestra, 1940; *A Stopwatch and an Ordinance Map* (men's chorus and drums) 1940; *Second Essay* for orchestra, 1942; *Capricorn Concerto*, 1944; *Four Excursions* (piano) 1944; Cello Concerto, 1945; *Knoxville: Summer of 1915* (voice and orchestra) 1947; Piano Sonata, 1948; Second Symphony, 1950; *Souvenirs* ballet suite for orchestra, 1953; *Prayers of Kierkegaard* for chorus, soprano solo, and orchestra, 1954; *Toccata Festiva* (organ and orchestra) 1960; *Die Natali* chorale preludes for Christmas, 1960; Piano Concerto, 1962; ballets for Martha Graham: *Cave of the Heart*, 1947; *Medea*, 1947; *Andromache's Farewell*, 1962; operas: *Vanessa*, performed at Metropolitan 1958; *A Hand of Bridge* (mini-opera)

Spoleto 1960; *Antony and Cleopatra,* commissioned for opening of the new Metropolitan Opera House 1966; many lieder, including *Hermit Songs,* 1953.

Romantic music, predominantly emotional, embodying sophisticated workmanship and complete care. Barber's aesthetic position may be reactionary, but his melodic line sings and the harmony supports it. His operas are less rewarding than his concert works and ballets.

BEESON, JACK born Muncie, Indiana 15 July 1921; studied at Eastman School of Music with Burrill Phillips, Bernard Rogers, and Howard Hanson 1939–44 (M.A. and M.M.), with Béla Bartók in New York 1944–45; married Nora Sigerist 1947; two children. Joined Columbia University opera workshop 1945, music faculty shortly after, became MacDowell Professor of Music in 1967. Received the prix de Rome and a Fulbright fellowship 1948–50; Guggenheim fellowship 1958–59; Marc Blitzstein award from the National Institute of Arts and Letters 1968. He is secretary of the Alice M. Ditson Fund and a board member of the American Composers' Alliance, Composers' Forum (chairman), American Music Center, Composers' Recordings, Inc. (vice-president), League of Composers-ISCM.

His works include the operas: *Jonah* (adapted from Paul Goodman) 1950; *Hello Out There* (after William Saroyan) Columbia University 1954; *The Sweet Bye and Bye* (libretto by Kenward Elmslie) Juilliard Opera Theatre 1957; *Lizzie Borden* (Richard Plant and Kenward Elmslie) New York City Opera 1965; *My Heart's in the Highlands* (after Saroyan) NET Opera Theatre television 1970. Other works include: for orchestra Symphony No. 1 in A, 1959; *Transformations,* 1959; *Fanfare,* 1963; *Commemoration* (band) 1960; chamber music: Fourth and Fifth Piano Sonatas, 1945 and 1946, revised 1951; Sonata for Viola and Piano, 1953; Two Diversions (piano) 1953; *Sketches in Black and White* (piano) 1958; Sonata Canonica for alto recorders, 1966; many songs, choral pieces, short piano works.

Here are unquestionably an operatic gift, a sense of the stage, and some expressivity in the vocal line.

BENNETT, ROBERT RUSSELL born Kansas City, Missouri 15 June 1894; studied with Carl Busch in Kansas City and Nadia Boulanger in Paris, also in Berlin, Vienna, and London; married Louise Edgerton Merrill 1919; one daughter. Played violin, piano, and trombone in Kansas

City 1908–16; later copyist, orchestrator, composer, conductor, and commentator on radio stations in New York, Hollywood, and Europe. Awarded Guggenheim fellowship and two Victor prizes for symphonic works; received the Edwin Franko Goldman medal 1965 for a band piece *That War in Korea,* the theme composition for a "Project 20" production of NBC, where he was musical director. He has orchestrated more than three hundred Broadway musicals including *Show Boat, Oklahoma, Kiss Me, Kate, South Pacific, My Fair Lady,* and *Camelot.* Some of his own compositions: *Abraham Lincoln,* 1931; *Sights and Sounds,* 1931; *Hold Your Horses,* 1933; Six Variations on a Theme by Jerome Kern, 1933; Concerto Grosso for Small Dance Band and Symphony Orchestra, 1934; *Maria Malibran* (opera) 1935; *Adagio Eroica,* 1935; Eight Etudes for Symphonic Orchestra, 1938; *Hexapoda,* 1941; A Symphony in D for the Dodgers, 1941; Concerto for Violin in A Major, 1944; *A Symphonic Story of Jerome Kern,* 1946; *Overture to an Imaginary Drama,* 1949; *Rose Variations,* 1955; Four Nocturnes, 1960.

He has composed successfully in all forms, but is known best for his effective scoring of music by others, largely in the popular field.

BERGER, ARTHUR VICTOR born New York 15 May 1912; B.S. in music New York University 1934; M.A. Harvard 1936; student at Longy School of Music, Cambridge 1934–36; studied with Nadia Boulanger 1937; married Esther Turitz 1937 (dec. 1960); married Ellen Phillips-born Tassman 8 December 1967. He has been an editor of the *Musical Mercury* 1934–37; music reviewer for the *Boston Transcript* 1934–37; instructor at Mills College (Oakland) 1939–41, at North Texas State College 1941, and Brooklyn College 1942–43; member of the Brandeis University faculty from 1953 and Naumberg Professor of music there from 1963; composer in residence Berkshire Music Center 1964. He received an award from the National Institute of Arts and Letters 1960; Fulbright research grant 1960–61; Naumberg recording award 1964; New York Music Critics' Circle award for his String Quartet 1962. Music reviewer with the *New York Sun* 1943–46; associate music critic *New York Herald Tribune* 1946–53; co-founder and member of the editorial board *Perspectives of New Music* from 1962, editor 1962–63. His compositions include: Two Episodes for piano, 1933; Woodwind Quartet, 1941; Serenade Concertante for orchestra, 1944–51; Three Pieces for Strings, 1945; *Ideas of Order* for orchestra, 1952; *Polyphony* for orchestra, 1956; Chamber Music for Thirteen Players, 1956; String Quartet, 1958; Chamber Concerto, 1960; Five Pieces for solo piano, 1968; Duos for violin and piano, No. 1, 1948; No. 2, 1950; for cello and piano, 1951; for oboe and clarinet, 1952; for piano and clarinet, 1957; for two pianos, 1961; and numerous solo piano pieces. He has published many articles and one book *Aaron Copland*, 1963.

Berger's highly intellectualized compositions, early modeled on Stravinsky's neoclassical period and later influenced by serialism, are often witty and entertaining, with their just-barely-concealed sidewalks-of-New-York charm. Nor do they lack nobility in their proportions.

BERGSMA, WILLIAM LAWRENCE born Oakland, California 1 April 1921; attended Stanford University 1938–40; taught Eastman School of Music 1940–44; A.B. University of Rochester 1942, M.M. 1943; married Nancy Nickerson 1946; two children. Formerly chairman of composition and assistant dean Juilliard School; since 1963 director School of Music, University of Washington, Seattle. Awards: Koussevitzky 1943–44, National Institute of Arts and Letters 1945; Society for the Publication of American Music 1945; Guggenheim fellow 1946 and 1951; Bearns prize 1943. Commissions: Town Hall 1942; Collegiate Chorale 1946; League of Composers 1953; Elizabeth Sprague Coolidge 1956; Wesleyan University 1956; Edwin Franko Goldman Memorial 1957; Portland Junior Symphony 1960; Harvard Musical Society 1961; Juilliard Foundation 1962; Mid-America Chorale 1963. Member National Institute of Arts and Letters.

His works include two symphonies, three string quartets, and a three-act opera *The Wife of Martin Guerre*, 1955, revised 1958; also choral works, concertos, and other compositions including the very successful *Music on a Quiet Theme* for orchestra, 1943.

A striking melodic gift, a cool mastery of the conventional techniques, and a relaxed emotional content all contribute to his music's unquestionable charm. A certain thinness, an understatement in harmony and orchestration, gives it distinction as well.

BERNSTEIN, LEONARD born Lawrence, Massachusetts 25 August 1918; A.B. Harvard 1939; was graduated from the Curtis Institute of Music 1941; studied piano with Helen Coates, Heinrich Gebhard, and Isabella Vengerova, conducting with Fritz Reiner and Serge Koussevitsky; married Felicia Montealegre Cohn 1951; two children. In

1942 he was assistant to Serge Koussevitsky at Berkshire Music Center; assistant conductor New York Philharmonic 1943–44; conductor of the New York City Center Orchestra 1945–48; musical adviser Israel Philharmonic Symphony Orchestra 1948–49. He was a member of the faculty of the Berkshire Music Center from 1948, head of its conducting department from 1951; from 1951–56 professor of music at Brandeis University. In 1957–58 he was co-conductor with Dmitri Mitropoulos of New York Philharmonic, its sole director from 1959–69. He has conducted at La Scala (Milan), Metropolitan Opera (New York), and Staatsoper (Vienna); also the major U.S. and European orchestras. Works include: Clarinet Sonata, 1942; song cycle *I Hate Music*, 1943; *Seven Anniversaries* for piano, 1943; Symphony No. 1 (*Jeremiah*) 1942; Five Pieces for Brass Instruments, 1947; Symphony No. 2 (*The Age of Anxiety*) 1949; *Four Anniversaries* for piano, 1948; song cycle *La Bonne Cuisine*, 1949; *Trouble in Tahiti* (one-act opera to his own libretto) 1952; score for musical show *On the Town*, 1944; ballets *Fancy Free*, 1944, and *Facsimile*, 1946; incidental music for *Peter Pan*, 1950; music for Broadway productions *Wonderful Town*, 1952; *Candide*, 1956; *West Side Story*, 1957; film score *On the Waterfront*, 1954; Serenade for violin and string orchestra with percussion, 1954; Symphony No. 3 for narrator, chorus, and orchestra (*Kaddish*) 1963; *Chichester Psalms* for mixed choir and instruments, 1965. Author: *The Joy of Music*, 1959; *Leonard Bernstein's Young People's Concerts for Reading and Listening*, 1962; *The Infinite Variety of Music*, 1966.

A successful composer in both pop and standard fields; as a conductor absolutely top-flight for both concert and opera, with brains, a vast repertory, a store of experience, and lots of skill. His own music tends to be derivative—chief sources Milhaud, Stravinsky, Mahler. Also an accomplished pianist, linguist, musical explicator through books and TV. As a conductor he has programmed U.S. music consistently and played it understandingly.

BLITZSTEIN, MARC born Philadelphia 2 March 1905; student at the University of Pennsylvania 1921–23, Curtis Institute 1924–26, and the Akademie der Kunste, Berlin 1927; married Eva Goldbeck 2 March 1933 (dec. 1936). He was a Guggenheim fellow from 1940–42, served in the U.S. Air Force 1942–45. He was co-founder with A. Copland, L. Engel, and V. Thomson of the Arrow Music Press, 1937. He received a National Institute of Arts and Letters award 1946, a Newspaper Guild award 1947; was elected to the National

Institute in 1959. His stage works, for most of which he wrote both book and lyrics, include *The Cradle Will Rock*, New York 1937; *I've Got the Tune*, radio song-play CBS 1937; *No for an Answer*, New York 1941; *Regina*, opera based on Lillian Hellman's *The Little Foxes*, New York 1949; other musico-dramatic productions include *Triple-Sec; The Harpies; The Condemned; Parabola and Circula; Reuben, Reuben* 1953; and *Juno* (based on Sean O'Casey's *Juno and the Paycock*), 1959. His most popular work was his adaptation of the Kurt Weill-Bertolt Brecht *Three-penny Opera*, Brandeis Festival 1952, which had a long run off-Broadway. He also wrote a symphonic poem *Freedom Morning*, 1943; a symphony with speaker, solo tenor, solo baritone, men's chorus, and orchestra *The Airborne*, 1946; a ballet *The Guests*, 1948; and a cantata *This Is the Garden*, 1957. He wrote incidental music for Orson Welles's *Julius Caesar*, 1937; *Danton's Death*, 1938; and *King Lear* with Luening and Ussachevsky, 1955; also *Androcles and the Lion*, 1946; *Midsummer Night's Dream* and *A Winter's Tale*, 1958. His films include *The True Glory; The Spanish Earth* with Virgil Thomson, 1937; and *Native Land*, 1941. *Sacco and Vanzetti*, an opera commissioned for the Metropolitan, was incomplete at his death in 1964.

A pupil of Rosario Scalero, Nadia Boulanger, and Arnold Schoenberg, Blitzstein was internationally schooled. He also had a strong *sens du théâtre* and a gift for clear prosodic declamation, especially of colloquial American. His operas are strongest when they parody musical styles, underlining character through Marxist satire of class conditionings.

BLOCH, ERNEST born Geneva, Switzerland 24 July 1880; studied in Geneva, Brussels, Frankfurt-am-Main; harmony with Emile Jacques Dalcroze, violin with Eugène Ysaÿe, composition with Iwan Knorr; married Marguerite Schneider, 1904; three children. Conducted concerts in Switzerland 1909–10; taught at Conservatoire in Geneva 1911–15. Came to the United States in 1916, naturalized 1924. Taught at the Mannes College of Music in New York 1917–19; founder of the Cleveland Institute of Music and its director from 1920–25; director of the San Francisco Conservatory 1925–30; professor at the University of California, Berkeley from 1939. Received New York Music Critics' Circle award 1954. Member (honorary) of the Accademia di Sta. Cecilia, Rome and of the American Academy of Arts and Letters; received gold medal from National Institute of Arts and Letters 1942. Early works include the opera *Macbeth*, Paris 1910;

Trois Poèmes juifs, 1913; the symphony *Israel;* Three Psalms; the rhapsody for cello and orchestra *Schelomo,* 1917; the Jewish Sacred Service, 1933. Other works include the First Violin Sonata, 1921; Quintet with piano, 1923; five string quartets; three suites for solo cello; *Voice in the Wilderness,* cello and orchestra, 1935; *Evocations* for orchestra; Concerto for Violin and Orchestra, 1937; Suite Symphonique, 1944; Concerto Symphonique, 1948; *Scherzo Fantasque,* 1948; Concertino, 1950; *Rhapsodie Hébraique,* 1951; Concerto Grosso No. 2, 1952; Sinfonìa Breve, 1952; Symphony for trombone and orchestra, 1954; Symphony in E flat, 1955; *Proclamation* for trumpet solo and orchestra, 1955; *Last Poems* for flute and orchestra. He died in Portland, Oregon 15 July 1959.

As a pedagogue he rendered important service to American composers. His own music, sincerely felt and of high technical quality, has had a worldwide public. *Schelomo,* which offers Jewish pathos with cello virtuosity, is a repertory work justifiably popular. Bloch's music in general is romantic in feeling, classical in form; when not Jewish-inspired it tends toward the neoclassical.

BOWLES, PAUL born New York 30 December 1910; studied with Aaron Copland in New York and Berlin 1930–32, with Virgil Thomson in Paris 1933–34; married Jane Sydney Auer 1938. In 1941 received Guggenheim fellowship, in 1959 a Rockefeller grant. Wrote incidental music for many plays including *Horse Eats Hat, Doctor Faustus, My Heart's in the Highlands, Love's Old Sweet Song, Twelfth Night, Liberty Jones, Roots in the Earth* (film score for United States Department of Agriculture), *Watch on the Rhine, Jacobowsky and the Colonel, The Glass Menagerie, Cyrano de Bergerac, Summer and Smoke, In the Summer House, Edwin Booth, Sweet Bird of Youth, The Milk Train Doesn't Stop Here Any More;* the ballets *Yankee Clipper, Pastorelas, Sentimental Colloquy;* an opera *The Wind Remains,* 1943, based on a García Lorca play; has also composed songs, extended vocal works, and a Sonata for Two Pianos and Percussion. He is the author of the following novels: *The Sheltering Sky,* 1949; *The Delicate Prey,* 1950; *Let It Come Down,* 1952; *The Spider's House,* 1955; *A Hundred Camels in the Courtyard,* 1962; *Their Heads Are Green and Their Hands Are Blue,* 1963; *Up Above the World,* 1966.

Bowles's fiction has a worldwide readership, deserved. His songs and chamber music, though less known, are expressive, distinguished, and picturesque, often with an ethnic background (Mexico, Spain, Morocco). His stage music benefits from a strong theatre sense. His songs can be quite delicious.

BRANT, HENRY DREFUSS born Montreal 15 September 1913, studied in New York at the Juilliard School 1930–34; married Maxine Picard 1938 (div.); married Patricia Gorman 1948; three children. His teaching positions include Columbia University, Bennington College, and since 1947 the Juilliard School of Music. Since 1940 he has written music to documentary films for various United States government departments, including the Office of War Information, Department of State, and Department of Agriculture. Since 1942 he has been active as composer, conductor, and arranger for various radio network programs. He is a member of the editorial board of the American Composers' Alliance; a recipient of the Prix Italia 1955, a Guggenheim fellowship 1946 and 1955, a National Institute of Arts and Letters grant 1955. He is best known as a composer of "spatial music in temporal polyphony," and his works include: *The Great American Goof* (ballet-play) 1940; *Origins* a percussion symphony, 1952; *Signs and Alarms,* 1953; *Rural Antiphonies,* 1953; *Millenium 2,* 1954; *Encephalograms,* 1954; *Ceremony,* 1954; *December* for Collegiate Chorale and instruments-spread; *Galaxies,* 1954; *Grand Universal Circus,* 1956; *Mythical Beasts* voice and instruments-spread; *Antiphony One* for orchestra in five groups in auditorium, 1960; *The Fire Garden,* 1960; *Atlantis* for band and orchestra, 1960; *Voyage Four,* "a spatial concert piece for eighty-three instrumentalists and one singer, led by three conductors," 1964; *Consort for True Violins* (eight violins built for this work) 1965; and *Windjammer* quintet (spread-formation music) 1969.

Henry Brant has a remarkable knowledge of instruments and their possibilities. His far-outness is of the fun-and-games variety—an antiphony of five orchestras playing at once but not without coordination, a symphony for toy instruments from the dime-store, and a surprisingly expressive achievement in the Concerto for Flute accompanied by ten other flutes (alto to piccolo). The instrumental virtuosities that his music can mobilize give it high color and a dazzling brilliance.

BROWN, EARLE A. JR. born Lunenburg, Massachusetts 26 December 1926, attended Northwestern University; from 1947–50 studied composition with Roslyn Brogue and the Schillinger system of composition and orchestration with Kenneth McKillop; married Carolyn Rice 28 June 1950. Taught the Schillinger technique in Denver, Colorado, expanding it to include the aleatoric; he also devised a system of notation using symbolic ideograms. He worked with John Cage and David Tudor 1952–54; was later an editor and recording engineer for Capitol Records; a Guggenheim fellow in 1965 and 1966; is presently director of the *Contemporary Sound Series* sponsored by Time Records and Composer in residence at the Peabody Conservatory in Baltimore, Maryland. Works include: *Folio Pieces,* 1952; two octets for magnetic tapes, 1953–54; *Pentathis* for 9 instruments, 1958; *Hodograph* for flute, piano, celesta, bells, vibraphone, and marimba, 1959; *Indices* for 12 players, 1960; *Light Music* for electric lights, electronic equipment, and variable numbers of instruments, 1961; *Available Forms I* for 18 players, Darmstadt 1961; *Available Forms II* for 98 players and 2 conductors, 1963; *Times Five* for 4 tapes and 5 instruments; and *Four Systems* for four amplified symbols, 1964; He has also composed traditional music for strings, pianos, percussion. His works have been published in Germany and are frequently played in European avant-garde concerts.

Here is far-outness manicured and groomed, always clear in sound, generally sparse in texture. Its most striking novelty is the use of serialized dynamics in fast-moving piano music—hard to perform, but an utterly brilliant effect.

CAGE, JOHN born Los Angeles 5 September 1912; studied at Pomona College 1928–30; privately with Richard Buhlig, Adolph Weiss, Henry Cowell, Arnold Schoenberg; married Xenia Kashevaroff 1935 (div.). Taught at Cornish School, Seattle, 1936–38; School of Design, Chicago 1941–42; New School for Social Research, New York 1955–60. From 1944 was musical director of the Merce Cunningham dance company; later president of the Cunningham Dance Foundation; a fellow at the Center of Advanced Studies, Wesleyan University 1960–61; composer in residence University of Cincinnati and University of Illinois (Urbana). Commissions include: from Ballet Society *The Seasons* (1947); Donaueschingen Musiktage a work for prepared pianos; Montreal Festivals Society an orchestral work. In 1951 he organized a group of musicians and engineers for making music directly on magnetic tape. He is a board member of the Foundation for Contemporary Performance Arts, a founding member of the New York Mycology Society, a member of the National Institute of Arts and Letters; Guggenheim fellow 1949; National Institute of Arts and

Letters award 1949; Woodstock Art Film Festival award for score *Works of Calder,* 1951. Other works include: *Metamorphosis* for piano, 1938; *Imaginary Landscapes* Nos. 1, 2, 4, 5, 1939; *Amores* for piano and percussion, 1943; *The Perilous Night* for piano, 1944; Six Melodies for violin and keyboard, 1950; *Music of Changes* for prepared piano, 1951; Music for Piano, 1952–53; *59½ Seconds* for a string player, 1953; *4 Minutes and 33 Seconds* silent music for piano in three movements, 1954; Concert for Piano and Orchestra, 1958; Aria, 1958; Music for Amplified Toy Piano, 1960; Suite for Toy Piano, 1960; Cartridge Music, 1960; *A Flower* for voice and piano, 1960; *Forever and Sunsmell,* song with percussion duet, 1960; *Seven Haiku* for piano, 1960; *In a Landscape* for piano and harp, 1960; *Music for the Marrying Maiden,* 1960; Music for Carillon No. 1, 1960, No. 3, 1961; *Music for Marcel Duchamp* (piano) 1961; *Atlas Eclipticalis* for orchestra, 1961; *Double Music* for percussion quartet (with Lou Harrison) 1961; *Experiences No. 1* for two pianos, 1961; *0'00"* "to be performed in any way by anyone," 1962; Sonata for clarinet, 1963. Multimedia works include Variation VII, 1967, and *HPSCHD,* 1969. Author: *Virgil Thomson: His Life and Music* (with Kathleen O'Donnell Hoover) 1959; *Silence,* 1961; *A Year from Monday,* 1967; *Notations,* 1969.

For a discussion of Cage and his works see Chapter 8.

CARPENTER, JOHN ALDEN born Park Ridge, Illinois 28 February 1876; A.B. Harvard 1897, honorary A.M. 1922; studied with Bernard Ziehn and Sir Edward Elgar; married Rue Winterbotham 20 November 1900 (dec. 1931); Ellen Waller Borden 31 January 1933. From 1897 employed by George B. Carpenter and Company, ship supplies, vice-president from 1909–36; director of the Illinois Children's Home and Aid Society; chevalier Légion d'Honneur 1921. Musical works include: *When Little Boys Sing* (with wife) 1904; *Improving Songs for Anxious Children* (with wife) 1907; Sonata for Violin and Piano, 1912; *Gitanjali* "song offerings," 1913; *Adventures in a Perambulator* suite for orchestra, 1914; Concertino for Piano and Orchestra, 1915; Symphony (Norfolk Festival) 1917; *The Birthday of the Infanta* ballet produced by Chicago Opera Company 1919–20; *Krazy Kat* ballet, 1922; *Skyscrapers* ballet produced by Metropolitan Opera 1926; *Song of Faith* for chorus and orchestra, 1932; *Patterns* for piano and orchestra, 1932; a symphonic poem *Sea Drift,* 1933; *Danza* for orchestra, 1935; Concerto for Violin and Orchestra, 1938; Symphony for 50th Anniversary of Chicago Symphony Orchestra, 1940;

Symphony No. II, 1942; symphonic suite *The Seven Ages*, 1945; and many songs. Died 26 April 1951.

Carpenter was an impressionist composer of superficial but perfectly real charm. His works embodying whimsy, gentle sentiments, and the picturesque are more striking than his monumental ones.

CARTER, ELLIOTT COOK JR. born New York 11 December 1908; A.B. Harvard 1930, A.M. 1932; studied with Walter Piston, in Paris with Nadia Boulanger 1932–34; married Helen Hibbett Jones 1939; one son. Teaching positions: Peabody Conservatory of Music 1946–48; Columbia University 1948–50; Salzburg Seminars 1958; Yale University 1960–62; at present Juilliard School of Music. Awarded Guggenheim fellowship 1945–46, 1950–51; on board of directors League of Composers 1939–52; board of directors International Society for Contemporary Music 1946–52; president United States Section 1952; board of directors American Composers' Alliance 1939–52; member of American Academy of Arts and Letters.

Principal works: Tarantella for male chorus and orchestra, 1937; *Pocahontas* (ballet) 1939, (suite) 1941; *The Defence of Corinth* for male chorus, 1941; First Symphony, 1943; *The Harmony of Morning*, 1945; Piano Sonata, 1945; *Holiday Overture*, 1945; *The Minotaur* (ballet) 1947; Woodwind Quintet, 1947; Sonata for Cello and Piano, 1948; *Emblems* for men's chorus and piano, 1948; Eight Etudes and a Fantasy for woodwind quartet, 1949; String Quartet No. 1, 1951; Sonata for Flute, Oboe, Cello, Harpsichord, 1952 (Naumburg award 1956); String Quartet No. 2, 1954; Variations for Orchestra, 1955; Double Concerto for harpsichord and piano, 1956; Piano Concerto, 1965; Concerto for Orchestra, 1970.

Music of unusual complexity and refinement at its most striking in chamber works, including the Double Concerto. The orchestral works, though punctilious, seem lacking in strength of line; but Carter's chamber music beginning with the Piano Sonata, 1945, is in my opinion the most interesting being composed today by anybody anywhere. And I mean intrinsically interesting, not merely attractive to the ear. His genius is to have combined intellectual elaboration and auditory delight with no loss of intensity to either. Researches in instrumental virtuosity commanded by an authentic musical temperament.

CHADWICK, GEORGE WHITEFIELD born Lowell, Massachusetts 1854; entered father's insurance business but shortly became a student at the New England Conservatory; taught briefly at Olivet College before going to Europe for further study (in Berlin with Haupt, in Leipzig with Jadassohn). Taught from 1882 at the New England Conservatory becoming in 1897 its director, a position he held until his death. He was also a church organist and a conductor of choral societies. His works include: the overtures *Rip Van Winkle*, 1879; *Thalia*, 1883; *The Miller's Daughter*, 1884; *Melpomene*, 1887; *Adonais*, 1899; *Euterpe*, 1906; five string quartets; a piano quintet; three symphonies; a symphonic ballad *Tam O'Shanter;* Symphonic Sketches; the operas *Judith, The Quiet Lodging, Tabasco,* and *The Padrone;* many smaller works for chorus and voice (*Dedication Ode, The Viking's Last Voyage*). He received an honorary A.M. from Yale in 1897, LL.D. from Tufts in 1905; member of the American Academy of Arts and Letters. He died in 1931.

Though a composer of vigorous gesture and stage-oriented, his operas never achieved the success they probably deserved. Choral works and some orchestral are still performed.

CHANLER, THEODORE WARD born Newport, Rhode Island 29 April 1902; studied piano with Hans Ebell, composition with Arthur Shepherd and Ernest Bloch at the Cleveland Institute of Music; also studied at Oxford University 1923–25 and with Nadia Boulanger in Paris; married Maria d'Acosta Sargent 31 October 1931. Notable works: Violin Sonata, 1927; Mass for two female voices and organ, 1930; the song cycles *Epitaphs*, 1937, and *The Children;* a piano suite *Five Short Colloquies*, 1936; a ballet *Pas de Trois; Ann Gregory* (for chorus); a fugue for two pianos *The Second Joyful Mystery;* many songs; and a chamber opera *The Pot of Fat*, 1955. Died 27 July 1961.

Chanler's chamber music, inspired by Fauré, expresses with distinction feelings really felt. His songs, among the finest of our time in English, are impeccable for prosodic declamation and imaginative in their use of accompanimental polyharmonies.

CHOU, WEN-CHUNG born Chefoo, China 29 June 1923; B.S. National Chungking University 1945; came to the United States in 1946, naturalized 1958. Attended New England Conservatory of Music 1946– 49; M.S. Columbia University 1954; studied composition with Edgard Varèse 1949–54; married Yi-an Chang 23 June 1962; one son. On faculty of Columbia since 1964; director of research program in classical and Chinese music 1955–57; composer in residence University of Illinois 1958–59; musical executor of Edgard Varèse estate. Received a grant from the Rockefeller Foundation 1955–57, Guggenheim fellowship 1957–58, 1959–60; has also received awards from the National Institute of Arts and Letters 1963, William and Norma Copley Foundation 1966.

His works include three *Landscapes* for orchestra: *All in the Spring Wind,* 1952–53; *And the Fallen Petals,* 1954; *In the Mode of Shang,* 1956; Three Folksongs (harp and flute) 1950; Suite for harp and wind quintet, 1951; Seven Poems of T'ang Dynasty for high voice and instrumental ensemble, 1951–52; *Two Miniatures from T'ang Dynasty* for chamber ensemble, 1957; *The Willows Are New* for piano, 1957; *To a Wayfarer* for clarinet and strings, 1958; *Soliloquy of a Bhiksuni* for trumpet with brass and percussion ensemble, 1958; *Poems of White Stone,* 1958–59; *Metaphors* for wind and symphony orchestra, 1961; *Riding the Wind,* 1964; *Cursive* for flute and piano, 1963; *The Dark and the Light* for piano, percussion, and strings, 1964; *Yu Ko* for nine players, 1965; *Pien* chamber concerto for piano, winds, and percussion.

Impressionist music of strong Chinese flavor, imaginative, poetic, and deliciously scored.

CLAFLIN, AVERY born Keene, New Hampshire 21 June 1898; attended Phillips Exeter Academy and Harvard; studied piano with John P. Marshall and composition with Archibald T. Davison; married Dorothea Carroll 2 December 1922; three children; chevalier Légion d'Honneur. His successful career in business was led in New York at the French-American Banking Corporation of which he became president. Compositions: four operas: *The Fall of Usher,* 1921; *Hester Prynne,* 1932; *La Grande Brétèche,* 1947; *Uncle Tom's Cabin,* 1966; for chorus: *Mary of Nazareth, Lament for April 15;* for orchestra: *Moby Dick Suite,* 1929; *Fishhouse Punch, Teen Scenes,* Four Pieces for Orchestra, *Larghetto and Shuffle;* also symphonies, a piano concerto, a ballet, and chamber music. Co-author (with Bernard Faÿ) of *The American Experiment,* 1929.

Claflin's operas are his most personal expression. Broadly conceived both as drama and as musical style, they have not yet come to please strongly today's somewhat finicky taste in stage music.

CONVERSE, FREDERICK SHEPHERD born Newton, Massachusetts 5 January 1871; studied with John Knowles Paine at Harvard (A.B.

1893), also in Munich; married Emma Cecil Tudor 1894; seven children. From 1899–1901 and 1931–38 taught at New England Conservatory of Music, from 1901–07 at Harvard; from 1911–14 was vice-president of the Boston Opera Company. Member of National Commission in Charge of Music in Training Camps 1918–19; member American Academy of Arts and Letters. He composed three symphonies, many symphonic and chamber works, also songs. Some of the major compositions: *Festival of Pan, La Belle Dame Sans Merci, The Mystic Trumpeter;* the following operas: *The Pipe of Desire* (first American work produced at the Metropolitan Opera) 1910; *The Sacrifice;* and *The Immigrants;* symphonic poem *Ormazd;* cantata *The Peace Pipe;* photo music drama *The Scarecrow;* symphonic poem *Flivver Ten Million;* tone poem *California;* orchestral suite *American Sketches,* 1929. Died 8 June 1940.

Of a great career, in its time, little remains.

COPLAND, AARON born Brooklyn, New York 14 December 1900; studied piano with Paul Wittgenstein and Clarence Adler, composition with Rubin Goldmark and Nadia Boulanger; Mus.Doc. (honorary) Princeton 1956. He was lecturer at the New School for Social Research, New York 1927–37; guest lecturer Harvard 1935–44; taught composition at the Berkshire Music Center from 1940; was dean from 1946; Charles Eliot Norton professor of poetry Harvard 1951–52. Co-founder with Roger Sessions of Copland-Sessions Concerts 1928–31; founder of the American Music Festivals at Yaddo, Saratoga Springs 1932. Received Guggenheim fellowship 1925–26; RCA Victor award 1930; Pulitzer prize 1944; New York Music Critics' Circle award 1945 (for *Appalachian Spring*); Oscar from Academy of Motion Picture Arts and Sciences for the score of *The Heiress* 1950; gold medal from National Institute of Arts and Letters 1956; honorary member of the Accademia di Sta. Cecilia, Rome. He is a director of the Koussevitzky Music Foundation, the Edward MacDowell Association, and the Walter W. Naumberg Foundation, a fellow of the American Academy of Arts and Sciences, and a member of the American Academy of Arts and Letters.

His works for orchestra include: First Symphony (with organ), 1925; *Music for the Theatre,* 1925; *A Dance Symphony,* 1925; Concerto for Piano and Orchestra, 1926; *Symphonic Ode,* 1929; Short Symphony, 1933; *Statements,* 1935; *El Salón México,* 1936; *Music for Radio,* 1937; *An Outdoor Overture,* 1938; *Quiet City,* 1940; *A Lincoln Portrait,* 1942; Third Symphony, 1946; Orchestral Variations, 1960; *Connotations* for orchestra, 1963; *Music for a Great City,* 1965; *Emblems* for band, 1965.

Ballets and operas: *Grogh,* 1925; *Hear Ye! Hear Ye!* 1934; *Billy the Kid,* 1938; *Rodeo,* 1942; *Appalachian Spring,* 1944; *Dance Panels,* 1965; *The Second Hurricane* (opera for high schools) 1937; *The Tender Land* (opera) 1954.

Scores for films: *The City,* 1939; *Of Mice and Men,* 1940; *Our Town,* 1940; *North Star,* 1943; *The Red Pony,* 1949; *The Heiress,* 1949.

Chamber music: Two Pieces for String Quartet, 1928; *"Vitebsk"* Trio, 1929; Piano Variations, 1930; Piano Sonata, 1941; Violin Sonata, 1943; *In the Beginning* (short oratorio) 1947; Twelve Poems of Emily Dickinson, 1950; Quartet for Piano and Strings, 1950; Piano Fantasy, 1957; Nonet for strings, 1962.

He is the author of *What to Listen For in Music,* 1939, revised 1957; *Our New Music,* 1941, revised 1968; *Music and Imagination,* 1952; *The Pleasures of Music,* 1959; *Copland on Music,* 1963.

As Leonard Bernstein said: "He is the best we have." For further comment see Chapter 6.

COWELL, HENRY DIXON born Menlo Park, California 11 May 1897; mostly self-educated; received honorary Mus. Doc. from Wilmington College 1953; married Sidney Hawkins Robertson 1941. Began career 1913 in San Francisco as pianist playing his own compositions; many European tours since 1923 and annually in United States. He was director of music at the New School for Social Research, New York 1930–36 and from 1940–65; also taught at Mills School for Teachers, New York 1941–45; lecturer in music Stanford University, Bennington College, and Mills College (Oakland). Other teaching positions: Adelphi College, 1949–51; Peabody Institute, Baltimore, and Columbia University (adjunct professor from 1953–65). Founder 1927 and editor of *New Music Quarterly.* From 1943–45 senior music editor Office of War Information. Received Guggenheim fellowship for research in non-European music Berlin 1931–32; award from National Institute of Arts and Letters 1948. Member of the National Institute of Arts and Letters, New Music Society (director in chief), Pan-American Association of Composers (executive board), League of Composers (executive board), American Composers' Alliance (president 1951), Contemporary Music Society (vice-president 1953).

Author: *New Musical Resources,* 1930; *American Composers on*

American Music, 1933; and with Sidney Cowell *Charles Ives and His Music,* 1955. He died 10 December 1965.

Cowell's works, too numerous for listing, include band, choral, piano, and chamber music, nineteen symphonies, seventeen pieces for various groupings entitled *Hymn and Fuguing Tune,* and an opera *The O'Higgins.* In early youth involved with Irish musical sources he later came to use in a convincing manner the music of Japan, India, Iran, Iceland, and other ethnic sources, including the Appalachian mountains and Southern farm regions of the United States. The variety of his sources and composing methods is probably the broadest of our time. And if his work, for all its grace, wit, and imagination, occasionally lacks intensity, it is never commercially oriented or otherwise lacking in sincerity.

For further comment see Chapter 9.

CRAWFORD, RUTH born East Liverpool, Ohio 3 July 1901; studied and taught piano at the School of Musical Art, Jacksonville, Florida; at the American Conservatory in Chicago; at Elmhurst College of Music. She spent her Guggenheim fellowship in Paris and Berlin 1930–31. In 1931 she married the musicologist Charles Seeger and settled in Washington; four children. As a busy mother she composed less than before, but she collected and transcribed much United States folk material. She was the music editor of *Our Singing Country* by John A. and Alan Lomax; author of *American Folksongs for Children.* Her works include: Nine Preludes for piano, 1924–28; Two Movements for Chamber Orchestra, 1926; Suite for String Quartet and Piano, 1927; Three Movements for Wind Instruments and Piano, 1928; *Study in Mixed Accents,* 1929; Chants for women's chorus, 1930; String Quartet, 1931; four *Diaphonic Suites* for flute, oboe, two clarinets, two cellos, 1931; Three Songs for contralto and seventeen instruments; *Rissolty Rossolty* for ten wind instruments, 1941; Suite for Wind Quintet. She died in Chevy Chase 18 November 1953.

An imaginative and inspired composer. Her String Quartet, a twelve-tone work, is a masterpiece for beauty of sound and sustained expressivity.

CRESTON, PAUL born New York 1 July 1906; completely self-taught in composition; maried Louise Gotto; two children. Concertized widely as pianist and accompanist; active as organist, conductor, teacher;

composer of more than ninety works including music for radio, television, and films. He has received the New York Music Critics' Circle award, Alice M. Ditson award, National Institute of Arts and Letters award, two Guggenheim fellowships, and a first prize (for his First Symphony) in the Paris International Referendum 1952. His works include five symphonies, thirteen concertos, especially for "neglected" instruments such as the marimba, saxophone, trombone, harp, and accordion, many works for piano and for chamber music combinations. Some of his more recent compositions are: *Chthonic Ode* (percussion, piano, and strings) 1966; *From the Psalmist* (contralto and orchestra) 1967; *Kalevala,* fantasy on Finnish folk songs for symphonic band, 1968; Missa "Cum Jubilo," 1968; and *The Northwest* for chorus and orchestra, 1969. He is the author of two textbooks: *Principles of Rhythm* and *Creative Harmony.*

Symphonically, the dance-movements are his best.

CRUMB, GEORGE HENRY (*See page 185.*)

DAVIDOVSKY, MARIO born Medanos, Buenos Aires, Argentina 4 March 1934; studied in Buenos Aires; after coming to the United States in 1960, with Otto Luening and Aaron Copland; married Elaine Blaustein 1962; one child. Since 1964 he has been associate director of the Columbia-Princeton Electronic Music Center; he was visiting lecturer at the University of Michigan School of Music in 1964; guest professor at Instituto di Tella, Buenos Aires 1965; is presently a professor of composition at Manhattan School of Music. Guggenheim fellowship 1961–63; Rockefeller fellowship 1965. Awards and commissions: Koussevitsky Foundation 1964; Library of Congress 1964; National Institute of Arts and Letters 1965; Brandeis University 1965; Aaron Copland award, Tanglewood 1966. Best known through works for small instrumental ensembles and for his electronic music: Electronic Study Nos. 1 and 2; *Synchronisms* Nos. 1, 2, and 3.

His work is well spoken of by experts in the electronic field.

DE KOVEN, HENRY REGINALD born Middletown, Connecticut 3 April 1861; was graduated from Oxford 1880; studied music in Stuttgart, Florence, Paris, and Vienna; married Anna Farwell 1884. Served as music critic on *New York World, Harper's Weekly,* and other papers. Founded and conducted the Washington Symphony Orchestra, president of the Manuscript Society 1897–98; member of the National Institute of Arts and Letters. He composed chiefly operas and operettas: *The Begum; Don Quixote; Robin Hood; The Fencing Master;*

The Algerian; Rob Roy; The Knickerbockers; The Tzigane; The Mandarin; The Highwayman; The Three Dragoons; Papa's Wife; Foxey Quiller; The Little Duchess; Maid Marian; Red Feather; Happyland; The Student King; The Snowman; The Golden Butterfly; The Beauty Spot; The Wedding Trip; Her Little Highness; The Canterbury Pilgrims (produced by Metropolitan Opera 1917); *A Masque of American Drama;* known also for his more than three hundred songs, including "Oh! Promise Me," and "A Recessional." He died 16 January 1920.

As a composer of operettas he was the most melodious of them all, more soaring even than Victor Herbert.

DELLO JOIO, NORMAN born New York 24 January 1913; studied at All Hallows Institute 1926–30, City College 1932–34, Institute of Musical Art 1936, Juilliard School 1939–41, Yale School of Music 1941; honorary Mus.Doc. from Lawrence College; member National Institute of Arts and Letters; married Grayce Baumgold 1942; three children. Has taught at Mannes College of Music and Sarah Lawrence College. Has received the following awards: Elizabeth Sprague Coolidge 1937; Town Hall Composition award 1941; Guggenheim fellowships 1943–44; grant from the National Institute of Arts and Letters 1945; New York Music Critics' Circle award 1949 and 1958; Pulitzer prize 1957. His works include: *On Stage* (ballet) 1944; *Ricercari* for piano and orchestra, 1946; *Variations–Chaconne–Finale* (orchestra) 1947; *Diversion of Angels* (ballet) 1948; Concerto for Clarinet and Orchestra, 1949; *New York Profiles* for orchestra, 1949; *The Triumph of St. Joan* (opera) 1950; *Psalm of David* for chorus and orchestra, 1950; *Song of Affirmation* for soprano, chorus, narrator, orchestra, 1951; *The Tall Kentuckian* (score for musical play) 1952; *Song of the Open Road* for chorus, 1952; *The Ruby* (opera) 1953; *The Lamentation of Saul,* 1954; *The Trial at Rouen* (opera) 1955; *Aria and Toccata* for two pianos, 1958; *To Saint Cecilia,* cantata, 1959; *Blood Moon* (opera) 1961; *Colloquies,* suite for violin and piano, 1964; Antiphonal Fantasy on a Theme by Vicenzo Albrici for organ, brass, and strings, 1966; Air for Strings, 1967; *Five Images* for piano four hands, 1967; *Proud Music of the Storm* for organ, brass, and chorus, 1967; and many film scores in the *Air Power* series (CBS for United States government).

A composer of warm lyrical outpouring with aspirations toward the lyric stage. His conditioning as a liturgical musician seems to hinder dramatic animation, though in ballet, films, songs, oratorio, and orchestral works, his music moves forward, speaks with authority. Even in the operas certain vocal solos can be eloquent.

DETT, ROBERT NATHANIEL born Drummondville, Quebec, Canada 11 October 1882; studied at Oberlin Conservatory (B.M. 1908, honorary Mus.Doc. 1926), Columbia University, Harvard, Eastman School of Music, Howard University (Mus. Doc. 1924), University of Pennsylvania. Won the Harmon medal in 1927 and several literary prizes. Teaching positions: Lane College, Jackson, Tennessee 1908–11; Lincoln Institute, Jefferson City, Missouri 1911–13; Hampton Institute, Virginia 1913–31; Samuel Houston College, Austin, Texas 1935; Bennett College, Greensboro, North Carolina 1937. He toured Europe 1929 as director of the Hampton Choir. Compositions include: two oratorios; *The Chariot Jubilee*, 1921; and *The Ordering of Moses* (Cincinnati Festival) 1937; piano works: *Magnolia Suite*, 1911; *In the Bottoms* suite (contains the popular *Juba Dance*) 1913; *Enchantment Suite*, 1922; *Cinnamon Grove Suite*, 1927; *Tropic Winter Suite*, 1938. For chorus: *Listen to the Lambs; O Holy Lord; Music in the Mine; Ave Maria; As Children Walk Ye; As by the Streams; Don't You Weep; Sit Down, Servant; Weepin' Mary; I'm So Glad*. Also published *Religious Folk Songs of the Negro*, 1926 and *The Dett Collection of Negro Spirituals*, four vols., 1936. He died in Battle Creek, Michigan 2 October 1943 where he was directing musical activities of the United Service Organizations.

Dett was a worthy and sincere musician, an honor to his people, and a composer of excellent music by any standard, much of which still lives.

DIAMOND, DAVID LEO born Rochester, New York 9 July 1915; studied at the Cleveland Institute of Music 1928–30; Eastman School of Music 1930–34; New Music and Dalcroze Institute, New York 1934–36; Fontainebleau summers 1937 and 1938; lecturer on American music at Salzburg Seminar 1949; taught composition at Metropolitan and Manhattan Music Schools, New York. Has received numerous awards and prizes and contributed to musical journals; works performed by many orchestras in United States and Europe. Compositions include: concertos, string quartets, chamber music, choral music, songs, scores for plays and motion pictures, six symphonies.

His string works are idiomatic, his songs melodious, his symphonies romantically inspired. The musical style in general is harmonious, the continuity relaxed. For all its seeming emotional self-indulgence, this is music of artistic integrity and real thought.

DLUGOSZEWSKI, LUCIA born Detroit 16 June 1931; attended Detroit Conservatory of Music and prepared for medical studies at Wayne State University; in New York studied piano with Grete Sultan, composition with Felix Salzer and Edgard Varèse; has taught at New York University, New School for Social Research, and Foundation for Modern Dance; received Tompkins literary award for poetry 1947; National Institute of Arts and Letters award 1966.

Since 1952 she has composed thirty works commissioned by Erick Hawkins Dance Company, Living Theatre, Menken-Maas Films, Connecticut College School of Dance, Ingram-Merrill Foundation, Foundation for Modern Dance, Center for Creative and Performing Arts at State University in Buffalo, and American Brass Quintet. Other works instrumental and vocal number nearly one hundred. She has invented over one hundred percussion instruments including the "timbre piano" and performed her own music in Paris, Montreal, New York, and on cross-continental tours.

She has published *A New Folder* poetry, 1969; with F.S.C. Northrup an extended article on philosophical aesthetics in *Main Currents,* 1970; and articles on modern dance in other magazines.

Far-out music of great delicacy, originality, and beauty of sound, also ingenious with regard to instrumental virtuosities and of unusually high level in its intellectual and poetic aspects. Typical of Miss Dlugoszewski's practicality and imagination, *Space Is a Diamond,* 1970, is an eleven-minute trumpet solo unaccompanied that seems virtually to exhaust the technical possibilities of the instrument without becoming didactic.

ELLINGTON, EDWARD KENNEDY ("DUKE") born Washington, D.C. 29 April 1899; studied music with Harry Grant; married Edna Thompson 1918; elected to National Institute of Arts and Letters 1970. First professional appearance as jazz player 1916; first appeared in New York 1922; Hollywood 1923; engaged by Cotton Club, New York 1927–32. Toured Europe 1933, 1950, 1958, 1960, 1962, 1964, 1965; Japan 1964, 1966. Presented annual concerts in New York 1943–50. Appeared in film *Check and Double Check,* 1930. Compositions include: *Mood Indigo, Solitude, Sophisticated Lady, Caravan, I Let a Song Go Out of My Heart, Do Nothing Till You Hear From Me, Don't*

Get Around Much Any More, In a Sentimental Mood, Black and Tan Fantasy, Creole Love Call; motion picture scores for *Anatomy of a Murder, Paris Blues, Assault on a Queen;* is said to have pioneered in wordless use of voice as a musical instrument in orchestration, also in use of miniature concerto form in building jazz arrangements around a soloist; certainly pioneered in extended compositions for jazz orchestra: *Reminiscing in Tempo,* 1935; *Black, Brown and Beige; A Tone Parallel to the History of the American Negro,* 1943; *New World A-Coming,* 1945; *Liberian Suite,* 1948; *Harlem,* 1950; A Concert of Sacred Music, 1965.

Bridging the chasm between "pop" and classical styles, though not yet fully achieved, has been consistently essayed by the "Duke." Though predominantly a big-band man, his position in blues, jazz, and swing is impregnable.

FARWELL, ARTHUR born St. Paul, Minnesota 23 April 1872; was graduated from the Massachusetts Institute of Technology 1893 with special studies in electrical engineering; studied composition 1893–99 with Homer Norris in Boston, Engelbert Humperdinck in Germany, and Alexandre Guilmant in Paris; married Gertrude Everts Brice 5 June 1917; six children; married Betty Richardson September 1939; one daughter. Was lecturer at Cornell University 1899–1901; established in 1901 the Wa-Wan Press for publishing Indian and Negro-based American music; from January 1909 was on the staff of *Musical America.* He was also supervisor of municipal concerts in New York 1910–13; director of Music School Settlement 1915–18; acting head of music department University of California 1918–19; holder of composer's fellowship Pasadena Music and Art Association 1921–25; from 1927–39 taught at Michigan State College. His works include: American Indian Melodies, 1901; *Dawn* and *The Domain of Hurakan,* 1901; *Navajo War Dance;* incidental music for *Joseph and His Brethren* and *The Gods of the Mountain;* music for pageants of Meriden, New Hampshire and Darien, Connecticut 1913; music for community masque *Caliban,* 1916, and *The Evergreen Tree,* 1917; music for the *Pilgrimage Play,* Hollywood 1921; Symphonic Hymn on *March! March!,* 1921; *Symbolistic Study No. 3,* 1922; *The Hako* for string quartet, 1922; *Rudolph Gott Symphony,* 1932; *The Hound of Heaven* for tenor, 1935; Piano Quintet in E minor, 1937; *Symbolistic Study No. 6; Mountain Vision* for two pianos and strings (National Federation of Music Clubs prize) 1939; forty Emily Dickinson songs,

1941–43; *Indian Scene* and *Navajo War Dance No. 2* for chorus, 1946; and the opera *Cartoon,* 1948. Died 20 January 1952.

Arthur Farwell's most vigorous music is inspired by American sources. The rest, though graceful, is French impressionism diluted.

FELDMAN, MORTON born New York 12 January 1926; studied composition with Wallingford Riegger and Stefan Wolpe; shaped his ideas on music through association in the early 1950s with John Cage, Earle Brown, Christian Wolff, and the pianist David Tudor. His *Projections* and *Projection 2* for flute, trumpet, violin, and cello, 1951, were among the first works to be drawn from the concept of indeterminacy and using graphic notation. In 1966 he was a Guggenheim fellow. Works include also: *Intersection 1,* 1951; *Marginal Intersection,* 1951; *Extension No. 4* for three pianos and Piece for Four Pianos, both 1957; *Durations* for chamber sextet, 1960–61; *Four Instruments,* 1965; Three Pieces for String Quartet and *Vertical Thoughts 2,* both 1968.

Feldman's music, school-of-Cage, is notable for its delicacy of sound and transparent textures.

FINE, IRVING GIFFORD born Boston 3 December 1915; A.B. Harvard 1937, A.M. 1938; studied piano with Frances L. Grover, composition with Edward Burlingame Hill, Walter Piston, and Nadia Boulanger, choral conducting with Archibald T. Davison, conducting with Serge Koussevitzky; married Verna Louise Rudnick 1941; three children. He taught in the Harvard music department 1939–50; was assistant conductor of the Harvard Glee Club 1942–45; from 1946 was on the Berkshire Music Center faculty at Tanglewood; in 1950 was co-director of the Salzburg Music Seminar. From 1950 was composer in residence, later professor at Brandeis University as well as chairman of the School of Creative Arts. Was recipient of a Fulbright research fellowship to France 1949; New York Music Critics' Circle award 1949; Koussevitzky Music Foundation commission 1949; Guggenheim fellowship 1950; Rodgers-Hammerstein commission 1952; Society for the Publication of American Music award 1954; National Institute of Arts and Letters award 1955. Composed cantatas, dances, choral and instrumental works including: Three Choruses from *Alice in Wonderland,* 1942; *The Hour Glass,* 1950; Nocturne for strings and harp, 1951; *Mutability,* 1952; String Quartet, 1952; *Old American Songs,*

1953; *Serious Song (Lament)* for string orchestra, 1955; *Children's Songs for Grown-Ups,* 1955; String Trio, 1956; *Blue Towers;* Diversion for Orchestra; Symphony, 1962. Died 23 August 1962.

Fine's was chiefly a lyrical output, whether written for voice or for instruments. Oriented toward French neo-Romantic art of the 1930s, his music seems to remember without really resembling it the music of Henri Sauguet.

FINE, VIVIAN born Chicago 28 September 1913; studied music with private teachers: piano, Djana Lavorie-Herz (Chicago), Abby Whiteside (New York); composition, Ruth Crawford (Chicago), Roger Sessions (New York); married Benjamin Karp 5 April 1935; two children. Was piano accompanist for Doris Humphrey and Charles Weidman in dance recitals; soloist in modern works for League of Composers, ISCM, Pan-American Association of Composers; lecture-recitalist 1965–68 at various universities including universities of Notre Dame, Wisconsin at Oshkosh, Bard College, William and Mary. A founder of American Composers' Alliance (vice-president 1961–65); musical director B. de Rothschild Foundation 1953–60; has taught at New York University (piano), Juilliard School of Music (literature and materials), New York State University at Potsdam (composition), Connecticut College School of Dance (composition for the dance); since 1964 at Bennington College (piano and composition). Received the Dollard award 1966; a Ford Foundation grant in the humanities 1970. Works include: Solo for Oboe, 1929; Four Pieces for Two Flutes, 1930; Four Songs with strings, 1933; Prelude and Elegiac Song for string orchestra, 1937; Dance Suite for orchestra, 1938; Sonatina for Oboe and Piano, 1939; Concertante for Piano and Orchestra, 1944; Capriccio for oboe and string trio, 1946; *The Great Wall of China* for voice, flute, cello, and piano, 1947; Divertimento for Cello and Percussion, 1951; Sonata for Violin and Piano, 1952; *A Guide to the Life Expectancy of a Rose* for soprano, tenor and chamber ensemble, 1956; String Quartet, 1957; *Valedictions* for soprano, tenor, chorus and chamber orchestra, 1959; Fantasy for cello and piano, 1962; *Morning* for narrator, chorus, and organ, 1962; *The Song of Persephone* for solo viola, 1964; *Dreamscope* for percussion ensemble, piano, three flutes, and cello, 1964; Concertino for piano and percussion, 1965; Chamber Concerto for Cello and Six Instruments, 1966; Quintet for String Trio, Trumpet, and Harp, 1967; *Paean* for narrator, chorus, and twelve brass instruments, 1969; also songs and short piano works. Dance works: *The Race of Life* for Doris Humphrey, 1937;

Opus 51 for Charles Weidman, 1938; *Tragic Exodus* for Hanya Holm, 1939; *Alcestis* for Martha Graham, 1960; *My Son, My Enemy* for José Limon, 1965. Two of these have been made into suites for orchestra: *The Race of Life* and *Alcestis*.

Miss Fine's music, combining emotional intensity with an intellectualized technique, has from the beginning been atonally oriented, though never serial. No rule-of-thumb, no simplified "method," no easy short-cut to popularity or fame mars the authenticity of its fine hand work.

FINNEY, ROSS LEE born Wells, Minnesota 23 December 1906; student at the University of Minnesota 1924–27; B.A. Carleton College 1927; studied at Harvard 1929, with Nadia Boulanger 1928, with Alban Berg 1932, with Gian-Francesco Malipiero 1937; married Gretchen Ludke 1930; two children. He was professor of music at Smith College 1929–48; taught concurrently at Mount Holyoke College 1940–44, at Hartt School of Music, Hartford, Connecticut 1941–42, at Amherst College 1946–47; since 1948 has been composer in residence at the University of Michigan. Awards: Johnson Foundation fellowship 1927; Connecticut Valley prize 1935; Guggenheim fellowship 1939–47; Pulitzer award 1939; Boston Symphony award 1955; Rockefeller Foundation grant 1956; National Institute of Arts and Letters award 1956. His works include: 4 piano sonatas; 3 sonatas for violin and piano; 2 sonatas for viola and piano; 2 sonatas for cello and piano; 6 string quartets; 3 symphonies; 2 piano trios; Eight Poems by Archibald MacLeish, 1935–57; Fantasy for Piano, 1939; Slow Piece, 1941; *Pale Star for This Year*, 1941; *Symphony-Communiqué*, 1942; Variation, Fuguing Tune, and Rondo, 1943; Duo for Violin and Piano, 1943; *Pilgrim Psalms*, 1945; *Poor Richard*, 1946; *Music to be Danced*, 1947; Waltzes, 1947; *Six Spherical Madrigals*, 1947; Violin Concerto, 1947; *Solemn Music*, 1948; *Three Love Songs*, 1948; Piano Quartet, 1948; Piano Concerto, 1948; 36 Songs, 1952; *Immortal Autumn*, 1952; Variations for Piano, 1952; *Hymn, Fuguing Tune*, and *Holiday*, 1966; Concerto for Percussion and Orchestra, 1967. Author of *The Game of Harmony*, 1947.

Finney's early chamber music, especially that involving strings, is thematically delicate and richly kaleidoscopic in harmony. His 12-tone works, both chamber and orchestral, tend toward a certain opacity of sound. All his music is brightly colored; at its best it glows like the celestial firmament, with a dispersed brilliance untouched by human feeling.

FLANAGAN, WILLIAM born Detroit, Michigan 14 August 1923; studied composition with Burrill Phillips and Bernard Rogers at the Eastman School of Music; with Arthur Honegger, Arthur Berger, and Aaron Copland at the Berkshire Music Center, with David Diamond in New York. At the same time he engaged in musical journalism, eventually as supplementary reviewer for the *New York Herald Tribune* 1957–60, during the 1960s for *Stereo Review*. His works include: Divertimento for string quartet, 1947; Passacaglia for piano, 1947; Piano Sonata, 1950; Divertimento for Classical Orchestra, 1948; Chaconne for violin and piano, 1948; *Song for a Winter Child* to words of Edward Albee, 1950; *A Concert Ode* for orchestra, 1951; a one-act opera after the Melville short story *Bartleby*, 1952–57; *The Weeping Pleiades* song cycle to words by A. E. Housman, 1953; *The Lady of Tearful Regret* for coloratura soprano and instruments to words by Albee, 1958; A Concert Overture, 1959; *Notations* for large orchestra, 1960; *Chapter from Ecclesiastes* for mixed chorus and string quintet, 1963; *Narrative for Orchestra*, 1964; *Another August* for soprano and orchestra (James Merrill) 1967. He wrote incidental music for Edward Albee's plays *The Sandbox*, 1961; *The Ballad of the Sad Cafe*, 1963; and *The Death of Bessie Smith*. The New York City Opera commissioned him in 1963 to write with Albee *The Ice Age;* libretto and music remain unfinished. He was working on *Silences* for a woman's voice and orchestra at the time of his sudden death on or about 31 August 1969.

A soaring lyric afflatus and an extreme beauty in the melodic materials give to Flanagan's music a distinction and an authenticity quite unusual.

FOSS, LUKAS born Berlin, Germany 15 August 1922; attended the Lycée Pasteur, Paris 1932–37; came to United States 1937, naturalized 1942; was graduated from the Curtis Institute of Music 1940; special studies at Yale 1940–41; studied also with Paul Hindemith, Julius Herford, Serge Koussevitzky, Fritz Reiner, Isabella Vengerova, Randall Thompson, Rosario Scalero, Felix Wolfes; married Cornelia Brendel 1952; two children. Formerly professor at University of California, Los Angeles; in 1963 became conductor and music director of Buffalo Philharmonic.

His best known works include: *The Jumping Frog* a short opera; a cantata *The Prairie;* Piano Concerto No. 2; *Song of Songs* for soprano and orchestra; *Song of Anguish;* String Quartet in G; *Parable of Death; Griffelkin* opera in three acts; Psalms; also piano pieces and ballets. He received a Pulitzer scholarship 1942; Guggenheim fellowship 1945; New York Critics' Circle award 1944; Prix de Rome 1950; Horblit award 1951; Naumberg recording award 1957; grant from National Institute of Arts and Letters 1957; New York Music Critics' Circle award (for *Time-Cycle* orchestral songs) 1961, and for *Echoi* (orchestra) 1963; member of National Institute of Arts and Letters.

A musician of perfect gifts and training, a first-class conductor, as a composer perhaps more accomplished than convincing, but highly ingenious and venturesome all the same.

FLOYD, CARLISLE born Latta, South Carolina 11 June 1926; B.M. Syracuse University 1946, M.M. (studying with Ernest Bacon) 1949; married Margery Kay Reeder 1957. Since 1947 he has taught piano and composition at Florida State University in Tallahassee. He has written the following operas, all to his own libretti: *Slow Dusk,* 1949; *Fugitives,* 1951; *Susannah,* 1955; *Wuthering Heights,* 1958; *The Passion of Jonathan Wade,* 1962; *The Sojourner and Mollie Sinclair,* 1963; *Markheim,* 1966; *Of Mice and Men,* 1970.

In *Susannah,* for all its orchestral ineptitude, Floyd has composed an opera of repertory status. Nothing he has written since has matched the eloquence of its straightforward text, its music, or its drama, though I do not know *Of Mice and Men,* recent and apparently successful.

GABURO, KENNETH born Somerville, New Jersey 5 July 1926; studied at Eastman School of Music (M.M.), Santa Cecilia (Rome), Tanglewood, Princeton, University of Illinois (D.M.A.); married Yvonne Stevens 14 September 1947 (div.), two sons; married Virginia Hommel 15 July 1964, one daughter. Taught at Kent State (Ohio), McReese (Louisiana), University of Illinois, and University of California, San Diego. Awards and fellowships: Gershwin Memorial, Sagalyn, University of Illinois, Fulbright, UNESCO, Guggenheim, Thorne, German Academy (Berlin). Commissions: Notre Dame University, Colgate University, Illinois Wesleyan University, Victor Alessandro, Magnavox Corporation, American Guild of Organists, Walter Trampler, Koussevitsky and Fromm foundations. Founded in 1964 New Music Choral Ensemble. Orchestral works: Three Interludes for String Orchestra, 1949; *On a Quiet Theme,* 1951; Elegy for Small Orchestra, 1956; *Antiphony I* for three string groups and tape, 1957; *Shapes and Sounds* for full orchestra, 1960; chamber music: Four Inventions for clarinet and piano, 1954; Music for Five Instruments, piano, trumpet, trombone, flute, clarinet, 1954; *Ideas and Transformations No. 1* (violin, viola), *No. 2* (violin, violoncello), *No. 3* (viola, violoncello), 1955; String Quartet in One Movement, 1956; *Line Studies* for flute, clarinet, trombone, viola, 1957; *Antiphony IV (Poised)* for piccolo, trombone, string bass, and electronics, 1967; *Antiphony V* for piano and electronics, 1969. For theatre: *The Snow Queen* (opera) 1952; *The Widow* (one–act opera) 1959; two tape operas (concrete and electronic); and music for plays (live and electronic). There is also electronic and concert music both for live players and on disk.

Gaburo's orchestral, chamber, and choral music is ravishing in sound on account of its high sensitivity to interval relations. His electronic and partly-electronic music is among the most original that exists. Gaburo is at once far-out and "musical," imaginative and advanced, a strong composer in no way casual. Pierre Boulez has remarked the originality of his vocal writing.

GERSHWIN, GEORGE born Brooklyn, New York 26 September 1898; studied piano with Charles Hambitzer, harmony and composition with Edward Kilenyi, Rubin Goldmark, Henry Cowell, and Joseph Schillinger. Among his musical comedies are: *La! La! Lucille,* 1919; music for *George White's Scandals,* 1920–24; *Our Nell,* 1923; *Sweet Little Devil,* 1923; *Lady, Be Good!* 1924; *Tip-Toes,* 1925; *Oh, Kay!* 1926; *Funny Face,* 1927; *Girl Crazy,* 1927; *Strike Up the Band,* 1930; *Of Thee I Sing,* 1931; *Let 'em Eat Cake,* 1933; *Pardon My English,* 1933.

His "serious" music includes: a String Quartet, 1919; *Blue Monday* later renamed *135th Street* (one-act opera) 1922; *Rhapsody in Blue,* 1924; Concerto in F for piano and orchestra, 1925; *An American in Paris,* 1928; *Second Rhapsody,* 1932; Variations on "I Got Rhythm," 1933; *Cuban Overture,* 1934; *Porgy and Bess* (opera) 1935; Preludes for Piano; many songs. He died 11 July 1937.

Lively rhythm, graceful harmony, and a fine melodic gift. Tops for his time in show music. *Porgy and Bess,* a white man's view of life among the blacks, has circled the globe. Its powerful charm puts it not far below Bizet's *Carmen,* which is after all a Frenchman's view of Spain.

GOULD, MORTON born Richmond Hill, Long Island 10 December 1913; attended local public schools; studied piano with Abby Whiteside, composition with Dr. Vincent Jones at New York University; played many concerts as child pianist composer, was published at six, also worked in vaudeville and radio; on staff of Radio City Music Hall at seventeen, later worked for NBC and WOR Mutual; has guest-conducted major symphony orchestras; married Shirley Uzin 1936; Shirley Bank 3 June 1945; four children.

His orchestral works include concertos for viola and for piano; three symphonies; Concerto for Orchestra, *Foster Gallery; American Salute;* four *American Symphonettes, Spirituals* for string choir and orchestra, *Cowboy Rhapsody, Homespun Overture, A Lincoln Legend; Minstrel Show;* Tap Dance Concerto. Stage works include the ballets *Interplay,* 1943, and *Fall River Legend,* 1947; *Delightfully Dangerous,* stage show in which he also appeared; Broadway musicals *Billion Dollar Baby, Arms and the Girl; Windjammer* film. Later orchestral works: *Inventions,* 1953; *Dance Variations,* 1953; Showpiece for Orchestra, 1954; *Cinerama Holiday,* 1954; *Declaration* symphonic narrative, 1957; *Jekyll and Hyde Variations,* 1957; *St. Lawrence Suite,* 1958; *Dialogues for Piano and Orchestra;* and many other "specialty" numbers. He has also appeared on television as musical commentator.

Among all our recent composers commercially or pop-concert oriented Gould is probably the one most often played by high-prestige conductors. At the same time his *American Salute* and *Cowboy Rhapsody* are virtually classical for bands and high school orchestras, his *Interplay* and *Fall River Legend* repertory dance works.

GRIFFES, CHARLES TOMLINSON born Elmira, New York 17 September 1884; studied piano locally, also organ; in Berlin from 1903 studied piano with Jedliczka and Galston, composition with Rufer and Humperdinck, gave private lessons, and played his compositions in public. He returned to America in 1907, taught music at the Hackley School for Boys in Tarrytown, New York. Influenced by the French impressionists, also by Mussorgsky and by Scriabin, he became a composer in the impressionist style, known especially for *The White Peacock* for piano (also for orchestra) 1917, and a tone poem *The Pleasure Dome of Kubla Khan,* 1919. Other works: *The Kairn of Koridwen* dance drama for five woodwinds, celesta, harp, and piano, 1917; *Shojo* Japanese pantomime drama for four woodwinds, four muted strings, harp, and percussion, 1917; *Poem* for flute and orchestra, 1919; two Sketches on Indian Themes for string quartet, published posthumously 1922; for piano: *Three Tone Pictures,* 1915;

Fantasy Pieces, 1915; *Roman Sketches,* 1917; Sonata in F, published 1921; and many songs. He died 8 April 1920.

Griffes's music is first-class all through and can be played anywhere. His death at thirty-five seems somehow unfair.

HANSON, HOWARD born Wahoo, Nebraska 28 October 1896; studied at Luther College, Wahoo; University of Nebraska; Institute of Musical Art, New York; Mus.B. Northwestern University 1916; Mus. Doc. (honorary) Northwestern University, Syracuse University, Horner Institute, Augustana College, and Theological Seminary, University of Nebraska, American Conservatory of Music, Columbia University, Capital University, Shurtleff College, Hartt College of Music; LL.D. from Wesleyan University, College of the Pacific; Litt.D. Keuka College; L.H.D. Drury College; married Margaret Elizabeth Nelson 1946. He was a member of the theory department College of the Pacific, San José, California 1916, dean of the Conservatory of Fine Arts 1919–21; director of the Eastman School of Music, Rochester from 1924; has served as guest conductor in major United States and foreign cities. Awards: Pulitzer prize 1944, George Foster Peabody award 1946, and many others. Fellow American Academy in Rome 1921–24; Royal Academy of Music in Sweden 1938; member of the National Institute of Arts and Letters.

Composer of a wide variety of excellent music, including symphonies, symphonic poems, choruses, solo vocal works, and concertos. His opera *Merry Mount* was produced at the Metropolitan in 1934. Though perhaps unduly attached to sequence-structure, Hanson is a Romantic composer of warm heart. He is also an excellent administrator and a master conductor.

HARRIS, ROY ELLSWORTH born Lincoln County, Oklahoma 12 February 1898; studied music with his mother, with Arthur Farwell, and with Nadia Boulanger; attended University of California 1919–20; received honorary Mus.Doc. Rutgers University 1941 and University of Rochester 1946; four marriages, six children. Received Guggenheim fellowship 1928, 1929, 1930; creative fellowship of the Pasadena Music and Arts Association 1930–31; awarded first honors for *Folk Song Symphony* 1940 by Committee for Appreciation of American Music; certificate of honor by National Association for Composers and Conductors 1940; Coolidge medal 1942. Teaching positions include:

Cornell University 1941–43; Colorado College 1943–48; Utah State Agricultural College 1948–49; Peabody College for Teachers, Nashville 1949–51; Pennsylvania College for Women, Pittsburgh 1951–56; University of Southern Illinois 1956–57; University of Indiana 1957; and most recently University of California, Los Angeles. In 1945 served as musical director with Office of War Information; member National Institute of Arts and Letters.

A prolific composer, he has written works in many different genres including chamber music, music for schools, bands, orchestra, chorus, and piano. He is best known for his early chamber music and for his Third Symphony, though there are eleven symphonies in all. Some of his more recent works include: *Symphonic Epigram;* Concert Piece for Orchestra, both 1954; Fantasia for Orchestra, 1954; Fantasy for Piano and Orchestra, 1954; *Ode to Consonance*, 1957; *Reverie and Dance*, 1958; *Folk Fantasy for Festivals* (for chorus) 1958; *Give Me the Splendid Silent Sun* cantata for baritone and orchestra, 1959; Fantasy for organ, brasses, and timpani, 1966; *Horn of Plenty* for orchestra, 1967.

Harris's best works have a deeply meditative quality combined with exuberance. Even without citation of folklore they breathe an American air. His music reflects high artistic aims and a sophistication of thematic, harmonic, and instrumental usage that identify it as work of distinction, with frequently great beauty in the texture.

HARRISON, LOU born Portland, Oregon 14 May 1917; student of Henry Cowell and Arnold Schoenberg. Has written on music for *View, Listen, Modern Music*, and the *New York Herald Tribune;* also taught at Mills College (Oakland), Black Mountain College, Greenwich House Music School in New York, and San José State College. Beside being a composer Harrison has been a playwright, conductor, poet, dancer, and maker of musical instruments. He has edited a number of Charles Ives's works, notably the Third Symphony, which he conducted in world premiere, New York 1946, and recorded. His compositions include an orchestral tribute *At the Tomb of Charles Ives;* three sonatas for harpsichord, 1946; *Solstice* for gamelan, 1950; a String Trio; a set of percussion Simfonies (sic); several concertos, notably for flute and for violin; *Canticles* for percussion; Suite for Violin, Piano, and Small Orchestra; Suite for Piano; Suite for Strings; Symphony on G; and the opera *Rapunzel*. Harrison is also an adept of Esperanto. He has written many of his own vocal texts including the

Political Primer for baritone, chorus, and orchestra (translated into Esperanto) and the third of three vocal works (one is choral) entitled *Peace Piece.*

The list of Harrison's works is long and highly varied as to instrumentation and musical format. One might be tempted to consider his finest works to be those of East Asian inspiration (Indian, Indonesian, Korean) were it not for the works inspired by the sweetness of Elizabethan England (the Masses, the string suites) and for the warmly eloquent Symphony on G. He is author of a pamphlet *About Carl Ruggles,* 1946.

Fuller discussion of Harrison's work will be found in Chapters 8 and 9.

HERBERT, VICTOR born Dublin, Ireland 1 February 1859; began his music education in Germany at the age of seven; married Therese Foerster 1886. Was principal cello player in court orchestra of Stuttgart and played in concerts throughout Europe before coming to United States as solo cellist with Metropolitan Opera 1886. Was associated with Thomas Seidl's and other orchestral organizations as conductor and soloist; bandmaster 22nd Regiment Band New York 1894; conductor Pittsburgh Orchestra 1898–1904, Victor Herbert's New York Orchestra from 1904. Founded in 1910 the American Society of Composers, Authors, and Publishers; member National Institute of Arts and Letters.

Best known for his operettas, writing thirty-five between 1894 and 1917; among them: *Prince Ananias, The Wizard of the Nile, The Serenade, Cyrano de Bergerac, The Ameer, The Viceroy, The Idol's Eve, The Fortune Teller, The Singing Girl, Babette, Mlle. Modiste, The Red Mill, Babes in Toyland, It Happened in Nordland.* His two grand operas were *Natoma* (Philadelphia 1911) and *Madeleine* (Metropolitan Opera 1914). Other works include *The Captive* cantata written for Worcester Festival, 1891; Serenade for strings, 1888; *Suite Romantique; Hero and Leander* symphonic poem; the suites *Woodland Fancies* and *Columbus;* two cello concertos. He died 26 May 1924.

Revered master, along with Reginald de Koven, of the Vienna-style American operetta. Songs like "Kiss Me Again" and "Gypsy Love Song" will not be soon forgotten.

HILL, EDWARD BURLINGAME born Cambridge, Massachusetts 9 September 1872; studied at Harvard (A.B. 1894) with John Knowles

Paine and F. F. Bullard, with G. W. Chadwick in Boston, with Arthur Whiting in New York, and with Widor in Paris; Mus.Doc. (honorary) University of New Hampshire 1952; married Alison Bixby 12 June 1900; three sons. Taught at Harvard from 1908 until his retirement in 1940; lectured in Paris, Lyon, and Strasbourg; chevalier Légion d'Honneur; member National Institute of Arts and Letters, fellow of the American Academy of Arts and Sciences.

Wrote mostly instrumental music for orchestra: four symphonies; several suites; *Launcelot and Guinevere* and *Lilacs* (symphonic poems); Concertino for Piano and Orchestra; Violin Concerto; Music for English Horn and Orchestra; Suite for Strings; and two *Stevensoniana* suites. Sonatas for various instruments, a quintet, and a String Sextet make up his chamber music. Author of *Modern French Music*, 1924. He died in 1960.

A sound impressionist composer, a master of orchestration, and a valued pedagogue. Walter Piston, Randall Thompson, Virgil Thomson, Arthur Berger, and Elliott Carter are among his pupils.

HILLER, LEJAREN ARTHUR born New York 23 February 1924; B.A. Princeton 1944, M.A. 1946, Ph.D. 1947; M.M. University of Illinois 1958; married Elizabeth Halsey 1945; two children. From 1947–52 he was a research chemist at E. I. du Pont de Nemours and Company Waynesboro, Virginia; in 1953 he joined the University of Illinois (Urbana) chemistry department, from 1958 was a professor of music, also director of the Experimental Music Studio. In 1969 he was Visiting Slee Professor of Music at the New York State University at Buffalo and co-director with Lukas Foss of the Center of the Creative and Performing Arts; is now a professor of music there. He is co-author with L. M. Isaacson of *Experimental Music*, 1950; with R. H. Herber *Principles of Chemistry*, 1960, and *Informationstheorie und Computermusik*, 1964. His compositions include: Fifth Piano Sonata, 1960; *Music for Time of the Heathen*, 1961; Fourth String Quartet, 1962; *Amplification for Tape Recorder and Band*, 1962; *Music for Man with the Oboe*, 1962; *Music for Spoon River Anthology*, 1962; Seven Electronic Music Studies, 1963; *Computer Cantata*, with R. A. Baker, 1963; *Machine Music for Piano, Percussion, and Tape*, 1964; *A Triptych for Hieronymus*, 1965; Suite for Two Pianos and Tape, 1966; *Algorithms I* for nine instruments and tape, 1967; and with John Cage *HPSCHD*, 1969.

He is reputed to be an authority in his field, which is mainly that of engineering-music.

HOVHANESS, ALAN born Somerville, Massachusetts 8 March 1911; studied at the New England Conservatory of Music 1932–34; taught at the Boston Conservatory 1948–51. Guggenheim fellowships, 1953–55; first world tour in 1959 conducting chiefly his own music; award from National Institute of Arts and Letters 1951; honorary doctorates from University of Rochester 1958 and Bates College, Maine 1959.

His works include: the concertos *Lousadzak* (piano) 1944; *Elibris* (flute) 1944; *Tzaikerk* (violin) 1945; *No. 1 Arevakap* (orchestra only) 1951; *Khaldis* (piano, four trumpets, percussion) 1952; *Talin* (viola) 1953; for other solo instruments including horn, trombone, accordion, trumpet; the two ballets *Hanna,* 1953 and *Ardent Song,* 1954; the cantatas *Avak the Healer,* 1946; *Thirtieth Ode of Solomon,* 1947; *Vartan Symphony,* 1950; Easter Cantata, 1953; *Shepherd of Israel,* 1953; *Glory to God,* 1954. Also incidental music for *The Flowering Peach,* 1955 and considerable music for NBC television films.

Hovhaness's music is mostly of Middle East inspiration, especially Armenian; some later works employ Japanese materials. A seemingly inexhaustible composer, his music too goes on and on. As with much music evoking Asia it adds no drama to the structure, but interests through sheer continuity and lovely sound. If like heaven it purports to be eternal, for mortals it can also on occasion seem interminable; but its variety from piece to piece is infinite.

IMBRIE, ANDREW WELSH born New York 6 April 1921; A.B. Princeton 1942; M.A. University of California, Berkeley 1947; married Barbara Cushing 1953; two children. From 1947 has taught at University of California, Berkeley; professor since 1960. Awards: New York Music Critics' Circle 1943–44; Alice M. Ditson fellow, Columbia 1946–47; Prix de Rome 1947–49; grant from National Institute of Arts and Letters 1950; creative award Brandeis University 1958; Naumberg award 1960; National Foundation on Arts and Humanities grant 1967–68; member National Institute of Arts and Letters.

Compositions include three string quartets, trios, sonatas, and songs; Serenade for flute, violin, piano, 1952; for orchestra: one symphony; *Ballad in D,* 1947; Concerto for Violin and Orchestra, 1954; Little Concerto, 1956; *Legend,* 1959; for chorus: *On the Beach at Night,* 1948; Introit, Gradual, and Offertory, 1956; an opera *Three Against Christmas.*

Characteristically a pupil of Roger Sessions, Imbrie composes music of a certain complexity, a shade hermetic, always well constructed. It also sounds well.

IVES, EDWARD CHARLES born Danbury, Connecticut 20 October 1874; studied solfeggio, harmony, counterpoint, and instrumentation with his father, organ with Dudley Buck, composition with Horatio W. Parker at Yale (B.A. 1898); married Harmony Twichell 1908; one daughter. He was organist at the Congregational Church, Danbury 1887; St. Thomas Church, New Haven 1893–94; Centre Church, New Haven 1894–98; organist and choir master First Presbyterian Church, Bloomfield, New Jersey 1898–1900; Central Presbyterian Church, New York 1900–02. Worked as clerk with Mutual Life Insurance Company 1898–1906; formed his own insurance firm, Ives and Myrick, in which he was active 1906–30. Member National Institute of Arts and Letters; Pulitzer prize 1947.

Composer of organ music, songs, four symphonies, four violin sonatas, two piano sonatas, other piano music, three orchestral suites, eleven volumes of chamber music including trios and string quartets; choral music with and without orchestra. These works include: Variations on "America" for organ, 1899; anthems, hymns, psalms, and choral works, 1888–1904; songs (about one hundred fifty) 1886–1925; *Intercollegiate* (march for military band) 1895; *Harvest Festival* (chorus, organ, trumpets, trombones) 1898; First String Quartet, *Revival Service*, 1896; First Symphony (D minor) 1898; Second Symphony, 1897–1902; First Piano Sonata, 1902–08; Third Symphony, 1911; Fourth Symphony, 1910–16; Symphony Holidays: *Washington's Birthday*, 1913; *Decoration Day*, 1912; *The Fourth of July*, 1912–13; *Thanksgiving Day*, 1904; Set for Theatre Orchestra, 1906–11; *Browning Overture*, 1905–12; *The Unanswered Question—a Cosmic Landscape* (orchestra) 1908; Second Piano Sonata subtitled *Concord, Massachusetts 1840–60* (*Emerson, Hawthorne, The Alcotts, Thoreau*) 1911–15; for various groups of instruments or chamber orchestras (some with voices): Largo Cantabile, 1904; Adagio (*The Innate*) 1908; *The Rainbow*, 1914; *The Pond, Halloween, From the Steeple and the Mountains*, 1904–14; *Gong on the Hook and Ladder— Firemen's Parade on Main Street*, 1912; *Calcium Light Night*, 1897; *Aeschylus and Sophocles*, 1922; *Over the Pavements*, 1906–13; *The Last Reader*, 1911; *Children's Day at the Camp Meeting*, Fourth Violin Sonata, 1915; Quarter-tone Music; Chorales for Strings, 1913–14; a war march *They Are There*, 1917; *Three Tone-Roads* (*On the Way* to Town Meetings, 1911–19; The Indians, 1912; On the Antipodes, 1915–23); works for chorus and orchestra: Lincoln, the Great Commoner, 1912; The Masses, 1915; An Election, 1920; General Booth's Entrance into Heaven, 1914; December, 1912; The New River, 1912; First Orchestral Set: Three Places in New England (Boston Common, Putnam's Camp in Redding, The Housatonic at Stockbridge) 1914; Second Orchestral Set: (An Elegy to Our Forefathers, The Rockstrewn Hills Join in the People's Outdoor Meeting, From Hanover Square North on a Tragic Day—a Theme of the People Again Arose) 1915.

A vast production impressive for both size and quality. For critical comment see Chapter 3.

KAY, HERSHY born Philadelphia 17 November 1919; was a student of cello at Curtis Institute 1936–40. He is best known as orchestrator of scores for Broadway shows: On the Town, 1944; A Flag Is Born, 1947; Peter Pan, 1950; Golden Apple, 1954; Sand Hog, 1955; Candide, 1956; Once Upon a Mattress, 1958; Juno, 1958; Livin' the Life, 1959; Happiest Girl in the World, 1961; Milk and Honey, 1961; 110 in the Shade, 1963; Kelly, 1965; Coco, 1969. Arranged ballet scores for Martha Graham 1947; Thief Who Loved a Ghost for Ballet Theatre 1950; for the New York City Ballet: Cakewalk, 1951; Western Symphony, 1954; Stars and Stripes, 1958; for the American Ballet Theatre Concert for Ballets USA, 1959, and L'Inconnue, 1965. His orchestrated film scores include Man with a Gun, 1955; King and Four Queens, 1956; South Seas (cinerama) 1958; Girl of the Night, 1960; Drat! The Cat!, 1965. Television scores include Valiant Years, 1962; FDR Series, 1964; and others for ABC and NBC. Composed the background music for Cyril Ritchard's Mother Goose recording, 1958. Completed opera The Good Soldier Schweik by Robert Kurka (dec.) 1959. Reconstructed and orchestrated Louis M. Gottschalk's Grande Tarantelle for piano and orchestra, 1957.

His original compositions may be minor but his contributions as orchestrator and arranger are important. Along with Robert Russell Bennett he represents the highest standard in the world for this kind of workmanship (commercial, of course).

KAY, ULYSSES born Tucson, Arizona 7 January 1917; B.M. University of Arizona 1938; M.M. Eastman School of Music 1940; student at Yale 1941–42; Columbia University 1946–49; honorary Mus.Doc.

Lincoln College 1963 and Bucknell University 1966; married Barbara Harrison 1949; 3 children. For many years editorial adviser Broadcast Music, Inc.; visiting professor University of California, Los Angeles 1966–67; teaches at Herbert Lehman College of the City University of New York. Member of the first official delegation of U.S. composers to the USSR 1958. Awards: Alice M. Ditson fellowship 1945; ABC prize 1946; Gershwin Memorial 1947; Julius Rosenwald fellowship 1948; prix de Rome 1949–50, 51–52; Fulbright fellowship, Italy 1950–51; Guggenheim fellowship 1964–65; member of Yaddo Corporation.

His works include: *The Boor, The Juggler of Our Lady* (operas); *Danse Calinda* (ballet); *The Quiet One* (film score); *New Horizons* overture; Suite for Strings; Concerto for Orchestra; Symphony in E; Three Pieces After Blake, soprano and orchestra; Serenade for Orchestra; *Triumvirate* for male chorus; the cantatas *Song of Jeremiah, Phoebus Arise, Inscriptions from Whitman;* and many other orchestral, choral, and chamber works.

A composer of taste, notably gifted for ballet and films.

KIRCHNER, LEON born Brooklyn, New York 24 January 1919; A.B. 1940 University of California, Berkeley; married Gertrude Schoenberg 1949; two children. Taught at University of Southern California and at Mills College (Oakland); in 1961 became Walter Bigelow Rosen Professor of music at Harvard. In 1942 he received the Prix de Paris; Guggenheim fellowships 1948–50; New York Music Critics' Circle awards 1949–50, 1959–60; Naumberg award 1954; grant from the National Institute of Arts and Letters 1951. Member of the National Institute of Arts and Letters, fellow of the American Academy of Arts and Sciences.

His compositions include: (for piano) Sonata, 1948; Little Suite, 1949; (chamber music) Duo for Violin and Piano, 1947; Sonata Concertante for violin and piano, 1952; two string quartets, 1949 and 1958; Trio for Violin, Cello and Piano, 1954; (orchestral) Piece for Piano and Orchestra, 1946; Sinfonìa, 1951; Piano Concerto, 1953; Toccata for Strings, Solo Winds, and Percussion, 1955; Concerto for Violin, Cello, Ten Winds, and Percussion, 1960; Music for Orchestra, 1969.

Kirchner's music, though it remembers Sessions and Schoenberg, is direct in its expression, strongly emotional, admirably structured for effect.

Twentieth-Century Composers

KLEINSINGER, GEORGE born San Bernardino, California 13 February 1914; studied at New York University with Philip James, at Juilliard with Jacobi and Wagenaar. Played piano in dance bands and served as music director in youth camps. He is best known for satirical works of colorful orchestration: *Tubby the Tuba* for narrator and orchestra, 1942; *Pan the Piper*, 1946; *Pee-Wee the Piccolo*, 1946; *Street Corner Concerto* for harmonica and orchestra, 1947; *Brooklyn Baseball Cantata*, 1948; and the chamber opera *Archy and Mehitabel*, 1954, in which a cat tells all to a cockroach. Many of these have enjoyed popularity. More classical works include a symphony, 1942; a cello concerto, 1946; and a violin concerto, 1953.

KUBIK, GAIL born South Coffeyville, Oklahoma 5 September 1914; Mus.B. Eastman School of Music; M.M. American Conservatory, Chicago 1935; graduate study at Harvard 1937–38; studied composition under Edward Royce, Bernard Rogers, Leo Sowerby, Walter Piston, Nadia Boulanger; Mus.Doc. (honorary) Monmouth College 1955; married Jessie Louise Mayer 1938; Joyce Mary Scott Paine 1946; Mary Gibbs Tyler 1952. Taught at Monmouth College 1934–36, Dakota Wesleyan University 1936–37, Columbia Teachers College 1938–40; staff composer and program adviser NBC 1940–41; composer-conductor of film and radio units United States Air Force 1943–46; professor of music University of Southern California 1946; guest lecturer Accademia di Santa Cecilia, Rome 1952. Awards include: Guggenheim fellowship 1944–45; prix de Rome 1950; Pulitzer prize 1952. Works include: four symphonies; Variations on a Thirteenth Century Troubador Song, 1935; *In Praise of Johnny Appleseed*, 1938; *Stewball Variations* (band) 1943; *War-Time Episode*, 1944; *A Mirror for the Sky* (folk opera) 1946; Piano Sonata 1947; *Profiles*, folk song sketches, 1948; *Boston Baked Beans* (opera) 1950; *Thunderbolt Overture*, 1953; *Scenario for Orchestra*, 1957; the following film scores: *Memphis Bells*, 1944; *Gerald McBoing Boing*, 1950; *Two Gals and a Guy*, 1951; *Transatlantic*, 1952; *The Desperate Hours*, 1955; *Down to Earth*, 1959.

An accomplished composer of music with energy in it, especially effective with films.

LEE, DAI-KEONG born Honolulu 2 September 1915; studied medicine at the University of Hawaii 1933–36; after coming to the United States studied with Roger Sessions, Frederick Jacobi, and Aaron Copland;

M.A. Columbia University 1951; Guggenheim fellowship 1945, 1951. His works include: *Prelude and Hula*, 1939; *Hawaiian Festival Overture*, 1940; *The Poet's Dilemma*, 1940; *Golden Gate Overture*, 1941; *Pacific Prayer*, 1943; Overture in C, 1945; Symphony No. 1, 1946; Concerto for Violin and Orchestra, 1947; *Open the Gates* (opera) 1951; Symphony No. 2, 1952; *Phineas and the Nightingale* (opera) 1951; score for musical comedy *Tea-House of the August Moon*, 1954; *Polynesian Suite* for orchestra, 1958; *Mele Ololi* for chorus, solo, and orchestra, 1960; *The Golden Lotus*, 1961; *The Gold of their Bodies*, 1963.

The music is sound enough but lacks charm; and since it lacks also the quirk which might give it intellectual distinction, I frankly do not quite know how to place it.

LEE, NOEL born Nanking, China 25 December 1924; B.A. Harvard 1948; New England Conservatory diploma 1948; also studied at the Conservatoire National de Musique, Paris 1949–51 and privately with Nadia Boulanger. Awards: Lili Boulanger Memorial 1953; National Institute of Arts and Letters 1959; Arthur Shepherd composition prize 1961. An expert pianist, he has led a sound career as concert and recording artist and as member of a piano-violin team with Paul Makanowitzky. Summers 1958 and 1959 he was visiting professor at Brandeis University. He lives in Paris.

Works include: Ballet Music for orchestra, 1950; Quintet, 1952; Capriccio (orchestra) 1952; Four Rhapsodies (chorus and orchestra) 1952; Fantasy in Four Movements, 1953; Variations (various instruments) 1953; *Paraboles* (tenor solo, chorus, orchestra) 1954; *Overture and Litanies* for strings, 1954; Five Songs on Poems of García Lorca, 1955; String Quartet, 1956; *Dialogues* for violin and piano, 1958; *Profile* (orchestra) 1958; Variations for Orchestra, 1960; also scores for films, much piano music, and some songs.

His music, essentially neo-Romantic, has charm, translucency, grace, and a Franco-American refinement. Even melodically (Ay! There's the rub!) it is not banal.

LOPATNIKOFF, NICOLAI born Reval, Russia 16 March 1903; studied music at the conservatories of Petrograd and Helsingfors; engineering diploma at Karlsruhe 1928; married Nora Laschinsky 1926 (dec.); married Sara Henderson Hay 1951. Came to United States in 1939, was naturalized; from 1945–69 taught at Carnegie-Mellon University,

Pittsburgh. Received award from Belaieff publishing house for Second
String Quartet 1921; from German Radio for First Symphony 1930;
won Twenty-Fifth Anniversary competition Cleveland Orchestra 1943;
Koussevitsky Foundation award 1944; Guggenheim fellowship 1945;
award from National Institute of Arts and Letters 1953; elected to
membership 1963. His compositions include three symphonies (1929,
1939, 1954); two piano concertos (1925, 1930); three string quartets;
chamber works and piano pieces; Opus Sinfonicum, 1933–41; Sinfoni-
etta, 1942; Violin Concerto, 1942; Concertino for Orchestra, 1945;
Two Russian Nocturnes for orchestra, 1945; *Variations and Epilogue*
for cello and piano, 1946; Concerto for Two Pianos and Orchestra,
1958; Music for Orchestra, 1959.
A neoclassic master.

LUENING, OTTO born Milwaukee 15 June 1900; studied at the State
Academy of Music in Munich 1915–1917, at the conservatoire in
Zurich 1917–20, and at the University of Zurich 1919–20; Mus.Doc.
(honorary) 1963; married Ethel Codd 13 April 1927; Catherine
Brunson 5 September 1959. Flutist and conductor of opera and orchestras in Munich and Zurich 1915–20; worked in opera department
of Eastman School of Music 1925–28, also as conductor of American
Opera Company, Rochester, New York. Taught at University of Ari-
zona 1932–34, Bennington College 1934–44, Barnard College and
Columbia University from 1944; co-director from 1959 of Columbia-
Princeton Electronic Music Center; from 1944 was musical director
of Brander Mathews Theatre, Columbia University. He is a member of
the National Institute of Arts and Letters, has been active in the
American Music Center, American Composers' Alliance, Composers'
Forum, League of Composers, National Federation of Music Clubs,
Society for the Publication of American Music. Received a Guggenheim fellowship 1930–32; David Bispham medal for American opera
1933; award from National Institute of Arts and Letters 1946.
His principal works include: First Music for Orchestra, *Kentucky
Concerto*, two Symphonic Fantasias, three string quartets, two violin
sonatas, suites and sonatas for various instruments; *Evangeline*
(opera). Since 1952 he has been active in the field of electronic
music, often in collaboration with Vladimir Ussachevsky. He has
composed eight works in collaboration with Ussachevsky, including:
Concerted Piece, for New York Philharmonic; *A Poem in Cycles and
Bells* for Los Angeles Philharmonic; and *Strange Voyage* for CBS
television. Luening's own electronic works include: Theatre Piece No.

11, ballet for Doris Humphrey; *Gargoyles* for violin and electronic sound; and *Synthesis* for electronic sound and symphony orchestra; also *Fantasy in Space, Incantation in Twelve Tones, Low Speed,* and *Moonflight.* His orchestral works have been widely performed. He is a member of the National Institute of Arts and Letters, a trustee of the American Academy in Rome, and a member of the educational advisory board of the Guggenheim Foundation.

A German-schooled fine all-round musician—instrumentalist, conductor, composer, teacher, and a handy man among the Foundations. There is nothing wrong about his music either, except that it is sometimes hard to remember. Could it be that constant labors in the professional vineyard have cost him a certain intensity of concentration on the creative act?

MacDowell, Edward Alexander born New York 18 December 1861; studied in Paris 1876–79 and at Frankfurt-am-Main 1879–81; became one of the main teachers at the Darmstadt Conservatory 1881; married Marian Nevins July 1884. From 1884–88 he lived in Wiesbaden returning to the States in 1888, lived in Boston until 1896, from then on in New York. In 1896 he was appointed to the first chair of music at Columbia University where he remained until his resignation in 1904. He was director of the Mendelssohn Glee Club of New York, 1896–98; president of the American Society of Musicians and Composers 1897–98; vice-president of the National Institute of Arts and Letters 1904–05; Mus. Doc. (honorary) Princeton 1896 and University of Pennsylvania 1902. His most important compositions, performed in major European and American cities, include: two orchestral suites, two piano concertos, four symphonic poems for orchestra, four piano sonatas, twelve virtuoso studies for piano, *Six Idylls after Goethe* for piano, *Six Poems after Heine* for piano, many other piano works including *Sea Pieces, Woodland Sketches, New England Idylls,* and *Fireside Tales;* over fifty songs. He died 23 January 1908.

Our nearest to a great master before Ives. His short works for piano still speak to us.

McPhee, Colin born Montreal, Canada 15 March 1901; studied composition with Gustav Strube at Peabody Conservatory and was graduated in 1921; in Canada studied piano with Arthur Friedheim in Toronto and played his own concerto 1924 with Toronto Symphony Orchestra; in Paris studied composition with Paul Le Flem and piano with Isidor Philipp. In 1926 he returned to the United States; in New York wrote his Concerto for Piano and Wind Octet, 1929; *Sea Shanty Suite* for male chorus, two pianos, and drums; and music for the films by Ralph Steiner H_2O and *Mechanical Principles*. From 1934–39 he lived on the island of Bali. His major work *Tabuh-Tabuhan* for two pianos and orchestra (written in Mexico 1936 and first played by Carlos Chávez with the National Orchestra of Mexico) is based on Balinese music; the attendant esteem brought him an Academy of Arts and Letters award. During his last six years he taught at the University of California, Los Angeles. His stay in Bali inspired three books: *A House in Bali*, 1946; *A Club of Small Men*, 1947; and *Music in Bali*, 1966, an authoritative work on the subject, supported by grants from the Bollingen, Guggenheim, and Huntington Hartford Foundations. Musical works include: *From the Revelation of St. John the Divine*, men's chorus and instruments; *Transitions*, orchestra; Symphony No. 2, 1958; *Four Iroquois Dances*, orchestra; *Invention* and *Kinesis*, piano; and a set for two pianos, *Balinese Ceremonial Music*. Died 7 January 1964.

A well-schooled neoclassical composer, McPhee remained essentially that, except for the orchestral evocation of Bali called *Tabuh-Tabuhan*. This work and the treatise *Music in Bali* lift him far above all present workers in the Indonesian field.

MENNIN, PETER born Erie, Pennsylvania 17 May 1923; studied at Oberlin Conservatory, Mus.B. 1942; M.M. Eastman School of Music 1945, Ph.D. 1947; studied composition with Howard Hanson, conducting with Koussevitzky; married Georganne Bairnson 1947; two children. From 1947 taught composition at Juilliard School of Music; director of Peabody Conservatory, Baltimore 1959–63; president of Juilliard since 1963. Has received award from National Institute of Arts and Letters; Guggenheim fellowship; Bearns prize, Columbia; first Gershwin Memorial award; Koussevitzky award; Naumberg award 1952; member of the executive committee International Music Council, Paris 1956; member National Institute of Arts and Letters.

Works include: seven symphonies (1941, 1944, 1946, 1948, 1950, 1958, 1963); String Quartet, 1941; Concertino for Flute, Strings, and Percussion, 1945; *Folk Overture*, 1945; Sinfonìa for Chamber Orchestra, 1946; Fantasia for Strings, 1947; Divertimento, 1947; Partita, 1949; *The Christmas Story* cantata, 1949; Violin Concerto, 1950; Second Quartet, 1950; Concertato for Orchestra (*Moby Dick*) 1952; Cello Concerto, 1956; Piano Concerto, 1958; Sonata Concertante for violin and piano, 1959; *Canto* for orchestra, 1963; Piano Sonata, 1967; *Cantata de Virtute*, 1969; early songs, choral and piano works.

A composer almost exclusively of serious symphonic and chamber music distinguished by straightforward thematic material, a soaring melodic line, and strong structures.

MENOTTI, GIAN-CARLO born Cadegliano, Italy 7 July 1911; studied composition with Rosario Scalero at the Curtis Institute of Music, was graduated in 1933; honorary B.M. 1945; since 1941 has taught at Curtis. Recipient of Guggenheim fellowship, 1946, 1947; Pulitzer prize, 1955. In 1958 he founded the Festival of Two Worlds in Spoleto, Italy; is still its director. His works include orchestral pieces, songs, and chamber music; but he is best known for his operas, which have been produced in chief opera houses of the world as well as on Broadway. These include: *Amelia al Ballo* (Philadelphia 1937); *The Old Maid and the Thief* (NBC 1939); *The Island God* (Metropolitan Opera 1942); *The Medium* (Columbia University 1946); *The Telephone* (Ballet Society 1947); *The Consul* (1950); *Amahl and the Night Visitors* (NBC-TV 1951); *The Saint of Bleecker Street*, 1954; *Maria Golovin,* 1958; *Labyrinth* television opera, 1963; *The Last Savage* (Paris Opéra-Comique 1963); *Martin's Lie* (CBS-Bath Festival 1964); *Help! Help! the Globolinks* a "children's opera" (Santa Fe, New Mexico 1969). Other works include: two ballets; *Sebastian,* 1944 and *Errand into the Maze,* 1947; Piano Concerto, 1945; *Apocalypse,* symphonic poem, 1951; Violin Concerto, 1952; a madrigal-ballet *The Unicorn, The Gorgon, and the Manticore,* 1956; *The Death of the Bishop of Brindisi* dramatic cantata, 1963.

Menotti, still an Italian citizen, is the author of highly effective operas in the *verismo* style with strong librettos written by himself in excellent American. Beneath occasional minor failures of literary taste, his stage sense is impeccable, his dramatic imagination fecund and highly original. His music, though rarely modernistic, is never inelegant or undistinguished.

MOORE, DOUGLAS STUART born Cutchogue, Long Island 10 August 1893; B.A. Yale 1915; Mus.B. Yale School of Music 1917; studied at the Schola Cantorum in Paris 1921, at the Cleveland Institute of Music 1924; married Emily Bailey 1920; two daughters. Received honorary Mus.Doc. from Cincinnati Conservatory of Music 1946, from University of Rochester 1947, from Yale 1955. He was director of music at the Cleveland Museum of Art 1921; from 1926 taught at Columbia University; became chairman of the music department in 1940; MacDowell Professor in 1943. Received Pulitzer scholarship 1925; Guggenheim fellowship 1934; Pulitzer prize in music 1951. He was a member of the board of directors American Academy in Rome, of the American Academy of Arts and Letters (president), and of the Edward MacDowell Association (director); associate fellow of Calhoun College, Yale.

His many works include: *Pageant of P. T. Barnum*, 1924; *Moby Dick* tone poem for orchestra, 1928; *Symphony of Autumn*, 1930; Overture on an American Tune, 1931; *White Wings* (opera) 1935; *The Headless Horseman* (opera) 1936; *The Devil and Daniel Webster* (opera) 1938; *Village Music*, 1942; *In Memoriam*, 1943; Symphony in A, 1945; *Farm Journal*, 1947; *The Emperor's New Clothes* (opera) 1948; *Giants in the Earth* (opera based on the book by D. E. Rolvaag) 1950; *The Ballad of Baby Doe* (opera) 1955; *Gallantry* (a "soap opera") 1958; *The Wings of the Dove* (opera based on Henry James's novel) 1961; *Carrie Nation* (opera) 1967. He was the author of *Listening to Music*, 1932; and *From Madrigal to Modern Music*, 1942. He died 25 July 1969.

Moore's chamber and orchestral music has modesty, grace, and sound construction. His operas have theatrical qualities and abundant melody.

MUMMA, GORDON born Framingham, Massachusetts 1935; plays French horn; was guest lecturer at Brandeis University Electronic Music Studio 1966; since 1966 has worked with the Merce Cunningham Dance Company; is an organizer of the ONCE festival and a member of the Sonic Arts Group, an ensemble performing live (non-recorded) electronic music. *Hornpieces*, 1964, exhibited the composer playing horn and reciting German poetry. His composition *Home* is described as an "unmultiplexed polyphase radio communication array." *Second Horn*, 1969, is for instruments and cybernetic console. *Runway*, 1969 in collaboration with David Behrman is a "collaboration in performance engineering which provides conversation between personages on the ground and others moving through the concert hall's sky."

John Cage admires his work; Merce Cunningham uses it.

NABOKOV, NICOLAS born Lubcha, Novogrudok district, Minsk government, Russia 17 April 1903; moved to St. Petersburg in 1911; after the

1917 revolution moved to southern Russia where he studied composition in Yalta with Vladimir Rebikov; in Berlin he studied with Paul Juon, later with Busoni. In Paris Diaghilev commissioned and produced a cantata–ballet to a text by the Russian poet Lomonossov. Moved to United States in 1933; taught at Wells College 1936–41, St. John's College, Annapolis 1941–44, and at Peabody Conservatory, Baltimore 1947–52. Was cultural advisor to United States Military Government Berlin 1945–47, in 1947 served in the International Broadcast Division of the State Department. In 1951 he became secretary-general of Congress for Cultural Freedom; organized Paris Festival of Twentieth-Century Music 1952, Rome Festival 1954, East-West Festival, Tokyo 1961; in 1963 became artistic director of West Berlin Festival. Five marriages: three sons. His works include: *Ode, or Meditation at Night on the Majesty of God, as revealed by the Aurora Borealis* (Ballets Russes, 1928); *Lyrical Symphony,* 1930; *Job* (oratorio) 1933; *Collectionneur d'echos* for soprano, bass, and percussion, 1933; *Union Pacific* (ballet) 1934; *Vie de Polichinelle* orchestral suite, 1934; *Le Fiancé* for orchestra, 1934; incidental music to *Samson Agonistes,* 1938; *Sinfonìa Biblica,* 1941; Symphonic Suite (marches for band) 1945; *The Return of Pushkin* for voice and orchestra, 1948; *Vita Nuova* for soprano, tenor, and orchestra, 1951; *Symboli Chrestiani* for bass-baritone and orchestra, 1953; cello concerto *Les Hommages,* 1953; *The Holy Devil,* opera about Rasputin (libretto by Stephen Spender) 1958; *The Last Flower* (ballet) 1959; *Don Quichotte* ballet in three acts (scenario by Nabokov and Balanchine) 1966; Third Symphony (*A Prayer*), 1968. He is the author of *Old Friends and New Music,* 1951, and *Igor Stravinsky,* 1964; autobiography in preparation.

Though his inspiration is basically lyrical, Nabokov is a composer of strong dramatic powers and unusual orchestral eloquence.

ORNSTEIN, LEO born Krementchug, Russia 11 December 1895; entered Imperial Conservatory of Music, Petrograd at age of nine; came to United States in 1907; studied with Bertha Fiering-Tapper and at Friends Seminary; married Pauline Mallet-Prevost 1918. First public concert as pianist in New York 1911; later appeared as soloist with major United States orchestras and toured in Europe; director Ornstein School of Music, Philadelphia. Works include: *Deux Impressions de Notre-Dame* for piano, 1914; *Danse Sauvage* for piano, 1915; *Poems of 1917* (ten works for piano) 1918; *À la Chinoise* for piano, 1918; *À la Mexicana* (three pieces for piano) 1920; *Arabesques* for piano, 1921; *Memories from Childhood* (piano cycle) 1925; *The Corpse*, voice and piano, 1928; many chamber works and songs.

As modernism of yesteryear, his *Danse Sauvage* of 1915 (sometimes known as *Wild Man's Dance*) can still be listened to.

PAINE, JOHN KNOWLES born Portland, Maine 9 January 1839; studied under Hermann Kotzschmar, made first appearance as organist in 1857; studied in Germany with Haupt and others 1858–61; artistic European tour 1866–67. Became first instructor in music at Harvard 1862, professor in 1875, continuing till his death; honorary A.M. and Mus.Doc. Works include: Mass, 1867; *St. Peter* oratorio; *Centennial Hymn* for chorus and orchestra, 1876; music to *Oedipus Tyrannus* (Sophocles) 1881; cantatas: *The Realm of Fancy, Phoebus Arise, The Nativity, Song of Promise;* two symphonies; two symphonic poems: *The Tempest; An Island Fantasy;* incidental music to *The Birds* (Aristophanes); *Columbus March and Hymn,* 1893; overture to *As You Like It;* opera *Azara,* 1901; *Hymn of the West,* 1904; chamber works; piano pieces; songs. Author of *The History of Music to the Death of Schubert,* 1907 posthumous. He died 25 April 1906.

Though best known for having established at Harvard America's first university music department, he also composed works of solid structure and some expressive life.

PARKER, HORATIO WILLIAM born Auburndale, Massachusetts 15 September 1863; educated at Auburndale and in Europe; was graduated from the Royal Conservatoire, Munich 1885; honorary A.M. Yale 1892, Mus.Doc. Cambridge University, England 1902; married Anna Ploessl 1886. Professor of music, Cathedral School of St. Paul, Garden City, Long Island 1885–87; organist Holy Trinity Church, New York 1888–93; Trinity Church, Boston 1893–1901; professor of music at Yale from 1894 till death; member of the American Academy of Arts and Letters. Works include *Hora Novissima* oratorio, 1898; *The Legend of St. Christopher,* 1898; *A Wanderer's Psalm,* 1900; Concerto for Organ and Orchestra, 1902; *Mona* (poem by Brian Hooker) opera performed by the Metropolitan 1911; *Fairyland* opera, 1914; *Cupid and Psyche* masque, 1916; cantatas *King Trojan, The Kobolds;* many choral pieces, chamber works, organ works, and songs. He died 18 December 1919.

A sound teacher, one gathers; but very little of his once impressive production is alive today. *Hora Novissima* survives in the choral societies and in England, also a few anthems. I find the melodic line not really firm and usually vassal to a quite conventional harmony.

PARTCH, HARRY born Oakland, California 24 June 1901; began composing at fourteen; in his twenties formulated his own theory of music; in 1930 wrote his first work using the new method, a piece for voice and viola adapted to the forty-three-tone scale. Much of his time has been spent in experimentation and in the designing and building of new instruments. He has received grants and commissions: from Carnegie Corporation 1934; Guggenheim fellowships 1943, 1945, 1950; Research Committee University of Wisconsin 1944–47; Fromm Foundation and University of Illinois School of Music 1956; and the University of Illinois Graduate School. Performers of his music must be trained to read his notation and play his instruments. Some of his works: *By the Rivers of Babylon*, 1930; *Barstow*, 1941; *The Letter*, 1943; *U.S. Highball*, 1943; *Intrusions*, 1949–59; *Plectra and Percussion Dances*, 1949–52; *Oedipus*, 1951; *The Bewitched*, 1955; *Windsong*, 1958; *Rotate the Body in all its Planes*, 1961; *Water, Water*, 1962; *And on the Seventh Day Petals Fell in Petaluma*, 1963–64. He is the author of *Genesis of a Music*, 1949.

A specialist in true intervals and their commas, he has built his own instruments for sounding these. His aim of producing music with true tunings is admirable. One regrets that his work sometimes lacks intellectual sophistication, though it can also be very beautiful.

PERSICHETTI, VINCENT born Philadelphia 6 June 1915; studied piano with Alberto Jonás and Olga Samaroff, composition with Roy Harris and Paul Nordoff; B.M. Combs Conservatory of Music 1936; conducting diploma from Curtis Institute 1939; M.M. Philadelphia Conservatory 1940, Mus.Doc. 1945; married Dorothea Flanagan 1941; two children. Head of composition at Philadelphia Conservatory from 1942; named head of composition at Juilliard 1948. From 1952 director of publications at Elkan-Vogel Company; from 1964 advisor to Ford Foundation. Received the Juilliard publication award 1943; Blue Network award 1945; grant from National Institute of Arts and Letters 1948; medal from the Italian government 1958; citation from the American Bandmasters' Association 1964. Compositions include eleven piano sonatas, seven symphonies, three string quartets, thirteen serenades for various instruments, seven band works, twelve choral works, twenty-five chamber works, thirty-three piano works, many songs.

Recent works include: Hymns and Responses for the Church Year, 1956; *Harmonium* song cycle for soprano and piano, 1959; Mass for mixed chorus, 1961; *Bagatelles* for band, 1962; *Spring Cantata* for women's voice and piano, 1964; *Stabat Mater* for chorus and orchestra, 1964; *Te Deum* for chorus and orchestra, 1964; *Introit* for strings, 1965; *Winter Cantata*, 1965. He is the author of William Schuman, 1954; *Twentieth-Century Harmony*, 1961.

Expert as a musical analyst, less strong as a composer, though his works have real grace and honest workmanship.

PISTON, WALTER born Rockland, Maine 20 January 1894; studied at the Massachusetts School of Art, Boston 1912–16; A.B. Harvard 1924, Mus.Doc. (honorary) 1953; married Kathryn Nason 1920. Awarded John Knowles Paine fellowship from Harvard 1924–26; studied with Nadia Boulanger in Paris; taught at Harvard 1926–60; Guggenheim fellowship 1935; Pulitzer prize 1948, 1961; member American Academy of Arts and Letters; fellow of American Academy of Arts and Sciences. Works include seven symphonies (1937, 1943, 1947, 1950, 1954, 1955, 1960); two violin concertos; five string quartets; various sonatas; one quintet; some choral and keyboard music; *The Incredible Flutist* (ballet) 1938; *Tunbridge Fair* for band, 1950; *Serenata* for orchestra, 1956; Concerto for Viola and Orchestra, 1957; Concerto for Two Pianos and Orchestra, 1959; *Three New England Sketches*, 1959; Symphonic Prelude, 1961; *Lincoln Center Festival Overture*, 1962. Author of *Harmony; Harmonic Analysis; Counterpoint; Orchestration*.

A neoclassical composer of Parisian cast, skilled technician of the orchestra, a valued pedagogue, and author of today's best book on harmony. For further comment see Chapter 9.

PORTER, QUINCY born New Haven, Connecticut 7 February 1897; studied with David Stanley Smith and Horatio Parker (A.B. Yale 1919, Mus.B. 1921); in Paris studied with Vincent d'Indy. Returning to United States worked as violinist in New York theatre orchestras and studied with Ernest Bloch; married Lois Brown 1926; two children. Taught at Cleveland Institute of Music 1922–28, 1931–32 and played viola in the Ribaupierre String Quartet; spent three years in Paris on Guggenheim fellowship 1928–31; professor at Vassar College and conductor of Vassar Orchestra 1932–38; dean New England Conservatory of Music 1938–42, director 1942–46; from 1946 to 1965 professor of music at Yale. Awards include: Coolidge medal 1943, Pulitzer prize 1953. Member National Institute of Arts and Letters. Works include: *Ukrainian Suite* (string orchestra) 1925; Suite in C minor (orchestra) 1926; *Poem and Dance* (orchestra) 1932; *Dance in Three-Time* (chamber orchestra) 1937; Symphony No. 1, 1938; Music for Strings, 1941; Fantasy on a Pastoral Theme (organ and string orchestra) 1942; Viola Concerto, 1948; Fantasy for Cello and Orchestra, 1950; *The Desolate City* (baritone and orchestra) 1950; Concerto Concertante for two pianos and orchestra, 1954; *New England Episodes* (symphonic suite) 1958; Symphony No. 2, 1964; ten string quartets, many chamber works, and some songs. He died 12 November 1966.

His string quartets are idiomatically conceived for the instruments, relaxed in structure, not unpleasing but not quite absorbing either.

POWELL, JOHN born Richmond, Virginia 6 September 1882; B.A. University of Virginia 1901; studied music with sister, piano and harmony with F. C. Hahr of Richmond, piano with Leschetizky in Vienna, composition with Nawratil, Vienna. Made debut as pianist in Berlin 1907; appeared later in Vienna, Paris, and London, continuing to perform for many years in leading cities of Europe and America. He married Louisa Burleigh 1928; was a member of the National Institute of Arts and Letters. Composed many orchestral works, choral settings, arrangements of folk songs, also two piano concertos, one violin concerto, three piano sonatas, and an opera *Judith and Holofernes*. Other works include *Rhapsodie Nègre* (piano and orchestra) 1918; *Sonata Virginianesque* (violin and piano) 1919; *In Old Virginia* (overture) 1921; *At the Fair* (suite for piano, also for orchestra) 1925; *Natchez on the Hill* (three country dances) 1932; *A Set of Three* (orchestra) 1935; Symphony in A, 1947; Symphony on Virginia Folk Themes, 1947. He died 15 August 1963.

A vigorous pianist and composer, quite a figure in the century's early decades.

READ, GARDNER JR. born Evanston, Illinois 2 January 1913; studied at Northeastern University 1930–32; Mus.B. Eastman School of Music 1936, M.M., 1937; Mus.Doc. (honorary) Doane College 1962; also studied with Copland at Tanglewood, Sibelius in Finland, Pizzetti in Rome; married Margaret Vail Payne 1940; one daughter. Received Cromwell traveling fellowship 1938–39; New York Philharmonic award for First Symphony; Paderewski Fund Competition award for Second Symphony; has conducted major orchestras in United States and lectured in Mexico. Has taught at St. Louis Institute of Music 1941–43, Kansas City Conservatory of Music 1943–45, Cleveland Institute of Music 1945, since 1948 at Boston University. Works include: Fantasy for Viola and Orchestra, 1944; Concerto for Cello and Orchestra, 1945; *Pennsylvania*, 1946; Partita, 1946; *A Bell Overture*, 1946; *Temptation of St. Anthony*, 1947; Symphony No. 3, 1948; *Arioso Elegiaco* for strings, 1951; *Toccata Giocosa*, 1953; Symphony No. 4, 1955; *Vernal Equinox*, 1955; *The Prophet*, 1960; choral and chamber music; songs. Editor of Birchard-Boston University Contemporary Music Series; author of *Thesaurus of Orchestral Devices*, 1952; *Style and Orchestration*, 1961; *Music Notation*, 1962, *Twentieth-Century Notation*, 1967.

A composer of picturesque music highly evocative, a master of orchestral device.

RIEGGER, WALLINGFORD born Albany, Georgia 29 April 1885; studied at Cornell University 1904–05; was graduated from the Institute of Musical Art, New York 1907; from 1907–09 studied at the Hochschule für Musik in Berlin; cello with Robert Hausmann, Anton Hekking; composition with Edgar Stillman Kelley; honorary Mus.Doc. Cincinnati Conservatory 1925; married Rose Schramm 1910; three children. From 1910–13 was cellist with the St. Paul Symphony Orchestra; conducted opera at Würzburg and Koenigsberg 1914–16, also the Blüthner Orchestra in Berlin 1916. He returned to America in 1917 and taught at the following institutions: Drake University, Ithaca Conservatory, Teachers College of Columbia University, New School for Social Research, Metropolitan Music School in New York, and Northwestern University; also acted as music director for the dance division of the WPA theatre project in New York. Received the Paderewski prize 1922; Elizabeth Sprague Coolidge prize 1924; Brandeis creative arts award 1961; was a member of the National Institute of Arts and Letters. He made some seven hundred choral arrangements under various pseudonyms. His original works include: *La Belle Dame Sans Merci*, 1923; *Rhapsody for Orchestra*, 1925; *Study in Sonority* for ten violins, 1927; Suite for Flute Alone, 1930; Canons for Woodwinds, 1921; Fantasy and Fugue for Organ and Orchestra, 1931; *Dichotomy*, 1932; Divertissement for flute, harp, and cello, 1933; Music for Brass Choir, 1949; two string quartets, 1940, 1949; Piano Quintet, 1950; *In Certainty of Song* (cantata) 1950; Nonet for brass, 1951; Woodwind Quintet, 1951; Sextet for Piano and

Winds, 1952; Variations for Piano and Orchestra, 1953; *Dance Rhythms,* 1955; Third and Fourth symphonies, 1947, 1957; *Festival Overture,* 1957. He died 2 April 1961.

Orchestral imagination and a poltergeist's musical wit give him a special place among U.S. composers. They even dominate the twelve-tone conformities of his middle period.

ROGERS, BERNARD born New York 4 February 1893; studied at the Institute of Musical Art 1919–21; married Anne Thacher 1934 (dec. 1935), one daughter; married Elizabeth Mary Clark 1938. From 1929 taught at Eastman School of Music. Received Loeb prize from Institute of Musical Art 1920; Pulitzer traveling scholarship 1921; Guggenheim fellowship 1927–29; Ditson prize 1946; Fulbright grant 1953; member of National Institute of Arts and Letters. His compositions include four symphonies; *Adonais,* 1927; *The Raising of Lazarus,* 1928; *The Marriage of Aude* lyric drama, 1931; *The Exodus,* 1933; Three Japanese Dances, 1934; *Once Upon a Time* five fairy tales for small orchestra, 1935; *The Colors of War,* 1939; *The Song of the Nightingale,* 1940; *The Dance of Salome,* 1940; *The Passion* (oratorio) 1944; *Characters from Hans Christian Andersen,* 1945; *The Warrior* (one-act opera given by the Metropolitan) 1947; *A Letter from Pete,* 1950; *The Veil* (opera given at University of Indiana) 1950; *Leaves from the Tale of Pinocchio* suite for narrator and orchestra, 1950. Died 24 May 1968.

A master of coloristic orchestration and a valued pedagogue.

ROREM, NED born Richmond, Indiana 23 October 1923; studied at Northwestern University 1940–42; Curtis Institute, Philadelphia 1942–43; B.A. Juilliard School of Music 1947, M.A. 1949. Slee Professor at Buffalo University 1959–61; professor of composition University of Utah 1965–67. Received Music Libraries' Association award 1948; Gershwin Memorial award 1949; Lili Boulanger Memorial award 1950; Fulbright fellowship 1951–52. Works include: *Mourning Scene from Samuel,* 1947; Lento for Strings, 1950; *Flight for Heaven,* 1950; Symphony No. 1, 1951; Piano Concerto No. 2, 1951; *Six Irish Poems,* 1951; *Another Sleep,* 1951; *Cycle of Holy Songs,* 1951; *From an Unknown Past,* 1951; *A Childhood Miracle* (opera) 1952; *Design for Orchestra,* 1954; Six Songs, 1954; *The Robbers* (opera) 1956; *Pilgrims* for strings, 1958; *Eagles* for orchestra, 1958; Symphonies No. 2 and No. 3, 1959; Eleven Studies for Eleven Instruments, 1959; *Last*

Day (opera) 1959; *Ideas for Easy Orchestra*, 1961; *King Midas*, 1961; *The Anniversary* (opera) 1962; *Lions* for orchestra, 1959; *Miss Julie* (opera) 1964; *Poems of Love and the Rain*, 1964; *Sun* voice and orchestra, 1966; *Paris Journal* chorus and orchestra; *Lovers* (chamber) 1966; *Letters from Paris* chorus and orchestra, 1969; Piano Concerto in Six Movements, 1970; and literally hundreds of songs, duets, choral pieces, and other short works. Author: *The Paris Diary of Ned Rorem*, 1966; *Music from Inside Out*, 1967; *The New York Diary of Ned Rorem*, 1967; *Critical Affairs: A Composer's Journal*, 1970. For comments see Chapter 9.

RUGGLES, CARL born Marion, Massachusetts 11 March 1876; studied in Boston with Joseph Claus; at Harvard with Walter Spalding and J. K. Paine; married Charlotte Snell 1908; one son. He founded and conducted the Winona, Minnesota Symphony Orchestra, 1912–17; from 1922–33 was active with Edgard Varèse in the International Composers' Guild and the Pan-American Association of Composers; in 1937 he joined the music faculty of the University of Miami, Florida. In his later years he has increasingly turned to painting, exhibiting in many museums. He is a member of the National Institute of Arts and Letters; now lives in Vermont. Works: *Toys* for soprano with piano accompaniment, 1919; *Men and Angels* symphonic suite for five trumpets and one bass trumpet, 1922, revised 1938 as *Angels* for four violins and three cellos or four trumpets and three trombones; *Men and Mountains* (*Men* and *Lilacs* from this suite are for strings only), *Marching Mountains* (for chamber orchestra, 1924, revised 1936); *Portals* for string orchestra, 1926; *The Sun-Treader* for orchestra, 1933; Polyphonic Composition for three pianos, 1940; *Evocations* four chants for piano, 1937 to 1945; *Organum* for orchestra, 1945; *Vox Clamans in Deserto* four songs for mezzo-soprano and chamber orchestra. He died 24 October 1971.

For comment see Chapter 3.

SALZMAN, ERIC born New York 8 September 1933; B.A. Columbia 1954; M.F.A. Princeton 1956; studied with Luening, Ussachevsky, Sessions, and Babbitt. Fellowships: Fulbright (Rome) 1956–58; Darmstadt summer 1957; Ford (for music criticism) 1964–65; Sang prize for criticism 1967. Critic presently with *Stereo Review*, formerly with *The New York Times*, later with *New York Herald Tribune;* sometime music director WBAI-FM. Taught at Queens College 1966–

68; presently director of Hunter College concerts "New Images of Sound."

Recent works include: *In Praise of the Owl and Cuckoo* for voice, guitar, and chamber ensemble, 1963; *Queens College* wiretap tape music, 1968; *Verses I, II, III, IV* for voice, guitar, multitrack tape, 1967; *Feedback* multimedia work (films by Stan Vanderbeek) 1967; *Foxes and Hedgehogs* (texts by John Ashbery) music theatre for voices, instruments, and tape, 1967; *The Peloponnesian War* dance–theatre work with Daniel Negrin, 1968; *Can Man Survive?* multimedia walk-through for centennial exhibition Museum of Natural History, New York, 1969; *The Nude Paper Sermon* tropes for actor, Renaissance consort, chorus, and electronics. Author: *Twentieth-Century Music: an Introduction,* 1967; also many articles published in United States and abroad.

The best critic in America for contemporary and far-out music, his own work, as can happen to critics, is in danger of neglect. It lies chiefly in the "live"-with-electronics realm, involves both speech and song, has imagination and humor.

SCHULLER, GUNTHER born New York City 22 November 1925; studied at the St. Thomas Choir School and Manhattan School of Music; married Marjorie Black 1948; two children. Worked as French horn player with Ballet Theatre and Cincinnati Symphony Orchestra; horn soloist of Metropolitan Opera orchestra 1945–59; taught at the Manhattan School of Music from 1950 and at Tanglewood summer school 1963; since 1967 president of the New England Conservatory of Music. Received creative arts award from Brandeis University 1960; National Institute of Arts and Letters award 1960; Guggenheim fellowship 1962; member National Institute of Arts and Letters. Works include: Concerto for Horn and Orchestra, 1944; Concerto for Cello and Orchestra, 1945; Atonal Jazz Study, 1948; Symphony for Brass and Percussion, 1950; Fantasy for Unaccompanied Cello, 1951; Recitative and Rondo for violin and piano, 1953; *Dramatic Overture,* 1956; Music for Violin, Piano, and Percussion, 1957; String Quartet, 1957; Woodwind Quintet, 1958; Concertino for Jazz Quartet, 1959; *Seven Studies on Themes of Paul Klee,* 1959; *Variants* (ballet with Balanchine) 1961; Music for Brass Quintet, 1961; *Contrasts,* 1961; Double Quintet, 1961; *Night Music,* 1962; *The Visitation* (opera) Hamburg 1965. He is the author of *Horn Technique,* 1962 and *Early Jazz: Its Roots and Music Development,* 1968.

Has sought as a composer to establish a musical "third world," or compromise between doctrinaire modernism and the more relaxed conventions. His music is practical, sounds well, has spontaneity. His opera *The Visitation* enjoyed a resounding success in Germany. His book on early jazz is by far the finest in its field.

SCHUMAN, WILLIAM HOWARD born New York 4 August 1910; B.S. Columbia University 1935, M.A. 1937; studied with Max Persin, Charles Haubiel, and Roy Harris; Mus. Doc. (honorary) Philadelphia Conservatory of Music 1952, Cincinnati College of Music 1953, Columbia University 1954; married Frances Prince 27 March 1936; two children. From 1935–46 taught at Sarah Lawrence College; from 1945–62 was president of Juilliard School of Music; from 1962–69 president of Lincoln Center for the Performing Arts; in 1944–45 was briefly director of publications at G. Schirmer, Inc. Awards include two Guggenheim fellowships, 1939–41; first Town Hall-League of Composers award 1942; first annual New York Critics' Circle award; first Pulitzer prize for music 1943; Columbia University Bicentennial Anniversary medal; first Brandeis University creative arts award in music; award from National Institute of Arts and Letters. He is a director of the Koussevitzky and Walter M. Naumberg foundations.

His compositions include: four string quartets; for orchestra: seven symphonies; *American Festival Overture; Circus Overture; Prologue* for chorus and orchestra; *This Is Our Time* cantata for chorus and orchestra; *Newsreel* for symphonic band; *William Billings Overture; New England Triptych; Prayer in Time of War; A Free Song* for chorus and orchestra; Concerto for Piano and Orchestra; Concerto for Violin and Orchestra; *George Washington Bridge; Credendum; In Praise of Shahn,* 1970; *The Mighty Casey* (opera); ballets: *Undertow, Judith, Night Journey;* many choral works.

For comment, see Chapter 9.

SESSIONS, ROGER HUNTINGTON born Brooklyn, New York 28 December 1896; A.B. Harvard 1915; Mus.Doc. Yale 1917; married Barbara Foster 1920; Elizabeth Franck 1936; two children. Taught at Smith College 1913–21, at Cleveland Institute of Music 1921–25; lived in Florence, Rome, and Berlin 1925–33. Other teaching positions: Boston University 1933–35; New Jersey College for Women 1935–37; Princeton University, where he has remained since 1935 with brief periods at Berkeley; now also at Juilliard; Charles Eliot Norton Professor at

Harvard 1969–70. Guggenheim fellowship 1926–28; Prix de Rome 1928–31; New York Music Critics' Circle award 1949–50; Naumberg Foundation prize 1949–50; Brandeis University award 1958; gold medal National Institute of Arts and Letters 1961; member American Academy of Arts and Letters; fellow American Academy of Arts and Sciences. Works: five symphonies (1927, 1946, 1957, 1958, 1964); three piano sonatas (1930, 1946, 1965); three string quartets (1936, 1951, 1957); incidental music for the *Black Maskers* (two suites) 1923; Concerto for Violin and Orchestra, 1935; Scherzino and March (piano) 1935; Duo for Violin and Piano, 1942; *Turn, O Libertad* (chorus, piano four hands) 1943; *The Trial of Lucullus* one-act opera (Bertolt Brecht) 1947; *Idyll of Theocritus* (soprano and orchestra) 1954; Concerto for Piano and Orchestra, 1956; String Quintet, 1958; Divertimento for orchestra, 1959; Psalm 140 (soprano and orchestra) 1963; *Montezuma* three-act opera (Berlin, 1964).

He is the author of *The Musical Experience of Composer, Performer and Listener*, 1950; *Harmonic Practice*, 1951; *Reflections on the Musical Life in the United States*, 1956.

For comment see Chapter 9.

SHAPEY, RALPH born Philadelphia 12 March 1921; studied violin with Emanuel Zetlin, composition with Stefan Wolpe; married Vera Shapiro 1957; one son. Has received the Brandeis creative arts award, Naumberg recording award, Copley Foundation award, Stern Foundation award, and Frank H. Beebe award. Assistant conductor of Philadelphia National Youth Orchestra 1938–42; musical director of orchestra and chorus University of Pennsylvania 1963–64; since 1964 on faculty University of Chicago and director of the Contemporary Chamber Players; since 1960 on board of directors of the International Society for Contemporary Music. Works include: *Challenge—The Family of Man* for orchestra, 1955; *Mutations* for piano, 1956; Duo for Viola and Piano, 1957; *Ontogeny* for orchestra, 1958; *Form* for piano, 1959; *Rituale* for orchestra, 1959; *Dimensions* for soprano and twenty-three instruments, 1960; *Incantations* for soprano and ten instruments, 1961. *Convocation* for chamber group, 1962; *Birthday Piece* for piano, 1962; Brass Quintet, 1963; String Quartet VI, 1963; *Sonance* for carillon, 1964; *Configurations* for flute and piano; *Evocations* for violin, piano, and percussion.

Far-out, non-serial composer admired by Varèse for his independence and artistic integrity. Nothing bogus about him.

SIEGMEISTER, ELIE born New York 15 January 1909; studied composition with Seth Bingham and Wallingford Riegger at Columbia University, B.A. 1927; with Nadia Boulanger at Ecole Normale de Musique, Paris (diploma 1931); and conducting with Albert Stoessel at Juilliard 1935–38; married Hannah Mersel 15 January 1930; three children. Organized American Ballad Singers 1939, was their director in nation-wide tours 1942–44; visiting lecturer at University of Minnesota 1948; conductor of the Hofstra Symphony Orchestra 1953–65, of the Pro Arte Symphony Orchestra 1965; since 1966 professor of music and composer in residence at Hofstra University, Long Island.

His works for orchestra include: *Ozark Set,* 1943; *Wilderness Road,* 1944; *Prairie Legend,* 1944; *Western Suite,* 1945; *Sunday in Brooklyn,* 1946; *From My Window,* 1949; *Cordura Suite,* 1959; Flute Concerto, 1960; *Dick Whittington and His Cat,* 1966; for symphonic band: Five American Folk Songs, 1948; *Deep Sea Chanty,* 1948; *Hootenanny,* 1950; *Three Cornered Suite,* 1954; for chorus: *The New Colossus,* 1949; *In Our Time,* 1965; *I Have a Dream,* 1967; operas: *Darling Corie,* 1952; *Miranda and the Dark Young Man,* 1954; *The Mermaid in Lock No. 7,* 1958; *The Plough and the Stars,* 1963; also chamber music, piano works, and incidental music for plays. Author of *Invitation to Music,* 1959; *Harmony and Melody,* 2 Vols., 1965.

Best known for his use of American folklore materials and populist subjects, Siegmeister has enjoyed considerable success both at home and abroad as a specialist of the backwoods background. His Irish opera *The Plough and the Stars* (after Sean O'Casey) was produced in French at Bordeaux 1970.

SUBOTNIK, MORTON born Los Angeles 1933; studied with Leon Kirchner and Darius Milhaud; was co-founder of Mills College (Oakland) Performance Group and San Francisco Tape Music Center; from 1966 was attached to the inter-media program at New York University School of the Arts; now associate dean of music California School of the Arts. *Silver Apples of the Moon* and *The Wild Bull* were commissioned by Nonesuch Records. *Electronic Chamber* is for electronic lights (sic), sound consoles, and eight players.

An electronic composer much respected by his colleagues.

STILL, WILLIAM GRANT born Woodville, Mississippi 11 May 1895; studied at Wilberforce University 1911–15, honorary M.M. 1936; also studied at Oberlin Conservatory of Music and New England

174

Conservatory; honorary Mus.Doc. Howard University and Oberlin College 1947; Litt.D. Bates College 1954; married Grace Dorothy Bundy 1915; four children; married Verna Arvey 1939; two children. Played violin, cello, and oboe in orchestras in Columbus, Ohio 1915; did arranging for orchestras and radio stations, and guest conducting with various orchestras. Received second Harmon award for contribution to American Negro culture; Guggenheim fellowship 1934; Rosenwald fellowship 1939. Compositions include: *From the Black Belt,* 1926; *Darker America,* 1927; *From the Journal of a Wanderer,* 1929; *Africa,* 1930; *Afro-American Symphony,* 1931; *Kaintuck,* 1936; *Dismal Swamp,* 1936; *Ebon Chronicle,* 1936; *And They Lynched Him on a Tree,* 1940; *Festive Overture,* 1945; four symphonies; symphonic band pieces; vocal works; ballets; and the following operas: *Blue Steel,* 1935; *Troubled Island,* 1938; *A Bayou Legend,* 1940; *A Southern Interlude,* 1942; *Costaso,* 1949; *Highway No. 1, U.S.A.,* 1963.

Old-school Negro writing based on spirituals, but not without distinction.

SWANSON, HOWARD born Atlanta 18 August 1909; as a child did manual labor on the railroad; later worked as a postal clerk. At Cleveland Institute of Music won Rosenwald fellowship; studied with Nadia Boulanger in Paris; remained in Paris until 1940; returning to New York worked for the Internal Revenue Department until 1945. His songs first attracted attention when Marian Anderson performed them in New York. His first orchestral success came with a Short Symphony conducted by Mitropoulos with New York Philharmonic which won New York Music Critics' Circle award 1952. Other works include Symphony No. 1, 1945; *Night Music* for small orchestra, 1950; Suite for Cello and Piano, 1949; songs and piano pieces.

A songful composer of straightforward inspiration and rather wonderful simplicity. No easily discernible Negro traits. Small production.

TALMA, LOUISE J. born New York 31 October 1906; B.M. New York University, M.A. Columbia; studied piano with Isidor Philipp and composition with Nadia Boulanger. Guggenheim fellowship 1946; now professor of music at Hunter College. Her works include: *Terre de France* song cycle, 1925; Three Madrigals, 1929; *La Belle Dame Sans Merci* for baritone, 1929; *Five Sonnets from the Portuguese* song cycle, 1934; Piano Sonata, 1943; Toccata for Orchestra, 1944;

Introduction and Rondo Giocoso, 1946; *The Divine Flame* (oratorio) 1948; *Let's Touch the Sky*, song cycle for chorus and woodwind, 1952; *The Alcestiad* (opera with libretto by Thornton Wilder) premiered in West Germany 1962.

Her music, though sincere, harmonious, and well constructed, has more grace than punch.

TAYLOR, JOSEPH DEEMS born New York 22 December 1885; A.B. New York University 1906; Mus.Doc. (honorary) New York University 1927, Dartmouth College and University of Rochester 1939, Cincinnati Conservatory 1941, Syracuse University 1944; Litt.D. Juniata College 1931. As a composer largely self-taught, though somewhat late he had lessons in New York with Oscar Coon 1908–11. Four marriages; one daughter. Member editorial staff *Nelson Encyclopedia* 1906–07, *Britannica* 1908; assistant editor *Western Electric News* 1912–16; assistant Sunday editor *New York Tribune* 1916 and its correspondent in France 1916–17; associate editor *Collier's Weekly* 1917–19; music critic *New York World* 1921–29; editor of *Musical America* 1927–1929; music critic *New York American* 1931–32; intermission commentator New York Philharmonic broadcasts 1936–43; president American Society of Composers, Authors, and Publishers 1942–48; member American Philosophical Society and American Academy of Arts and Letters. He died in 1966.

His many works include: *A Kiss in Xanadu* pantomime, 1923; *Through the Looking Glass* orchestral suite, 1922; *Portrait of a Lady* rhapsody for eleven instruments, 1924; *Jurgen* for orchestra, 1925; operas: *The King's Henchman* (Metropolitan 1927); *Peter Ibbetson* (Metropolitan 1931); *Ramuntcho* (Philadelphia 1942); *Christmas Overture*, 1943; *Elegy for Orchestra*, 1944; *Restoration* suite for orchestra, 1950; *The Dragon*, 1954; also incidental music for stage and screen, many choral works, piano pieces, and songs.

Author: *Of Men and Music*, 1937; *The Well-Tempered Listener*, 1940; *Pictorial History of the Movies*, 1943; *Music to My Ears*, 1949; *Some Enchanted Evenings*, 1953; *The One-Track Mind*, 1953.

His theatrical works, including the three operas, all show stage sense, but they lack memorable melody. His more modest efforts have charm and wit.

TCHEREPNIN, ALEXANDER born St. Petersburg, Russia 21 January 1899; studied at St. Petersburg Conservatoire; Mus.Doc. (honorary)

Roosevelt University 1953; married Lee Hsien-Ming 1937; three children. Lived in Paris from 1921; appeared in London 1922 as pianist and composer; subsequently toured extensively in Germany, Australia, United States, China, Japan. Later lived in Tokyo where he and his pupils published their own music; returned to Paris 1938, remained for the duration of the war. From 1949–64 taught at De Paul University in Chicago. His works include five symphonies; five piano concertos; operas: *Swat* (Ostrovsky); *Ol-Ol* (after Andreyev); *Sevat* (Ostrovsky); *Vanka* (Sologub) 1933; *Die Hochzeit der Sobeide*, 1933; *The Farmer and the Fairy*, 1952; twelve ballets; five cantatas; many works for large and small orchestra; piano pieces; songs; choral works for the Russian liturgy. Among the recent works: *Symphony-Prayer*, 1960; Serenade for Strings, 1965. Author of *An Anthology of Russian Music*.

A fecund and expert composer internationally successful in classical forms and also theatrically. Initially inspired by the Russian Romantic masters, he developed in France from medieval sources an original approach to modality and rhythm, later in East Asia was influenced by classical Chinese music. His work has at all periods been filled with poetry and bravura.

Himself the son of the nineteenth-century Russian composer Nicolai Tcherepnin, two of his three sons, Serge (born 1941) and Ivan (born 1943), are Harvard-trained American composers of far-out orientation including the electronic.

THOMPSON, RANDALL born New York 21 April 1899; A.B. Harvard 1920, M.A. 1922, Mus.Doc. (honorary) University of Rochester 1933. Studied composition with Ernest Bloch 1920–21; fellow at the American Academy in Rome 1922–25; married Margaret Quayle Whitney 1927; four children. Awards: Damrosch fellowship 1922; Guggenheim fellowship 1929–31; Elizabeth Sprague Coolidge medal 1941; Alice M. Ditson award 1944. He taught at Wellesley College, was also organist and choir director 1927–29; lecturer in music at Harvard 1929; professor of music and director of chorus at the University of California, Berkeley 1937–39; director of Curtis Institute of Music 1939–41; professor of music University of Virginia 1941–45; professor of music Princeton 1945–48; from 1948–67 professor at Harvard. He has been a director of the International Society for Contemporary Music (United States section) 1934–35; member board of directors League of Composers; is a fellow of the American Academy of Arts and Sciences; member National Institute of Arts and Letters.

Works include: symphonies, choral works, string quartets, operas. Also: *The Last Words of David*, 1949; *A Trip to Nahant* fantasy for orchestra, 1954; *Mass of the Holy Spirit*, 1955; *Ode to the Virginian Voyage*, 1956.

Widely known for his choral works (his *Alleluia* has sold over a million copies), he is the author also of a most effective symphony, No. 2, and one of our most indigenous-sounding string quartets.

Editor's Note:
The summary below is longer than any other here included because the text omits reference to Thomson's non-theatrical works.

THOMSON, VIRGIL GARNETT born Kansas City, Missouri 25 November 1896; A.B. Harvard 1922; honorary degrees from Syracuse, Rutgers, Park, Fairfield, Roosevelt; Academic Medal New York University; studied piano with G. Lichtenwalter, H. Gebhard; organ with Clarence D. Sears, Wallace Goodrich, Nadia Boulanger; conducting (choral) with A. T. Davison, (orchestral) Chalmers Clifton; composition with E. B. Hill, Rosario Scalero, Nadia Boulanger. Fellowships (Harvard) J. K. Paine, Naumburg; (Paris) Ecole Normale de Musique; (New York) Juilliard, Guggenheim, Fulbright. Assistant instructor Harvard 1920–21, 1922–23, 1924–25; organist and choirmaster King's Chapel, Boston 1922–23; lived in Paris 1925–40. Pulitzer prize in music; gold medal National Institute of Arts and Letters; Brandeis University award; David Bispham medal for American opera; special citation New York Music Critics' Circle (of which he was founder and first chairman).

Has conducted major orchestras in United States, Latin America, and Europe; opera in Chicago, New York, Paris. Visiting professorships Colorado College, State University of Buffalo, University of California in Los Angeles, Carnegie-Mellon, Trinity (Hartford); lectureships University of Southern California, Stanford, Smith, Emory. Commissions: Louisville, Dallas, Kansas City, New York Philharmonic orchestras; Ballet Caravan; Alice M. Ditson; Kansas City Festival; Library of Congress; New York State College (Potsdam); Goucher College; Smithsonian Institution; Koussevitzky and Ford foundations (for Metropolitan Opera). Was associated 1935–36 in federal theatre projects with John Houseman, Orson Welles, and Joseph Losey; from 1932–38 with A. E. Austin, Jr. in Hartford (opera, concerts, ballet, plays) also with Lincoln Kirstein, L. Christensen, G. Balanchine (ballet); Sir Frederick Ashton (opera). Fellow American Academy of Arts and Sciences, member American Academy of Arts and Letters, Honorable Order of Kentucky Colonels, officier Légion d'Honneur.

Chief works: operas: *Four Saints in Three Acts,* 1928 (produced 1934) and *The Mother of Us All,* 1947 (librettos by Gertrude Stein); *Lord Byron* (Jack Larson) 1968; ballet: *Filling Station,* 1937; films: *The Plough that Broke the Plains,* 1936 and *The River,* 1937 (both by Pare Lorentz); *Tuesday in November,* 1945 (by J. Houseman and N. Ray); *Louisiana Story,* 1949 (by Robert Flaherty); *The Goddess,* 1957 (by Paddy Chayevsky); *Power Among Men,* 1958 (United Nations film by Thorold Dickinson); *Journey to America,* 1964 (by John Houseman); incidental music for plays by Shakespeare, Sophocles, Euripides, Giraudoux, Truman Capote, directed by or starring Leslie Howard, Orson Welles, Joseph Losey, Tallulah Bankhead, Peter Brook, Alfred Lunt, Audrey Hepburn, Alfred Drake, Katherine Hepburn, collaborating frequently with John Houseman (opera, plays, films, TV); orchestral: two symphonies; six suites from films; twelve portraits; three landscapes—*The Seine at Night, Wheat Feld at Noon, Sea Piece with Birds;* three concertos (cello, flute, harp); suite *In Homage to an Earlier England; A Solemn Music and a Joyful Fugue; The Feast of Love* (with baritone); Storm and Love Scene from Byron's *Don Juan* (with tenor); Five Songs to Poems of William Blake (with baritone); Mass for Solo Voice (mezzo) or unison choir with orchestra or piano; Eleven Chorale-Preludes by Brahms orchestrated by V.T.; band: *Ode to the Wonders of Nature* (brasses); *At the Beach* (trumpet solo); *A Solemn Music;* divers fanfares and portraits; chamber: Sonata da Chiesa for five instruments; two string quartets; one violin sonata; Sonata for Flute Alone; Serenade for flute and violin; Three Portraits for Four Clarinets; eight portraits for violin alone, four for violin and piano, forty for piano; three arranged for violin and piano (S. Dushkin), four for cello and piano (L. Silva); choral: Missa Brevis (with percussion): *Dance in Praise* (with orchestra); *The Nativity* (with orchestra); Missa Pro Defunctis (with large orchestra); *Crossing Brooklyn Ferry* (Whitman) orchestra or piano; *Seven Choruses from the Medea of Euripides* (with percussion); *Scenes from the Holy Infancy;* and many shorter pieces; organ: Variations and Fugues on Sunday School Tunes (four sets); *Pange Lingua* (for large organ); also smaller pieces: (voice with instruments) Four Poems of Thomas Campion for mezzo with clarinet, viola, harp; *Stabat Mater* in French for soprano with string quartet; *Five Phrases from the Song of Solomon* for soprano or mezzo with percussion; *Capital Capitals* (Gertrude Stein) for four male soloists with piano; *Collected Poems* (Kenneth Koch) duet for soprano and baritone with small orchestra; piano: four short sonatas; two books of études; many portraits (forty published); *Ten Easy Pieces and a Coda; Synthetic Waltzes* (two pianos); and *Walking Song* (two pianos); a large number of songs in English and French, one group in Spanish, two extended vocal works in French—*Air de Phèdre* (Racine) and *Oraison Funèbre* (Bossuet).

Has written on music for *Vanity Fair, Boston Transcript, Modern Music, New York Review of Books;* chief critic *New York Herald Tribune* 1940–54. Books: *The State of Music,* 1939 and 1961; *The Musical Scene,* 1945; *The Art of Judging Music,* 1948; *Music Right and Left,* 1951; *Virgil Thomson* (autobiography) 1966; *Music Reviewed 1940–1954,* 1967; and *American Music Since 1910,* 1971.

For discussion of Thomson's operas see Chapter 10 by Victor Yellin (in this volume).

USSACHEVSKY, VLADIMIR born Hailar, Manchuria 3 November 1911 (21 October old style); came to United States 1930, attended Pomona College (California) and Eastman School of Music (M.A., Ph.D.) where he was a pupil of Howard Hanson and Bernard Rogers; married Elisabeth Kray 1944. Has taught at Columbia University since 1947, experimented with tape music since 1951; founded with Otto Luening, Roger Sessions, and Milton Babbitt in 1959 the Columbia-Princeton Electronic Music Center, of which he is co-director. Has received a Guggenheim fellowship twice, and an award from the National Institute of Arts and Letters.

Has written piano, vocal, chamber, and orchestral music; since 1952 chiefly electronic music. Works: *Underwater Valse,* 1952; *Sonic Contours,* 1952; Piece for Tape Recorder, 1955; *Metamorphosis,* 1956; *Studies in Sound,* 1955; *Wireless Fantasy,* 1960; *Of Wood and Brass,* 1965; Computer Piece, 1968. With Luening has written: *Incantation for Tape Recorder,* 1953; *A Poem in Cycles and Bells* for tape and orchestra, 1954; *Rhapsodic Variations* for tape recorder and orchestra, 1954; *A Ballad of Identity,* 1954; Concerted Piece for Tape Recorder and Orchestra, 1960. Theatre and film music: *King Lear* with Luening (for Orson Welles) 1956; *No Exit* (film) 1964; *Line of Apogy* (film) 1966; *An Incredible Voyage* (CBS-TV with Luening, Smiley, and Shields) 1967; *Two Images of a Computer Piece* (film) 1969.

Ussachevsky is an electronics man, convinced and consecrated. His music for classical instruments is gentle, sweet, and strongly personal. His tape music, whether playful or strong, tends to recall the Romantic masters—charmingly, for such is his nature. His larger works composed with Otto Luening for tape and orchestra have a place in the history of this combo.

VARÈSE, EDGARD born Paris 22 December 1883; early education in mathematics and science; studied music in Turin; in Paris at Schola Cantorum under Roussel and d'Indy, at the Conservatoire under Widor. Came to United States in 1915, naturalized 1926; married Louise Norton 1921. Founded and directed International Composers' Guild 1921–27; conducted choruses and orchestras in United States and Europe. Received Brandeis award 1962, Edward Mac-Dowell gold medal 1965. Member Acoustical Society of America, American Academy of Arts and Letters, Swedish Academy. Works: *Offrandes* for voice and orchestra, 1922; *Hyperprism* for wind instruments and percussion, 1923; *Octandre* for eight instruments, 1924; *Integrales* for orchestra and percussion, 1925; *Amériques,* 1926 (composed 1919); *Arcana,* 1927; *Ionisation* for forty-one percussion instruments and two sirens, 1931; *Ecuatorial,* 1934; *Density 21.5* for flute alone, 1935; *Deserts* for tape and orchestra, 1954; *Poème électronique,* 1958; *Nocturnal* for soprano, chorus, and orchestra, 1961; *Nuit* symphonic poem unfinished at death, 1965.

For comment see Chapter 5.

WARD, ROBERT born Cleveland, Ohio 13 September 1917; studied at Eastman School of Music (B.Mus. 1939); certificate from Juilliard Graduate School 1946; studied composition with Bernard Rogers, Howard Hanson, Frederick Jacobi, and Aaron Copland; conducting with Albert Stoessel and Edgar Schenkman; married Mary Benedict 1944; five children. Taught at Juilliard where he was assistant to the president 1954–56; music director of Third Street Music Settlement School 1952–56; executive vice-president and managing editor of Galaxy Music Corporation and Highgate Press; also served as chairman of the board of directors and president of the American Composers' Alliance. He has been a guest conductor with many orchestras and for some years conducted the Doctor's Orchestra in New York; at present is director of North Carolina School of the Arts. Awards include the Juilliard publication award 1942; Alice M. Ditson fellowship 1944; National Institute of Arts and Letters award 1946; Guggenheim fellowship 1950–51. His works include four symphonies; many pieces for orchestra and band; choral and vocal music; *He Who Gets Slapped* (opera based on the play by Leonid Andreyev); *The Crucible* (opera based on the play by Arthur Miller) 1961; and *The Lady from Colorado* (operetta to a libretto by Bernard Stambler) 1964.

His most successful work *The Crucible* is theatrically sound but not striking as music.

WEBER, BEN BRIAN born St. Louis 23 July 1916; studied at the University of Illinois 1934–35, at De Paul University 1937; received award from the National Institute of Arts and Letters 1950; Guggenheim fellowships 1950, 1953; Fromm Foundation awards 1953, 1955. Works include: Five Bagatelles for piano, 1938; Three Piano Pieces, 1946; Fantasia (Variations) for piano, 1946; Second Piano Suite, 1948; *Concert Aria After Solomon* (soprano and chamber ensemble), 1949; *The Pool of Darkness* ballet for Merce Cunningham, 1950, arranged as *Episodes* for piano 1955; Sonata da Camera for violin and piano, 1950; Symphony on Poems of William Blake (baritone and small orchestra) 1952; Two Pieces for String Orchestra, 1951; String Quartet No. 2, 1952; Serenade for harpsichord, flute, oboe, and cello, 1954; Concerto for Violin and Orchestra, Rome Festival 1954; Prelude and Passacaglia, 1954; Concertino for flute, oboe, clarinet, and string quartet, 1956; Serenade for Strings, 1956; *Rhapsodie Concertante* (viola and small orchestra) 1957; Three Songs for Soprano and Strings, 1959; Concerto for Piano and Orchestra, 1961; song cycle *The Ways*, 1962; Suite for Piano Four-Hands, 1964; *The Enchanted Midnight* (orchestra) 1967; *Dedication* for violin and orchestra, 1970.

Music of great sincerity and emotional depth couched in a modified serialism easily acceptable.

WEISGALL, HUGO born Ivancice, Czechoslovakia 13 October 1912; came to United States in 1920, naturalized 1926; did undergraduate work at Johns Hopkins University; Ph.D. 1940; studied at Peabody Conservatory 1927–30; Curtis Institute, Philadelphia 1936–39; also with Roger Sessions; married Nathalie Shulman 1942; two children. Conductor of Har Sinai Temple Choir 1931–42; Y-Alliance Orchestra 1935–42; Baltimore String Symphony 1936–38; Maryland N.Y.A. Orchestra 1940–41, guest conductor of many orchestras in United States and Europe. In 1942 enlisted in United States Army and served as assistant military attaché to governments in exile, London; cultural attaché to American Embassy, Prague 1946–47. Director of the Baltimore Institute of Musical Arts 1949; taught composition at

Cummington School of Arts 1948; and at Jewish Theological Seminary in New York; presently at Queens University, New York. Awards include Bearns prize 1931; National Institute of Arts and Letters award 1952; Guggenheim fellowship 1955–56. Works include: songs, 1929; *Quest* (ballet) 1937; *One Thing Is Certain* (ballet) 1939; Hymn for chorus and orchestra, 1941; *Overture, American Comedy,* 1942; Soldier Songs, 1944–45; *Outpost* (ballet) 1947; *The Tenor* (opera) 1949–50; *The Stronger* (opera) 1952; Three Symphonic Songs, 1952; *Six Characters in Search of an Author* (opera) 1959; *Athaliah* (opera) 1964; *Nine Rivers from Jordan* (opera) 1968.

Musical style possibly over-complex for opera, which is nevertheless where his finest work lies.

WOLFF, CHRISTIAN born Nice, France 8 March 1934; in 1941 came to United States; studied piano in New York, composition with John Cage; majored in classical languages at Harvard, received his Ph.D. in comparative literature 1963, joined the department of classics 1962. Arithmetical progressions of rhythmic values and a similar use of rests form the basis of his musical structures. He used three pitches only in his Duo for Violin and Piano; four in his Trio for Flute, Cello, and Trumpet; nine in a piano piece called *For Piano I.* From 1957 he offered to performers some free choice in the course of playing his works. His compositions include: Trio for Flute, Cello, and Trumpet, 1951; *Nine* for nine instruments, 1951; *For Six or Seven Players,* 1959; *Summer* for string quartet, 1961; *Duo for Violinist and Pianist,* 1961; *For Five or Ten Players,* 1962; *In Between Pieces* for three players, 1963; *For One, Two or Three People,* 1964; Septet for Any Instruments, 1964; *From One to Three Performers;* solo pieces for piano, also for two pianos and for four hands.

A Cage disciple so devoted to musical purity that throughout his educative years he avoided all classic musical education. His pieces are quiet, short, and very beautiful.

WOLPE, STEFAN born Berlin, Germany 25 August 1902; studied there at the Staatliche Hochschule für Musik 1919–24 and privately with Feruccio Busoni, Anton Webern, and Herman Scherchen; married Olga Okuniewska 1927, one daughter; married Irma Schoenberg 1934; married Hilda Morley 1948; came to United States in 1938, naturalized 1944. Professor of composition Palestine Conservatory 1934–38; other teaching positions of theory and composition: Settlement Music

School, Philadelphia 1939–42; Contemporary Music School, New York 1948–52; Philadelphia Academy of Music 1949–52; Black Mountain College 1952–56; Chatham Square Music School, New York 1957–63; since 1957 head of the music department at C.W. Post College, Long Island. Awards: National Institute of Arts and Letters 1949; Rothschild Foundation for Arts and Science 1953; Fulbright fellowship 1956–57; Fromm Foundation award 1960; Guggenheim fellow 1962–63; New York Music Critics' Circle award 1963; Thorne-Ketchum Foundation award 1965, 1966, 1967, 1968; Brandeis University award 1966; member National Institute of Arts and Letters. Works include: *Zeus and Elida* (opera) 1929; *Strange Stories* (theatre piece) 1929; March and Variations for two pianos, 1931; Ten Songs from the Hebrew, 1938; Sonata for Oboe and Piano, 1938; Sonata for Violin and Piano, 1949; Quartet for Trumpet, Tenor Saxophone, Percussion, and Piano, 1950; *Enactments for Three Pianos*, 1950–53; Symphony, 1956; Piece in Two Parts for Flute and Piano, 1960; Piece for Piano and Sixteen Instruments, 1960; Piece for Two Instrumental Units, 1962; Piece in Two Parts for flute, violin, and piano, 1963; Piece in Two Parts for violin alone, 1964; Chamber Piece No. 1 for fourteen instruments, 1964–65.

A remarkable teacher, a composer sometimes of high complexity, usually serial, always inspired.

WUORINEN, CHARLES born New York City 9 June 1938; B.A. Columbia 1961, M.A. 1963; has taught at Columbia since 1964; from 1962 has been co-director of the Group for Contemporary Music at Columbia; was visiting lecturer at Princeton 1967–68. Among his awards are a 1954 New York Philharmonic Young Composers award, 1958 MacDowell Colony fellowship, an Alice M. Ditson fellowship, four BMI Student Composers awards, three Bearns prizes, two Lili Boulanger Memorial awards, a National Institute of Arts and Letters award, and a Pulitzer prize 1970. He is president of the Serious Music Society, a director of Composers' Recordings, Inc., on board of governors of American Composers' Alliance. His works include three symphonies, a violin concerto, chamber and electronic music. Among the recent works: Trio No. 1 for flute, cello, and piano, 1961; Invention for Percussion Quintet, 1962; Octet, 1962; *Duuiensela* for cello and piano, 1962; *The Prayer of Jonah*, 1962; Second Trio: Peace for Stefan Wolpe, 1962; Chamber Concerto for cello and ten players, 1963; Composition for Violin and Ten Instruments, 1964; Chamber Concerto for flute and ten players, 1964; *Orchestral and Electronic Exchanges,*

1965; Chamber Concerto for oboe and ten players, 1965; Piano Concerto, 1966; *Janissary Music* for one percussionist, 1966; *Harpsichord Divisions,* 1966; *John Bull, Slave Regina Versus Septem,* 1966.

A composer of amazing fecundity but still unclear profile.

YOUNG, LAMONTE born Bern, Idaho 14 October 1935; studied at University of California, Los Angeles 1956–57 and Berkeley 1957–60; composition with Stockhausen in Darmstadt 1959; lectured at New School for Social Research, New York 1961. He has received a Guggenheim fellowship, a grant from the Foundation for the Contemporary Performing Arts, an award from the National Institute of Arts and Letters. His works: *Poem for Chairs, Tables, and Benches,* 1960; two stage spectacles for voice, song, and strings: *The Tortoise Droning Selected Pitches from the Holy Numbers for the Two Black Tigers, the Green Tiger, and the Hermit* (1964) and *The Tortoise Recalling the Drone of the Holy Numbers as They Were Revealed in the Dreams of the Whirlwind and the Obsidian Gong, Illuminated by the Sawmill, the Green Sawtooth Ocelot, and the High-Tension Line Stepdown Transformer* (1964); also a number of piano pieces. He is the editor of *An Anthology* of music, art, and poetry, 1963.

A leader of the "indeterminacy" school.

ADDENDUM

CRUMB, GEORGE HENRY born Charleston, West Virginia 24 October 1929; Mus.Bac. Mason College 1950; M.Mus. University of Illinois 1952; Fulbright Fellow at Hochschule für Musik, Berlin 1955–56; Doc. Mus.Arts University of Michigan 1959; married Elizabeth May Brown 2 May 1949; three children. Taught at Hollins College (Virginia) 1958–59, University of Colorado 1959–64, University of Pennsylvania 1965 to the present, Creative Associate in Music State University at Buffalo 1964–65. Fellowships, awards and commissions: Guggenheim 1967, Broadcast Music, Inc. composition prize 1957, Rockefeller Foundation grant 1964, Koussevitzky Foundation commission 1964, Bowdoin College 1965, University of Chicago 1966, Pulitzer Prize 1968.

Chief works: String Quartet, 1954; Sonata for Solo Violoncello, 1955; Variazioni for large orchestra, 1959; Five Pieces for piano, 1962; *Night Music I* for soprano, keyboard, and percussion, 1963; *Night Music II* for violin and piano, 1964; Madrigals for solo voice and instruments; *Eleven Echoes of Autumn* for violin, alto flute, clarinet, and piano, 1965; *Echoes of Time and the River,* 1967; *The Ancient Voices of Children* for soprano or mezzo, boy soprano, oboe, mandolin, harp, electric piano, and percussion, 1970.

The later music is highly imaginative as timbre and ultraromantic in its fluidity. An unquestioned brilliance of instrumentation and an assured professionalism have also helped create for Crumb a situation of leadership among today's forty-year-old far-outs. His romanticism may be real; no doubts are possible regarding his technique and talent.

A Suggested Reading List

Antheil, George, *Bad Boy of Music*. Garden City, New York, Double-day, Doran, 1945.

Berger, Arthur, *Aaron Copland*. New York, Oxford University Press, 1953.

Blesh, Rudi, and Janis, Harriet, *They All Played Ragtime*. New York, Knopf, 1950; revised with additions, paperback, New York, Oak Publications, 1966.

Broder, Nathan, *Samuel Barber*. New York, G. Schirmer, 1954.

Cage, John, *Silence: Lectures and Writings*. Middletown, Conn., Wesleyan University Press, 1961; M.I.T. Press, Cambridge, Mass. and London paperback 1966.

————, *A Year from Monday*. Middletown, Conn., Wesleyan University Press, 1969; also in paperback.

Chase, Gilbert, *America's Music: From the Pilgrims to the Present* (2nd edition, revised). New York, McGraw-Hill, 1966.

Cohn, Arthur, *The Collector's Twentieth Century Music in the Western Hemisphere*. Philadelphia and New York, Lippincott, 1961.

Copland, Aaron, *Our New Music*. New York, Whittlesey House, 1941; revised edition entitled *The New Music*, 1968.

————, *Copland on Music*. New York, W. W. Norton, 1963.

Cowell, Henry, *New Musical Resources*. New York, Knopf, 1930; reissued with preface and notes by Joscelyn Godwin, New York, Something Else Press, 1969.

————, *American Composers on American Music*, Stanford University Press, 1933.

Cowell, Henry and Sidney, *Charles Ives and His Music*. New York, Oxford University Press, 1955.

Harrison, Lou, *About Carl Ruggles* (with a note by Henry Cowell). Yonkers, N.Y., Alicat Book Shop, 1946.

Hitchcock, H. Wiley, *Music in the United States: A Historical Introduction*. Englewood Cliffs, N.J., Prentice-Hall, 1969.

Hoover, Kathleen and Cage, John, *Virgil Thomson: His Life and Music*. New York and London, Thos. Yoseloff, 1959.

Ives, Charles, *Essays Before a Sonata* (edited by Howard Boatwright). New York, W. W. Norton, 1961.

Maisel, Edward M., *Charles T. Griffes: The Life* . . . New York, Knopf, 1943.

Mellers, Wilfrid, *Music in a New Found Land: Themes and Developments in the History of American Music*. London, Barrie and Rockcliffe, New York, Knopf, 1964.

Ouellétte, Fernand, *Edgard Varèse*. Paris, Seghers, 1966; translated from the French by Derek Coltman, New York, The Orion Press, 1968.

Pound, Ezra, *Antheil and the Treatise on Harmony* (reprint of the 1927 edition with a new introduction by Ned Rorem). New York, Da Capo Press, 1968.

Reis, Claire R. *Composers in America: Biographical Sketches of Contemporary Composers with a Record of Their Works*. New York, Macmillan, 1947.

————, *Composers, Conductors and Critics*. New York, Oxford University Press, 1955.

Rorem, Ned, *The Paris Diary of Ned Rorem*. New York, Braziller, 1966.

————, *Music and People*. New York, Braziller, 1968.

Rosenfeld, Paul, *Musical Impressions* (selected from Paul Rosenfeld's criticism, edited and with an introduction by Herbert A. Leibowitz). New York, Hill and Wang, 1969.

Schuller, Gunther, *Early Jazz: Its Roots and Musical Development*. New York, Oxford University Press, 1968.

Smith, Julia, *Aaron Copland: His Work and Contribution to American Music*. New York, E. P. Dutton, 1955.

Thomson, Virgil, *The State of Music* (2nd edition, revised). New York, Random House, 1962.

————, *Virgil Thomson*. New York, Knopf, 1966.

————, *Music Reviewed: 1940–1954*. New York, Random House, 1967.

Yates, Peter, *Twentieth Century Music: Its Evolution from the End of the Harmonic Era into the Present Era of Sound*. New York, Random House, 1967.

A Suggested Reading List

Gelatt, Roland; Foss, Lukas; Hamilton, David, "The New Music: its Sources, its Sounds, its Creators." *High Fidelity*, September 1968.

Kostelanetz, Richard, "The American Avant-Garde Part I: Milton Babbitt, Part II: John Cage." *Stereo Review*, April and May, 1969.

Luening, Otto, "The Unfinished History of Electronic Music." *Music Educator's Journal*, November 1968.

Peyser, Joan, "The Troubled Time of Marc Blitzstein." *Columbia University Forum*, Winter 1966.

The files of *Modern Music*, Minna Lederman editor, published quarterly by the League of Composers from the 1920's through 1947, are a gold mine of writing by and about American composers.

Stereo Review, from 1962 to the present, has published extended, scholarly, and informative studies of American composers including Ives, Ruggles, Copland, Hanson, Harris, Barber, Thomson, Gershwin, Gottschalk, virtually everybody major in the field.

INDEX

Index

Index